Android Apps Security

Sheran Gunasekera

Apress·

Android Apps Security

ISBN-13 (pbk): 978-1-4302-4062-4

ISBN-13 (electronic): 978-1-4302-4063-1

President and Publisher: Paul Manning
Lead Editor: Steve Anglin
Development Editor: Tom Welsh, Douglas Pundick
Technical Reviewer: Michael Thomas
Editorial Board: Steve Anglin, Mark Beckner, Ewan Buckingham, Gary Cornell, Morgan Ertel, Jonathan Gennick, Jonathan Hassell, Robert Hutchinson, Michelle Lowman, James Markham, Matthew Moodie, Jeff Olson, Jeffrey Pepper, Douglas Pundick, Ben Renow-Clarke, Dominic Shakeshaft, Gwenan Spearing, Matt Wade, Tom Welsh
Coordinating Editor: Brigid Duffy
Copy Editor: Jill Steinberg
Compositor: SPi Global
Indexer: SPi Global
Artist: SPi Global
Cover Designer: Anna Ishchenko

Distributed to the book trade worldwide by Springer Science+Business Media New York, 233 Spring Street, 6th Floor, New York, NY 10013. Phone 1-800-SPRINGER, fax (201) 348-4505, e-mail orders-ny@springer-sbm.com, or visit www.springeronline.com.

For information on translations, please e-mail rights@apress.com, or visit www.apress.com.

Apress and friends of ED books may be purchased in bulk for academic, corporate, or promotional use. eBook versions and licenses are also available for most titles. For more information, reference our Special Bulk Sales–eBook Licensing web page at www.apress.com/bulk-sales.

Any source code or other supplementary materials referenced by the author in this text is available to readers at www.apress.com. For detailed information about how to locate your book's source code, go to www.apress.com/source-code/.

For Tess and Shana

—Sheran

Contents at a Glance

Contents

About the Author

Sheran Gunasekera is a security researcher and software developer with more than 13 years of information security experience. He is director of research and development for ZenConsult Pte. Ltd., where he oversees security research in both the personal computer and mobile device platforms. Sheran has been very active in BlackBerry and Mobile Java security research and was the author of the whitepaper that revealed the inner workings of the first corporate-sanctioned malware application deployed to its subscribers by the UAE telecommunications operator Etisalat. He has spoken at many security conferences in the Middle East, Europe and Asia Pacific regions and also provides training on malware analysis for mobile devices and secure software development for both Web and mobile devices. He also writes articles and publishes research on his security-related blog, `http://chirashi.zenconsult.net`.

About the Technical Reviewer

Michael Thomas has worked in software development for over 20 years as an individual contributor, team lead, program manager, and Vice President of Engineering. Michael has over 10 years experience working with mobile devices. His current focus is in the medical sector using mobile devices to accelerate information transfer between patients and health care providers.

Acknowledgments

I'd like to thank the editors, reviewers, and staff at Apress who worked tirelessly to help get this book published. They were the driving force behind this book in more ways than one. They put up with more than they should have. I am not a model author.

I'd also like to thank my dear friends and colleagues, Michael Harrington and Shafik Punja, without whom I would not have had the opportunity to publish this book. Thanks guys, this has been a great experience.

–Sheran Gunasekera

## Chapter 1

Android Architecture

Google entered the mobile phone market in a style that only multibillion-dollar companies can afford: it bought a company. In 2005, Google, Inc. purchased Android, Inc. At the time, Android was relatively unknown, despite having four very successful people as its creators. Founded by Andy Rubin, Rich Miner, Chris White, and Nick Sears in 2003, Android flew under the radar, developing an operating system for mobile phones. With a quest to develop a smarter mobile phone that was more aware of its owner's preferences, the team behind the Android operating system toiled away in secrecy. Admitting only that they were developing software for mobile phones, the team remained quiet about the true nature of the Android operating system until the acquisition in 2005.

With the full might of Google's resources behind it, Android development increased at a rapid pace. By the second quarter of 2011, Android had already captured nearly a 50% market share in mobile phone operating systems shipped to end users. The four founders stayed on after the acquisition, with Rubin taking the lead as Senior Vice President of Mobile. The official launch of version 1.0 of Android took place on September 23, 2008, and the first device to run it was the HTC Dream (see Figure 1-1).

Figure 1-1. An HTC Dream (Courtesy Michael Oryl)

One of the unique features of the Android operating system that has allowed it to grow rapidly has been that the binaries and source code are released as open source software. You can download the entire source code of the Android operating system, and it takes up approximately 2.6 GB of disk space. In theory, this allows anyone to design and build a phone that runs Android. The idea of keeping the software open source was followed until version 3.0. Versions of Android including and higher than 3.0 are still closed source. In an interview given to *Bloomberg Businessweek*, Rubin said that the version 3.x code base took many shortcuts to ensure it was released to market quickly and worked with very specific hardware. If other hardware vendors adopted this version of Android, then the chances for a negative user experience would be a possibility, and Google wished to avoid this.[1]

Components of the Android Architecture

The Android architecture is divided into the following four main components (see Figure 1-2):

1. The kernel

2. The libraries and Dalvik virtual machine

3. The application framework

4. The applications

---

[1] *Bloomberg Businessweek*, "Google Holds Honeycomb Tight," Ashlee Vance and Brad Stone, www.businessweek.com/technology/content/mar2011/tc20110324_269784.htm, March 24, 2011.

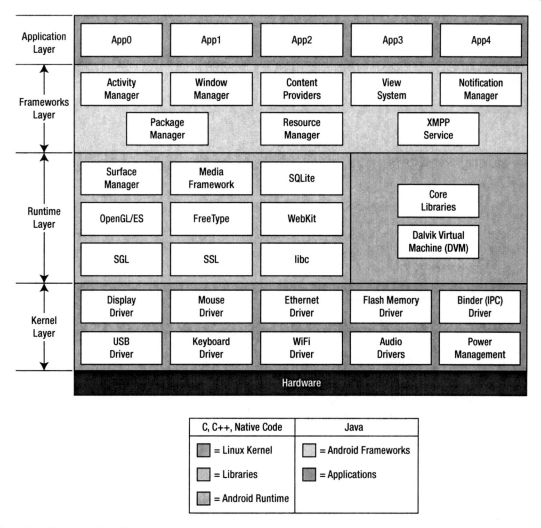

Figure 1-2. *The Android architecture*

The Kernel

Android runs on top of a Linux 2.6 kernel. The kernel is the first layer of software that interacts with the device hardware. Similar to a desktop computer running Linux, the Android kernel will take care of power and memory management, device drivers, process management, networking, and security. The Android kernel is available at `http://android.git.kernel.org/`.

Modifying and building a new kernel is not something you will want to consider as an application developer. Generally, only hardware or device manufacturers will want to modify the kernel to ensure that the operating system works with their particular type of hardware.

The Libraries

The libraries component also shares its space with the runtime component. The libraries component acts as a translation layer between the kernel and the application framework. The libraries are written in C/C++ but are exposed to developers through a Java API. Developers can use the Java application framework to access the underlying core C/C++ libraries. Some of the core libraries include the following:

- *LibWebCore*: Allows access to the web browser.
- *Media libraries*: Allows access to popular audio- and video-recording and playback functions.
- *Graphics libraries*: Allows access to 2D and 3D graphics drawing engines.

The runtime component consists of the Dalvik virtual machine that will interact with and run applications. The virtual machine is an important part of the Android operating system and executes system and third-party applications.

The Dalvik Virtual Machine

Dan Bornstein originally wrote the Dalvik virtual machine. He named it after a small fishing village in Iceland where he believed one of his ancestors once originated. The Dalvik VM was written primarily to allow application execution on devices with very limited resources. Typically, mobile phones will fall into this category because they are limited by processing power, the amount of memory available, and a short battery life.

WHAT IS A VIRTUAL MACHINE?

A virtual machine is an isolated, guest operating system running within another host operating system. A virtual machine will execute applications as if they were running on a physical machine. One of the main advantages of a virtual machine is portability. Regardless of the underlying hardware, the code that you write will work on the VM. To you as a developer, this means that you write your code only once and can execute it on any hardware platform that runs a compatible VM.

The Dalvik VM executes .dex files. A .dex file is made by taking the compiled Java .class or .jar files and consolidating all the constants and data within each .class file into a shared constant pool (see Figure 1-3). The dx tool, included in the Android SDK, performs this conversion. After conversion, .dex files have a significantly smaller file size, as shown in Table 1-1.

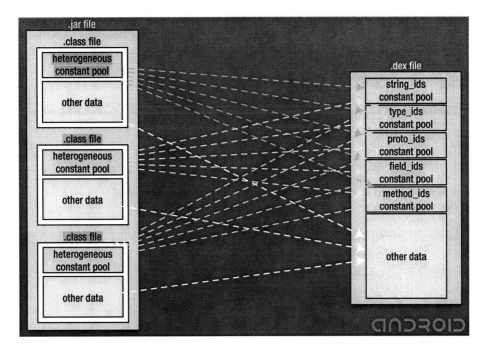

Figure 1-3. *Conversion of a .jar file to a .dex file*

Table 1-1. *A File Size Comparison (in Bytes) of .jar and .dex Files*

Application	Uncompressed .jar	Compressed .jar	Uncompressed .dex
Common system libraries	21445320 = 100%	10662048 = 50%	10311972 = 48%
Web browser app	470312 = 100%	232065 = 49%	209248 = 44%
Alarm clock app	119200 = 100%	61658 = 52%	53020 = 44%

The Application Framework

The application framework is one of the building blocks for the final system or end-user applications. The framework provides a suite of services or systems that a developer will find useful when writing applications. Commonly referred to as the API (application programming interface) component, this framework will provide a developer with access to user interface components such as buttons and text boxes, common content providers so that apps may share data between them, a notification manager so that device owners can be alerted of events, and an activity manager for managing the lifecycle of applications.

As a developer, you will write code and use the APIs in the Java programming language. Listing 1-1, taken from Google's sample API demos (http://developer.android.com/resources/samples/ApiDemos/index.html), demonstrates how to use the application framework to play a video file. The import statements in bold allow access to the core C/C++ libraries through a Java API.

Listing 1-1. A Video Player Demo (Courtesy Google, Inc.)

```
/*
 * Copyright (C) 2009 The Android Open Source Project
 *
 * Licensed under the Apache License, Version 2.0 (the "License");
 * you may not use this file except in compliance with the License.
 * You may obtain a copy of the License at
 *
 *      http://www.apache.org/licenses/LICENSE-2.0
 *
 * Unless required by applicable law or agreed to in writing, software
 * distributed under the License is distributed on an "AS IS" BASIS,
 * WITHOUT WARRANTIES OR CONDITIONS OF ANY KIND, either express or implied.
 * See the License for the specific language governing permissions and
 * limitations under the License.
 */


package com.example.android.apis.media;


import com.example.android.apis.R;
import android.app.Activity;
import android.os.Bundle;
import android.widget.MediaController;
import android.widget.Toast;
import android.widget.VideoView;

public class VideoViewDemo extends Activity {

    /**
     * TODO: Set the path variable to a streaming video URL or a local media
     * file path.
     */
    private String path = "";
    private VideoView mVideoView;

    @Override
    public void onCreate(Bundle icicle) {
        super.onCreate(icicle);
        setContentView(R.layout.videoview);
        mVideoView = (VideoView) findViewById(R.id.surface_view);

        if (path == "") {
            // Tell the user to provide a media file URL/path.
            Toast.makeText(
                    VideoViewDemo.this,
                    "Please edit VideoViewDemo Activity, and set path"
                            + " variable to your media file URL/path",
                    Toast.LENGTH_LONG).show();

        } else {
```

```
        /*
         * Alternatively,for streaming media you can use
         * mVideoView.setVideoURI(Uri.parse(URLstring));
         */
        mVideoView.setVideoPath(path);
        mVideoView.setMediaController(new MediaController(this));
        mVideoView.requestFocus();

        }
    }
}
```

The Applications

The application component of the Android operating system is the closest to the end user. This is where the Contacts, Phone, Messaging, and Angry Birds apps live. As a developer, your finished product will execute in this space by using the API libraries and the Dalvik VM. In this book, we will extensively look at this component of the Android operating system.

Even though every component of the Android operating system can be modified, you will only have direct control over your own application's security. This does not, however, give you free rein to ignore what happens if the device is compromised with a kernel or VM exploit. Ensuring your application does not fall victim to an attack because of an unrelated exploit is also your responsibility.

What This Book Is About

Now that you've got an overall understanding of the Android architecture, let's turn to what you will *not* learn in this book. First, you are not going to learn how to develop Android apps from scratch in this book. You will see many examples and source code listings; and while I will explain each section of code, you might have additional questions that you might not find answered in this book. You are required to have a certain degree of experience and skill at writing Java applications for the Android platform. I also assume that you have already setup your Android development environment using the Eclipse IDE. In this book, I will focus on how you can develop more secure applications for the Android operating system.

Android has had its fair share of security setbacks and a burgeoning list of malware that is worth examining and learning from. Armed with where to look and how to tackle security aspects of developing for Android will not necessarily make you a better coder, but it will start you on your way to becoming more responsible with your end users' privacy and security.

I've tried to write this book in a manner that will help you understand the concepts of security in relation to the applications you develop. In most cases, the best way I find I can achieve this is by teaching through example. Therefore, you will usually find me asking you to write and execute source code listings first. I will then follow up with an explanation of the specific concept that we are covering. With this in mind, let's take a look at some of the security controls available on the Android operating system.

Security

Security isn't a dirty word, Blackadder!

—General Melchett, *Blackadder IV*

Security is a vast subject and is applicable to many areas depending on what context it is taken in. I wrote this book to cover a small component of a small component of security. It is written to give you a good understanding of Android application security. However, what does that really mean? What are we trying to secure? Who will benefit from this? Why is it important? Let's try to answer those questions and possibly come up with a few new ones.

First, let's identify who you really are. Are you a developer? Maybe you're a security practitioner conducting research. Alternatively, maybe you're an end user interested in safeguarding yourself from an attack. I'd like to think that I fit into each of these categories. No doubt, you will fit into one or more of them. The vast majority, however, will fit into one category: an end user who wants to use the features of a well-written application in a manner that does not compromise her privacy and security. If you're a developer, and I'm guessing you are if you've picked this book up, this is your target audience: the end user. You write applications to distribute to your users. You may choose to sell them or give them away for free. Either way, you are writing applications that will end up installed on someone else's device, possibly thousands of miles away.

Protect Your User

Your application should strive to provide the best functionality possible while taking care to protect your users' data. This means thinking about security before you begin development.

Your user might not always know about the security practices you employ "under the hood" of your application, but one breach in your application is all it will take to ensure that all his Twitter and Facebook followers find out. Planning and thinking about security prior to the development phase of your application can save you the embarrassment of bad reviews and the loss of paying customers. The end user is almost never quick to forgive or forget.

As we go along, you will learn principles and techniques to identify sensitive user data and create a plan to protect this data. The goal is to eliminate or vastly reduce any unintentional harm your application could cause. So, what are you really protecting the end user from?

Security Risks

Mobile device users face some unique risks when compared with desktop computer users. Aside from the higher possibility of losing or having their device stolen, mobile device users risk losing sensitive data or having their privacy compromised. Why would this be different from desktop users? First, the quality of data stored on a user's mobile device tends to be more personal. Apart from e-mail, there are instant messages, SMS/MMS, contacts, photos, and voicemail. "So what?" you say. "Some of these things exist on a desktop computer." True, but consider this: The data on your mobile device is most likely going to be of higher value than that on your desktop because you carry it around with you all the time. It is a converged platform of both your computer and mobile phone that contains a richer collection of personal data. Because the level of user interaction is higher on the smartphone, the data is always newer than on your desktop computer. Even if you have configured real-time sync to a remote location, that still only protects you from a loss of data and not a loss of privacy.

Consider also that the format of data stored on mobile devices is fixed. Every phone will have SMS/MMS, contacts, and voicemail. Phones that are more powerful will have photos, videos, GPS locations, and e-mail, but all of it is common regardless of the operating system. Now consider how important all of this information is to an end user. To a user who has no backups, losing data of this nature can be unthinkable. Losing important phone numbers, precious moments of her daughter's first steps caught on video, or important SMS messages can be catastrophic to the everyday phone user.

What about the user who combines both business and personal activities on his phone? What would you do if someone copied an entire file of passwords for your office server farm from your phone? Or if an e-mail containing trade secrets and confidential pricing for proposals leaked out onto the Internet? What if you lost the address of your child's school? Consider a stalker gaining access to this information and more, such as your home address and phone number.

It is clear when you think about it that the data stored on the phone is, in most cases, far more valuable than that of the device itself. The most dangerous type of attack is the one that takes place silently and remotely; an attacker does not need physical access to your phone. These types of attacks can happen at any time and can often happen because of weak security elsewhere on the device. These lapses in security might not be because your application is insecure. They could be due to a bug in the kernel or web browser. The question is this: can your application protect its data from attackers even when they gain access to the device through different routes?

Android Security Architecture

As we discussed previously, Android runs on top of the Linux 2.6 kernel. We also learned that the Android Linux kernel handles security management for the operating system. Let's take a look at the Android Security Architecture.

Privilege Separation

The Android kernel implements a privilege separation model when it comes to executing applications. This means that, like on a UNIX system, the Android operating system requires every application to run with its own user identifier (uid) and group identifier (gid).

Parts of the system architecture themselves are separated in this fashion. This ensures that applications or processes have no permissions to access other applications or processes.

WHAT IS PRIVILEGE SEPARATION?

Privilege separation is an important security feature because it denies one of the more common types of attacks. In many cases, the first attack that is performed is not the most effective one. It is usually the stepping-stone or gateway to a bigger attack. Often, attackers will exploit one component of a system first; and once there, they will try to attack a more important component in the system. If both these components are running with the same privileges, then it is a very trivial task for the attacker to hop from one component to the next. By separating privileges, the attacker's task becomes more difficult. He has to be able to escalate or change his privileges to that of the component he wishes to attack. In this manner, the attack is stopped, if not slowed.

Because the kernel implements privilege separation, it is one of the core design features of Android. The philosophy behind this design is to ensure that no application can read or write to code or data of other applications, the device user, or the operating system itself. Thus, an application might not be able to arbitrarily use the device's networking stack to connect to remote servers. One application might not read directly from the device's contact list or calendar. This feature is also known as *sandboxing*. After two processes have run in their own sandboxes, the only way they have to communicate with each other is to explicitly request permission to access data.

Permissions

Let's take a simple example. We have an application that records audio from the built-in microphone of the device. For this application to work correctly, the developer has to make sure to add a request for the RECORD_AUDIO permission in the application's AndroidManifest.xml file. This allows our application to request permission to use the system component that handles audio recording. But who decides whether to grant or deny access? Android allows the end user to perform this final approval process. When the user installs our application, he is prompted with the screen shown in Figure 1-4. It is worthwhile to note that no prompt for permissions will take place when the application is executing. Instead, the permission will need to be granted at install time.

If we do not explicitly set our need for the RECORD_AUDIO permission, or if the device owner does not grant us the permission after we request it, then an exception will be thrown by the VM and the application will fail. It is up to the developer to know to request the permission and handle the scenario where permission is not granted by catching the relevant exception. To request this permission, the following tag must be included in the AndroidManifest.xml file of the project:

```
<uses-permission android:name="android.permission.RECORD_AUDIO" />
```

The full list of permissions is given in this book's appendix.

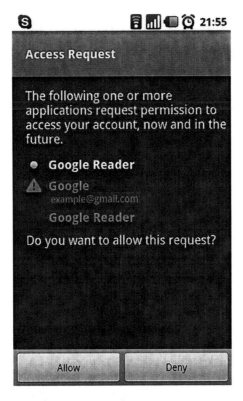

Figure 1-4. *The Android permissions request screen*

Application Code Signing

Any application that is to run on the Android operating system must be signed. Android uses the certificate of individual developers in order to identify them and establish trust relationships among the various applications running in the operating system. The operating system will not allow an unsigned application to execute. The use of a certification authority to sign the certificate is not required, and Android will happily run any application that has been signed with a self-signed certificate.

Like permissions checks, the certificate check is done only during installation of the application. Therefore, if your developer certificate expires after your application is installed on the device, then the application will continue to execute. The only difference at this point would be that you would need to generate a new certificate before you could sign any new applications. Android requires two separate certificates for debug versions of your application and release versions of your application. Generally, the Eclipse environment running the Android Development Tools (ADT) is already setup to help you generate your keys and install your certificate, so that your applications can be automatically packaged and signed. The Android emulator behaves identically to the physical device. Like the physical device, it will only execute signed applications. We will cover application code signing in detail, as well as publishing and selling your applications online.

Summary

As we've seen so far, Android received a tremendous boost in resources and attention thanks to Google's takeover of Android. This same care and attention has helped propel Android to one of the most rapidly growing smartphone operating systems in the world today. Android's open source model has helped its numbers grow, mainly because many different hardware manufacturers can use the operating system on their phones.

We've also seen that the core of Android is based on the Linux kernel. The kernel's two main tasks are (1) to serve as a bridge between hardware and operating system, and (2) to handle security, memory management, process management, and networking. The kernel is usually one of the main components that will be modified when different hardware manufacturers start adopting Android to work with their hardware.

The next layer that goes around the Android kernel is the runtime layer that comprises the core libraries and the Dalvik virtual machine. The Dalvik VM is a fundamental part of executing your applications on the Android platform. As you will see in the following chapters, the Dalvik VM has some unique features when it comes to executing applications securely and efficiently in a resource-constrained environment.

The next upper layers to be added are the frameworks and applications, respectively. You can think of the framework layer as yet another bridge between the Java API and the native code and system processes running below. This is where all the Android Java APIs live. Any libraries that you wish to import in your program are imported from here. The applications layer is where your applications will finally live and work. You will share this space with other developer applications and Android's bundled applications such as the Phone, Calendar, E-mail, and Messaging applications.

We then looked briefly at the security risks, how you have the responsibility to protect your end user, and some of the ways in which Android facilitates this. The three areas we looked at were privilege separation, permissions, and application code signing. In the next chapters, we will explore what you can do to not only make use of these features, but also add in your own levels of security and end-user protection.

## Chapter 2

Information: The Foundation of an App

The basis of all meaningful applications is information, and we design and build applications to exchange, create, or store it. Mobile applications are no different. In today's well-connected mobile landscape, information exchange is the name of the game. To illustrate this point, imagine an Android phone without mobile network or WiFi coverage. While there would still be uses for such a phone, you would have lost access to some of the more important applications on your device. For example, e-mail, instant messaging, web browsing, and any other application that require the Internet would now be nonfunctional.

In later chapters, we will focus our efforts on examining information in transit and how to secure it. In this chapter, we will focus mostly on what happens to information that is stored.

Securing Your Application from Attacks

When created or received, data needs to be stored somewhere. How this information is stored will ultimately reflect on how secure your application really is. Releasing your application to the public should be approached with the same caution and paranoia as launching a website on the Internet. You should assume that your application will be either directly or indirectly attacked at some time and that the only thing standing between your end user's privacy and data protection is your application.

Indirect Attacks

As dramatic as that last sentence sounds, it is not without basis. Before we go further, let's take a look at whether my fear mongering is justified. In the latter part of 2010 and early 2011, two vulnerabilities were discovered in Android versions 2.2 and 2.3, respectively. The vulnerability is essentially the same one, in which an attacker can copy any file that is stored on the device's SD

Card without permission or even without a visible cue that this is happening. The vulnerability works as shown in Figure 2-1.

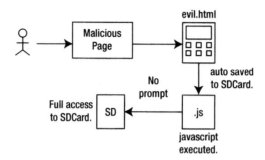

Figure 2-1. Data theft vulnerabilities

The following are the most noteworthy points:

1. A user visits a malicious website hosting a file, such as `evil.html`.

2. Due to one part of the vulnerability, the `evil.html` file is downloaded and saved to the device SD Card without prompting the user.

3. Due to another part of the vulnerability, the saved file can be made to execute JavaScript code as soon as it is saved. Once again, there is no prompt to the end user.

4. Due to the final part of this vulnerability, the executed JavaScript from the preceding point, because it is running under the "local" context of the device, will have full access to upload files stored on the SD Card to a website of the attacker's choosing.

For the sake of argument, assume that your application writes all saved information to the SD Card for storage under its own directory. Because of the vulnerability just discussed, the data used by your application is at risk of being stolen. Any Android device that runs your application and the vulnerable firmware versions poses a risk of data theft to its end user. This is an example of an indirect attack on your application.

How vulnerable your application is to an indirect attack depends largely on how much effort you put into architecting *and* considering security aspects *before* you begin writing a single line of code. You may ask the question, "I'm just a small app developer planning to sell my app for a low price online, so do I really need to waste time doing so much planning beforehand?" And I would answer you with a resounding, "Yes!" Whether you are part of a team of thirty developers or an individual working from home, a well-architected application is something you should always strive to create. I hope that this is what you will learn from this book.

Direct Attacks

Direct attacks are significantly different and can take many different forms. A direct attack can be classified as one that is targeted directly at your application. Thus, the attacker is looking to leverage weaknesses in your application design to either collect sensitive information on your application's users or to attack the server that your application talks to. Take, for instance, a mobile-banking application. An attacker may go after the mobile applications belonging to a specific bank. If the application design is weak–for example, if that sensitive user data is stored in clear text, or the communication between application and server is not secured by SSL–then an attacker can craft special attacks that only target these weaknesses. This is a direct attack on a specific application. I will cover direct attacks in more detail in Chapter 9 of this book.

Project 1:"Proxim" and Data Storage

Let's get started with a simple example called Proxim. I've been contracted to write an application that can send an SMS to specific, defined contacts when a user is within certain proximity to a set of GPS coordinates. For instance, with this application, a user can add his wife as a contact and have the application SMS her every time he is within three miles of his workplace and house. This way, she knows when he is close to home and the office.

You can download and examine the entire source code for the Proxim application from the Source Code/Download area of the Apress website (www.apress.com). For the sake of clarity, let's take a look at the most important areas.

The data-storage routine is shown in Listing 2-1.

Listing 2-1. The Save Routine, SaveController. java

```
package net.zenconsult.android.controller;

import java.io.File;
import java.io.FileNotFoundException;
import java.io.FileOutputStream;
import java.io.IOException;

import net.zenconsult.android.model.Contact;
import net.zenconsult.android.model.Location;
import android.content.Context;
import android.os.Environment;
import android.util.Log;

public class SaveController {
        private static final String TAG = "SaveController";

        public static void saveContact(Context context, Contact contact) {
                if (isReadWrite()) {
                        try {
File outputFile = new File(context.getExternalFilesDir(null),contact.getFirstName());
FileOutputStream outputStream = new FileOutputStream(outputFile);
                                outputStream.write(contact.getBytes());
                                outputStream.close();
```

```
                    } catch (FileNotFoundException e) {
                            Log.e(TAG,"File not found");
                    } catch (IOException e) {
                            Log.e(TAG,"IO Exception");
                    }

            } else {
                    Log.e(TAG,"Error opening media card in read/write mode!");
            }
    }

    public static void saveLocation(Context context, Location location) {
            if (isReadWrite()) {
                    try {
File outputFile = new File(context.getExternalFilesDir(null),location.getIdentifier());
FileOutputStream outputStream = new FileOutputStream(outputFile);
                            outputStream.write(location.getBytes());
                            outputStream.close();

                    } catch (FileNotFoundException e) {
                            Log.e(TAG,"File not found");
                    } catch (IOException e) {
                            Log.e(TAG,"IO Exception");
                    }

            } else {
                    Log.e(TAG,"Error opening media card in read/write mode!");
            }
    }

    private static boolean isReadOnly() {
            Log.e(TAG,Environment
                            .getExternalStorageState());
            return Environment.MEDIA_MOUNTED_READ_ONLY.equals(Environment
                            .getExternalStorageState());
    }

    private static boolean isReadWrite() {
            Log.e(TAG,Environment
                            .getExternalStorageState());

            return Environment.MEDIA_MOUNTED.equals(Environment
                            .getExternalStorageState());
    }
}
```

Each time a user selects the Save Location button or the Save Contact button, it triggers the preceding code. Let's take a look at the Location (see Listing 2-2) and Contact (see Listing 2-3) classes in more detail. While we could implement one main save routine, I am keeping it separate in case there is a need to act on different objects in a different manner.

Listing 2-2. The Location Class, Location.java

```java
package net.zenconsult.android.model;

publicclass Location {
        private String identifier;
        privatedouble latitude;
        privatedouble longitude;

        public Location() {

        }

        publicdouble getLatitude() {
                return latitude;
        }

        publicvoid setLatitude(double latitude) {
                this.latitude = latitude;
        }

        publicdouble getLongitude() {
                return longitude;
        }

        publicvoid setLongitude(double longitude) {
                this.longitude = longitude;
        }

        publicvoid setIdentifier(String identifier) {
                this.identifier = identifier;
        }

        public String getIdentifier() {
                return identifier;
        }

        public String toString() {
                StringBuilder ret = new StringBuilder();
                ret.append(getIdentifier());
                ret.append(String.valueOf(getLatitude()));
                ret.append(String.valueOf(getLongitude()));
                return ret.toString();
        }

        publicbyte[] getBytes() {
                return toString().getBytes();
        }

}
```

Listing 2-3. The Contact Class, Contact.java

```java
package net.zenconsult.android.model;

publicclass Contact {
        private String firstName;
        private String lastName;
        private String address1;
        private String address2;
        private String email;
        private String phone;

        public Contact() {

        }

        public String getFirstName() {
                return firstName;
        }

        publicvoid setFirstName(String firstName) {
                this.firstName = firstName;
        }

        public String getLastName() {
                return lastName;
        }

        publicvoid setLastName(String lastName) {
                this.lastName = lastName;
        }

        public String getAddress1() {
                return address1;
        }

        publicvoid setAddress1(String address1) {
                this.address1 = address1;
        }

        public String getAddress2() {
                return address2;
        }

        publicvoid setAddress2(String address2) {
                this.address2 = address2;
        }

        public String getEmail() {
                return email;
        }
```

```java
publicvoid setEmail(String email) {
        this.email = email;
}

public String getPhone() {
        return phone;
}

publicvoid setPhone(String phone) {
        this.phone = phone;
}

public String toString() {
        StringBuilder ret = new StringBuilder();
        ret.append(getFirstName() + "|");
        ret.append(getLastName() + "|");
        ret.append(getAddress1() + "|");
        ret.append(getAddress2() + "|");
        ret.append(getEmail() + "|");
        ret.append(getPhone() + "|");
        return ret.toString();
}

publicbyte[] getBytes() {
        return toString().getBytes();
}
}
```

The Location and Contact classes are standard classes designed to hold data specific to each type. Each of them contains toString() and getBytes() methods that return the entire contents of the class as either a String or an array of bytes.

If we were to manually add a Contact object, then we would most likely use code similar to what is shown in Listing 2-4.

Listing 2-4. Code that Adds a New Contact Object

```java
final Contact contact = new Contact();
contact.setFirstName("Sheran");
contact.setLastName("Gunasekera");
contact.setAddress1("");
contact.setAddress2("");
contact.setEmail("sheran@zenconsult.net");
contact.setPhone("12120031337");
```

Assume for the moment that the code in Listing 2-4 is called when a user fills in the screen to add a new contact to the application. Rather than seeing hardcoded values, you will use the getText() methods from each of the EditText objects that are displayed on your main View.

If you execute the code SaveController.saveContact(getApplicationContext(), contact))in your Android simulator, the SaveController will take the newly created Contact and store it in the external media source (refer back to Listing 2-1).

> **Note**   It is always good practice to use the `getExternalFilesDir()` method to find the
> location of the SD Card on an Android device. Because Android can run on a large number of
> devices with different specifications, the location of the SD Card directory may not always be in
> `/sdcard`. The `getExternalFilesDir()` method will query the operating system for the correct
> location of the SD Card and return the location to you.

Let's take it a line at a time, beginning with the constructor for the `saveContact()` method:

```
public static void saveContact(Context context, Contact contact) {
        if (isReadWrite()) {
                    try {
```

The preceding snippet expects a `Context` object and a `Contact` object. Each application on
Android has its own `Context`. A `Context` object holds application-specific classes, methods,
and resources that can be shared among all the classes within an application. For example, a
`Context` object will contain information about the location of the SD Card directory. To access it,
you have to invoke the `Context.getExternalFilesDir()` method. After the method accepts the
parameters, it will check to see if the SD Card on the device is mounted and if it is writeable. The
`isReadWrite()` method will execute and return a `true` or `false` value to indicate this:

```
File outputFile = new File(context.getExternalFilesDir(null),contact.getFirstName());
```

This code creates a `File` object that points to the location of the SD Card directory. We use the
first name of the `Contact` object as the file name:

```
FileOutputStream outputStream = new FileOutputStream(outputFile);
outputStream.write(contact.getBytes());
outputStream.close();
```

Using this code, we create a `FileOutputStream` that points to the location of our `File` object.
Next, we write the contents of our `Contact` object to the output stream using the `getBytes()`
method to return an array of bytes. Finally, we close the `FileOutputStream`.

When execution completes, we should have a file with the name "Sheran" written to the SD Card
directory on the device. I'm using the Android simulator on Mac OS X Snow Leopard. Therefore,
when I navigate to the location of the simulator, I can see the screen shown in Figure 2-2.

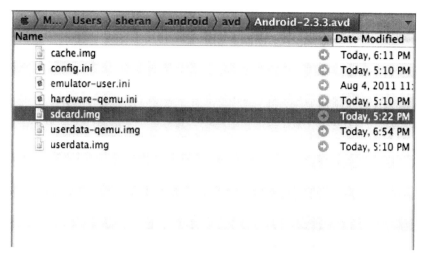

Figure 2-2. The SD Card image file on Max OS X

When this image is mounted by navigating to Android/data/net.zenconsult.android/files, the newly created contact file name is visible (see Figure 2-3).

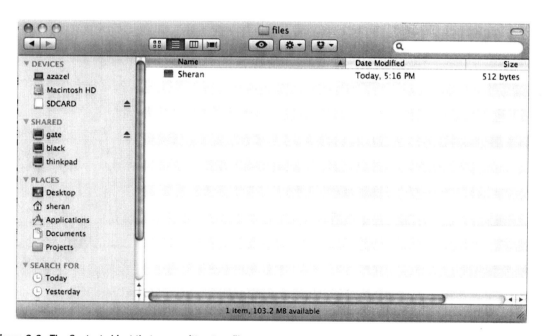

Figure 2-3. The Contact object that was written to a file

If we open the file up in a text editor, we can see the plain text data that was saved from the application (see Figure 2-4).

Figure 2-4. The contents of the Contact object

Classification of Information

One of the things I struggled with when starting out in mobile-application development was the fact that I'd get into code writing from the get go. I'd make up the features in my head and code them as I went along. All too often, I would later spend time revising my code and going back to write a plan midstream. This had devastating effects on my deadlines and deliverables. It also had a detrimental effect on the security of my applications.

I have since learned that writing up a brief outline of the project that I am about to embark on will help me think of things ahead of time. While this seems like an obvious thing, there are many developers that I have spoken with who fail to follow this simple step. One other thing that I have also begun doing religiously is finding time to look at the information or data that my application will be handling. For instance, I use a table like the one shown in Table 2-1 to classify the data that my application handles. The table is very basic; however, by putting it down on paper, I am able to visualize the types of data my application will handle—moreover, I'm able to formulate a plan to secure that information.

Table 2-1. Data Classification Table

Data Type	Personal?	Sensitive?	Create	Store	Send	Receive
Name	Yes	No	X	X	x	
E-mail Address	Yes	Yes	X	X	x	
Phone No.	Yes	Yes	X	X		
Address	Yes	Yes	X	X		

If you look at the data classification table in Table 2-1 closely, you will realize that some of the headings are very subjective. Different people will have different opinions on what constitutes sensitive or personal information. Nevertheless, it is usually best to try and zero in on a common frame of reference as to what constitutes sensitive and personal information. In this section, you will try to do that by taking a look at the table header first, and then going over each of the columns:

> *Data Type*: You will be handling this data within your application. It is self-explanatory.
>
> *Personal?*: This column indicates whether the data type is classified as personal information.

Sensitive?: This column indicates whether the data type is classified as sensitive information.

Create: Does your application allow this user to create this data type?

Store: Does your application store this data type either on the device or remotely on a server?

Sent: Is this data type sent across the network to another party or server?

Receive: Is this data type received over the network from another party?

What Is Personal Information?

Personal information can be classified as data that is known to you and a limited number of people within your social circle. Personal information is usually something that is private to you, but that you would be willing to share with close friends and family members. Examples of personal information can be your phone number, address, and e-mail address. The effects of having this information compromised and leaked will usually not cause significant physical or emotional harm to yourself or your family members. Instead, it may give rise to situations that will greatly inconvenience you.

What Is Sensitive Information?

Sensitive information is worth much more than personal information. Sensitive information is usually information that you will not share with anyone under most circumstances. Data of this type includes your passwords, Internet banking credentials (such as PIN codes), mobile phone number, Social Security number, or address. If sensitive information is compromised, then the effects may cause you either physical or emotional harm. This information should be protected all the time, regardless of whether it is in transit or in storage.

Caution   How can the loss of sensitive information cause you physical or emotional harm? Consider losing your online banking credentials. An attacker can cause you immense financial (physical and emotional) harm by stealing all your money. A stalker that gets hold of your phone number or address can pose a grave threat to you or your family's physical well being.

Analysis of Code

If we go back to the indirect attack that we discussed earlier in this chapter, it is evident that data kept in clear view on an SD Card is a significant risk and should be avoided at all costs. Data theft or exposure has been one of the leading causes of financial and reputational loss for corporations. But just because you're writing an application for a single user of a smartphone does not mean you should treat data theft lightly. In the case of Proxim, this weakness of clear text data storage exists. Anyone who has access to the device's SD Card will be able to copy personal information, such as names, addresses, phone numbers, and e-mail addresses.

We can trace the flaw in the original code to the point where we save the data. The data itself is not obscured or encrypted in any way. If we were to encrypt the data, then the personal information would still be safe. Let's take a look at how we can implement encryption in our original Proxim code. Chapter 5 will cover public key infrastructure and encryption in depth; so for the purposes of this exercise, we will cover a very basic example of Advanced Encryption Standard (AES) encryption. Public Key encryption or Asymmetric encryption is a method of encrypting or obfuscating data by using two different types of keys. Each user has two keys, a public and a private one. His private key can only decrypt data that is encrypted by the public key. The key is called public because it is freely given away to other users. It is this key that other users will use to encrypt data.

Where to Implement Encryption

We will encrypt our data just before we save it to the SD Card. In this way, we never write the data to the SD Card in a format that can be read by anyone. An attacker that collects your encrypted data has to first use a password to decrypt the data before having access to it.

We will use AES to encrypt our data using a password or key. One key is required to both encrypt and decrypt the data. This is also known s symmetric key encryption. Unlike public key encryption, this key is the sole one used to both encrypt and decrypt data. This key will need to be stored securely because, if it is lost or compromised, an attacker can use it to decrypt the data. Listing 2-5 shows the encryption routine.

Listing 2-5. An Encryption Routine

```
privatestaticbyte[] encrypt(byte[] key, byte[] data){
            SecretKeySpec sKeySpec = new SecretKeySpec(key,"AES");
            Cipher cipher;
            byte[] ciphertext = null;
            try {
                    cipher = Cipher.getInstance("AES");
                    cipher.init(Cipher.ENCRYPT_MODE, sKeySpec);
                    ciphertext = cipher.doFinal(data);
            } catch (NoSuchAlgorithmException e) {
                    Log.e(TAG,"NoSuchAlgorithmException");
            } catch (NoSuchPaddingException e) {
                    Log.e(TAG,"NoSuchPaddingException");
            } catch (IllegalBlockSizeException e) {
                    Log.e(TAG,"IllegalBlockSizeException");
            } catch (BadPaddingException e) {
                    Log.e(TAG,"BadPaddingException");
            } catch (InvalidKeyException e) {
                    Log.e(TAG,"InvalidKeyException");
            }
            return ciphertext;

    }
```

```java
public class SaveController {
        private static final String TAG = "SaveController";

        public static void saveContact(Context context, Contact contact) {
                if (isReadWrite()) {
                        try {
                                File outputFile = new File(context.getExternalFilesDir↵
(null),contact.getFirstName());
                                FileOutputStream outputStream = new FileOutputStream↵
(outputFile);
                                byte[] key = Crypto.generateKey↵
("randomtext".getBytes());
                                outputStream.write(encrypt(key,contact.getBytes()));
                                outputStream.close();

                        } catch (FileNotFoundException e) {
                                Log.e(TAG,"File not found");
                        } catch (IOException e) {
                                Log.e(TAG,"IO Exception");
                        }

                } else {
                        Log.e(TAG,"Error opening media card in read/write mode!");
                }
        }

        public static void saveLocation(Context context, Location location) {
                if (isReadWrite()) {
                        try {
                                File outputFile = new File(context.getExternalFilesDir↵
(null),location.getIdentifier());
                                FileOutputStream outputStream = new FileOutputStream↵
(outputFile);
                                byte[] key = Crypto.generateKey↵
("randomtext".getBytes());
                                outputStream.write(encrypt(key,location.getBytes()));
                                outputStream.close();

                        } catch (FileNotFoundException e) {
                                Log.e(TAG,"File not found");
                        } catch (IOException e) {
                                Log.e(TAG,"IO Exception");
                        }

                } else {
                        Log.e(TAG,"Error opening media card in read/write mode!");
                }
        }
```

```
    private static boolean isReadOnly() {
        Log.e(TAG,Environment
                    .getExternalStorageState());
        return Environment.MEDIA_MOUNTED_READ_ONLY.equals(Environment
                    .getExternalStorageState());
    }

    private static boolean isReadWrite() {
        Log.e(TAG,Environment
                    .getExternalStorageState());

        return Environment.MEDIA_MOUNTED.equals(Environment
                    .getExternalStorageState());
    }

    private static byte[] encrypt(byte[] key, byte[] data){
        SecretKeySpec sKeySpec = new SecretKeySpec(key,"AES");
        Cipher cipher;
        byte[] ciphertext = null;
        try {
                cipher = Cipher.getInstance("AES");
                cipher.init(Cipher.ENCRYPT_MODE, sKeySpec);
                ciphertext = cipher.doFinal(data);
        } catch (NoSuchAlgorithmException e) {
                Log.e(TAG,"NoSuchAlgorithmException");
        } catch (NoSuchPaddingException e) {
                Log.e(TAG,"NoSuchPaddingException");
        } catch (IllegalBlockSizeException e) {
                Log.e(TAG,"IllegalBlockSizeException");
        } catch (BadPaddingException e) {
                Log.e(TAG,"BadPaddingException");
        } catch (InvalidKeyException e) {
                Log.e(TAG,"InvalidKeyException");
        }
        return ciphertext;

    }
}
```

Exercise

ADD ENCRYPTION AT OBJECT CREATION TIME

There are many ways to encrypt the data in our Proxim application. What I have done is to encrypt it at storage time. Your exercise is to rewrite the Proxim application so that the data is encrypted as soon as it is created.

Tip   Do not modify the SaveController.java file. Look elsewhere.

WRITE A DECRYPTION ROUTINE FOR THE PROXIM APPLICATION

Use the Android API reference and write a simple decryption routine based on the same principle as the encryption routine. Create a new class called `LoadController` that will handle the loading of information from the SD Card.

Summary

Storing plain text or other easily read data on mobile devices is something you should avoid doing at all costs. Even though your application itself might be written securely, an indirect attack that originates from a completely different area on the device can still collect and read sensitive or personal information written by your application. Follow the following basic steps during application design:

1. First, determine what data types are stored, created, or exchanged by your application. Next, classify them into personal or sensitive data, so that you will be aware of how to treat the data during application execution.

2. Have a collection of encryption routines that you can reuse in your applications. It is best to keep this collection as a separate library that you can include in your project.

3. Generate a different key for each application that you write. Write a good key-generator algorithm that creates lengthy and unpredictable secret keys.

4. Encrypt data either at creation or storage time.

## Chapter 3

Android Security Architecture

In Chapter 2, we looked at a simple example of how we can protect information using encryption. However, that example did not make use of Android's built-in security and permissions architecture. In this chapter, we will take a look at what Android is able to offer the developer and end user with regard to security. We will also look at some direct attacks that can take place on applications and how to take the necessary safeguards to minimize the loss of private data.

The Android platform has several mechanisms that control the security of the system and applications, and it attempts to ensure application isolation and compartmentalization at every stage. Each process within Android runs with its own set of privileges, and no other application is able to access this application or its data without explicit permissions provided by the end user. Even though Android exposes a large number of APIs to the developer, we cannot use all of these APIs without requiring the end user to grant access.

Revisiting the System Architecture

Let's start by looking at the Android architecture once more. We covered the Android system architecture in Chapter 1, where you will recall that each process runs in its own isolated environment. There is no interaction possible between applications unless otherwise explicitly permitted. One of the mechanisms where such interaction is possible is by using permissions. Again in Chapter 1, we looked at a simple example of how we needed to have the `RECORD_AUDIO` permission set, so that our application can make use of the device's microphone. In this chapter, we will look at the permissions architecture in a little bit more detail (see Figure 3-1).

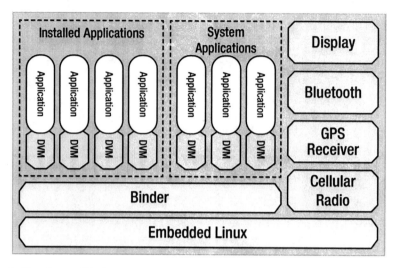

Figure 3-1. The Android system architecture

Figure 3-1 depicts a simpler version of the Android architecture than the one presented in Chapter 2; specifically, this figure focuses more on the applications themselves.

As we saw previously, Android applications will execute on the Dalvik virtual machine (DVM). The DVM is where the *bytecode*, or the most fundamental blocks of code, will execute. It is analogous to the Java Virtual Machine (JVM) that exists on personal computers and servers today. As depicted in Figure 3-1, each application—even a built-in system application—will execute in its own instance of the Dalvik VM. In other words, it operates inside a walled garden of sorts, with no outside interaction among other applications, unless explicitly permitted. Since starting up individual virtual machines can be time consuming and could increase the latency between application launch and startup, Android relies on a preloading mechanism to speed up the process. The process, known as Zygote, serves two functions: it acts first as a launch pad for new applications; and second, as a repository of live core libraries to which all applications can refer during their life cycles.

The Zygote process takes care of starting up a virtual machine instance and preloading and pre-initializing any core library classes that the virtual machine requires. Then, it waits to receive a signal for an application startup. The Zygote process is started up at boot time and works in a manner similar to a queue. Any Android device will always have one main Zygote process running. When the Android Activity Manager receives a command to start an application, it calls up the virtual machine instance that is part of the Zygote process. Once this instance is used to launch the application, a new one is forked to take its place. The next application that is started up will use this new Zygote process, and so on.

The repository part of the Zygote process will always make the set of core libraries available to applications throughout their life cycles. Figure 3-2 shows how multiple applications make use of the main Zygote process's repository of core libraries.

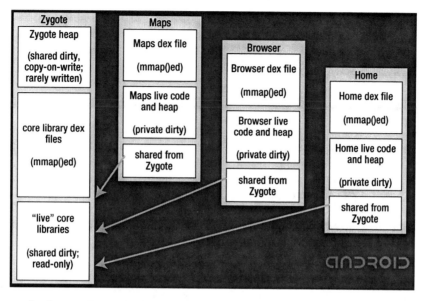

Figure 3-2. How applications use Zygote's repository of core libraries

Understanding the Permissions Architecture

As we discussed in Chapter 1, applications running on the Android operating system all run with their own set of user and group identifiers (UID and GID, respectively). The constrained manner in which applications execute make it impossible for one application to read or write data from another. To facilitate information sharing and interprocess communication among applications, Android uses a system of permissions.

By default, an application has no permissions to perform any types of activities that would cause damage or drastically impact other applications on the device. It also has no ability to interact with the Android operating system, nor can it call any of the protected APIs to use the camera, GPS, or networking stacks. Finally, a default application does not have the ability to read or write to any of the end user's data. The Linux kernel handles this task.

In order for an application to access high-privileged APIs or even gain access to user data, it has to obtain permission from the end user. You, as the developer, have to understand what permissions your application will require before you release it to the public. Once you make a list of all your required permissions, you will need to add each one of them to your AndroidManifest.xml file. Then, when installing an application for the first time, the end user is prompted by the device to grant or deny specific permissions as required by the application. Therefore, a good practice is to develop your application in a manner that will fail modularly if a user does not provide a specific permission. For example, let's say you've written an application that uses GPS Location inquiries, accesses user data, and sends SMS messages. The end user grants your application two of the three permissions, but leaves out SMS message sending. You should be able to write your application such that the functionality requiring SMS sending will disable itself (unless omitting this permission breaks your entire application). This way, the end user can still use your application with reduced functionality.

Before exploring permissions further, you need to familiarize yourself with a couple of topics that are used in the context of Android software development and security: *content providers* and *intents*. Although you most likely have heard these terms mentioned before, let's go over them here to make sure your understanding is complete.

Content Providers

Content providers are synonymous with data stores. They act as repositories of information from which applications can read and write. Since the Android architecture does not allow for a common storage area, content providers are the only way that applications can exchange data. As a developer, you might be interested in creating your own content providers, so that other applications can gain access to your data. This is as easy as subclassing the `ContentProvider` object in the `android.content` package. We will cover the creation of a custom `ContentProvider` objects in more detail in subsequent chapters of this book.

In addition to allowing the creation of your own content providers, Android provides several content providers that allow you to access the most common types of data on the device, including images, videos, audio files, and contact information. The Android provider package, `android.provider`, contains many convenience classes that allow you to access these content providers; Table 3-1 lists these.

Table 3-1. Content Provider Classes

Class Name	Description
AlarmClock	Contains an intent action and extras that can be used to start an activity to set a new alarm in an alarm clock application.
Browser	
Browser.BookmarkColumns	Column definitions for the mixed bookmark and history items available at BOOKMARKS_URI.
Browser.SearchColumns	Column definitions for the search history table, available at SEARCHES_URI.
CallLog	Contains information about placed and received calls.
CallLog.Calls	Contains the recent calls.
ContactsContract	The contract between the contacts provider and applications.
ContactsContract.AggregationExceptions	Constants for the contact aggregation exceptions table, which contains aggregation rules overriding those used by automatic aggregation.
ContactsContract.CommonDataKinds	Container for definitions of common data types stored in the ContactsContract.Data table.
ContactsContract.CommonDataKinds.Email	A data kind representing an e-mail address.
ContactsContract.CommonDataKinds.Event	A data kind representing an event.

(continued)

Table 3.1 (*continued*)

Class Name	Description
ContactsContract.CommonDataKinds. GroupMembership	Group membership.
ContactsContract.CommonDataKinds.Im	A data kind representing an IM address. You can use all columns defined for ContactsContract.Data, as well as the following aliases.
ContactsContract.CommonDataKinds.Nickname	A data kind representing the contact's nickname.
ContactsContract.CommonDataKinds.Note	Notes about the contact.
ContactsContract.CommonDataKinds.Organization	A data kind representing an organization.
ContactsContract.CommonDataKinds.Phone	A data kind representing a telephone number.
ContactsContract.CommonDataKinds.Photo	A data kind representing a photo for the contact.
ContactsContract.CommonDataKinds.Relation	A data kind representing a relation.
ContactsContract.CommonDataKinds.SipAddress	A data kind representing an SIP address for the contact.
ContactsContract.CommonDataKinds. StructuredName	A data kind representing the contact's proper name.
ContactsContract.CommonDataKinds. StructuredPostal	A data kind representing a postal address.
ContactsContract.CommonDataKinds.Website	A data kind representing a web site related to the contact.
ContactsContract.Contacts	Constants for the Contacts table, which contains a record per aggregate of raw contacts representing the same person.
ContactsContract.Contacts.AggregationSuggestions	A read-only subdirectory of a single contact aggregate that contains all aggregation suggestions (other contacts).
ContactsContract.Contacts.Data	A subdirectory of a single contact that contains all of the constituent raw contactContactsContract.Data rows
ContactsContract.Contacts.Entity	A subdirectory of a contact that contains all of its ContactsContract.RawContacts, as well as ContactsContract.Data rows.
ContactsContract.Contacts.Photo	A read-only subdirectory of a single contact that contains the contact's primary photo.
ContactsContract.Data	Constants for the data table that contains data points tied to a raw contact.
ContactsContract.Directory	Represents a group of contacts.
ContactsContract.Groups	Constants for the Groups table.

(*continued*)

Table 3.1 (*continued*)

Class Name	Description
ContactsContract.Intents	Contains helper classes used to create or manage intents that involve contacts.
ContactsContract.Intents.Insert	Convenience class that contains string constants used to create contact intents.
ContactsContract.PhoneLookup	Table that represents the result of looking up a phone number (e.g., for caller ID).
ContactsContract.QuickContact	Helper methods to display QuickContact dialogs that allow users to pivot on a specific Contacts entry.
ContactsContract.RawContacts	Constants for the raw contacts table, which contains one row of contact information for each person in each synced account.
ContactsContract.RawContacts.Data	A subdirectory of a single raw contact that contains all of its ContactsContract.Data rows.
ContactsContract.RawContacts.Entity	A subdirectory of a single raw contact that contains all of its ContactsContract.Data rows.
ContactsContract.RawContactsEntity	Constants for the raw contacts entities table, which can be thought of as an outer join of the raw_contacts table with the data table.
ContactsContract.Settings	Contact-specific settings for various Accounts.
ContactsContract.StatusUpdates	A status update is linked to a ContactsContract.Data row and captures the user's latest status update via the corresponding source.
ContactsContract.SyncState	A table provided for sync adapters to use for storing private sync state data.
LiveFolders	A LiveFolder is a special folder whose content is provided by a ContentProvider.
MediaStore	The Media provider contains meta data for all available media on both internal and external storage devices.
MediaStore.Audio	Container for all audio content.
MediaStore.Audio.Albums	Contains artists for audio files.
MediaStore.Audio.Artists	Contains artists for audio files.
MediaStore.Audio.Artists.Albums	Subdirectory of each artist containing all albums on which a song by the artist appears.
MediaStore.Audio.Genres	Contains all genres for audio files.
MediaStore.Audio.Genres.Members	Subdirectory of each genre containing all members.
MediaStore.Audio.Media	
MediaStore.Audio.Playlists	Contains playlists for audio files.

(*continued*)

Table 3.1 (*continued*)

Class Name	Description
MediaStore.Audio.Playlists.Members	Subdirectory of each playlist containing all members.
MediaStore.Files	Media provider table containing an index of all files in the media storage, including nonmedia files.
MediaStore.Images	Contains metadata for all available images.
MediaStore.Images.Media	
MediaStore.Images.Thumbnails	Allows developers to query and get two kinds of thumbnails: MINI_KIND (512 × 384 pixels) and MICRO_KIND (96 × 96 pixels).
MediaStore.Video	
MediaStore.Video.Media	
MediaStore.Video.Thumbnails	Allows developers to query and get two kinds of thumbnails: MINI_KIND (512 × 384 pixels) and MICRO_KIND (96 × 96 pixels).
SearchRecentSuggestions	A utility class providing access to SearchRecentSuggestionsProvider.
Settings	Contains global system-level device preferences.
Settings.NameValueTable	Common base for tables of name/value settings.
Settings.Secure	Secure system settings containing system preferences that applications can read, but are not allowed to write.
Settings.System	System settings containing miscellaneous system preferences.
SyncStateContract	The ContentProvider contract for associating data with any data array account.
SyncStateContract.Constants	
SyncStateContract.Helpers	
UserDictionary	A provider of user-defined words for input methods to use for predictive text input.
UserDictionary.Words	Contains the user-defined words.

Accessing a content provider requires prior knowledge of the following information:

- The content provider object (`Contacts`, `Photos`, `Videos`, etc.)
- The columns required from this content provider
- The query to fetch this information

As stated previously, content providers act in a similar manner to a Relational Database, such as Oracle, Microsoft SQL Server, or MySQL. This becomes evident when you first try to query one. For example, you access the `MediaStore.Images.Media` content provider to query for images.

Let's assume that we want to access each of the image names stored on the device. We first need to create a content provider URI to access the external store on the device:

```
Uri images = MediaStore.Images.Media.EXTERNAL_CONTENT_URI;
```

Next, we need to create a receiver object for the data we will be fetching. Simply declaring an array does this:

```
String[] details = new String[] {MediaStore.MediaColumns.DISPLAY_NAME};
```

To traverse the resulting dataset, we need to create and use a managedQuery and then use the resulting Cursor object to move through rows and columns:

```
Cursor cur = managedQuery(details,details, null, null null);
```

We can then iterate over the results using the Cursor object we created. We use the cur.moveToFirst() method to move to the first row and then read off the image name, like so:

```
String name = cur.getString(cur.getColumnIndex(MediaStore.MediaColumns.DISPLAY_NAME));
```

After that, we advance the cursor to the next record by calling the cur.moveToNext() method. To query multiple records, this process can be wrapped in either a for loop or do/while block.

Note that some content providers are controlled, and your application will need to request specific permissions before attempting to access them.

Intents

Intents are types of messages that one application sends to another to control tasks or transport data. Intents work with three specific types of application components: activity, service, and broadcast receiver. Let's take a simple example where your application requires the Android device browser to start up and load the contents of a URL. Some of the main components of an Intent object include the intent action and the intent data. For our example, we want our user to view the browser, so we will use the Intent.ACTION_VIEW constant to work with some data that is at the URL, http://www.apress.com. Our Intent object will be created like this:

```
Intent intent = new Intent(Intent.ACTION_VIEW, Uri.parse(http://www.apress.com);
```

To invoke this intent, we call this code:

```
startActivity(intent);
```

To control which applications can receive intents, a permission can be added to the intent prior to dispatching it.

Checking Permissions

We've very briefly covered content providers and intents, including how the Android operating system controls access to these objects through the use of permissions. In Chapter 1, we looked at how an application can request the end user for specific permissions to interact with the system. Let's look at how permission checks really take place and where.

A validation mechanism will handle permission checks within the Android operating system. When your application makes any API call, the permission validation mechanism will check if your application has the required permissions to complete the call. If a user grants permission, the API call is processed; otherwise, a SecurityException is thrown.

API calls are handled in three separate steps. First, the API library is invoked. Second, the library will invoke a private proxy interface that is part of the API library itself. Finally, this private proxy interface will use interprocess communication to query the service running in the system process to perform the required API call operation. This process is depicted in Figure 3-3.

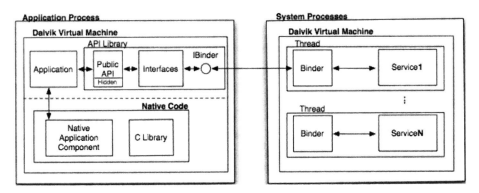

Figure 3-3. *The API call process*

In some instances, an application may also use native code to conduct API calls. These native API calls are also protected in a similar manner because they are not allowed to proceed unless they are called through Java wrapper methods. In other words, before a native API call can be invoked, it has to go through a wrapped Java API call that is then subject to the standard permission-validation mechanism. All validation of permissions is handled by the system process. Additionally, applications that require access to the BLUETOOTH, WRITE_EXTERNAL_STORAGE, and INTERNET permissions will be assigned to a Linux group that has access to the network sockets and files associated with those permissions. This small subset of permissions has its validation performed at the Linux kernel.

Using Self-Defined Permissions

Android allows developers to create and enforce their own permissions. As with system permissions, you need to declare specific tags and attributes within the AndroidManifest.xml file. If you write an application that provides a specific type of functionality accessible by other developers, you can choose to protect certain functions with your own custom permissions.

In your application's AndroidManifest.xml file, you have to define your permissions as follows:

```
<manifest xmlns:android="http://schemas.android.com/apk/res/android"
    package="net.zenconsult.mobile.testapp" >
    <permission android:name="net.zenconsult.mobile.testapp.permission.PURGE_DATABASE"
        android:label="@string/label_purgeDatabase"
        android:description="@string/description_purgeDatabase"
        android:protectionLevel="dangerous" />
    ...
</manifest>
```

You define the name of your permission in the android:name attribute. The android:label and android:description attributes are required. They are pointers to strings that you define in your AndroidManifest.xml file. The strings will identify what the permission is and describe what this permission does to end users that browse the list of permissions present on the device. You will want to set these strings with something descriptive, as in this example:

```
<string name=" label_purgeDatabase ">purge the application database </string>
<string name="permdesc_callPhone">Allows the application to purge the core database of
the information store. Malicious applications may be able to wipe your entire application
information store.</string>
```

The android:protectionLevel attribute is required. It categorizes the permission into one of the four levels of protection discussed earlier.

Optionally, you can also add an android:permissionGroup attribute to have Android group your permission along with either the system groups or with groups you have defined yourself. Grouping your custom permission with an already existing permissions group is best because this way, you can present a cleaner interface to the end user when browsing permissions. For example, to add the purgeDatabase permission into the group that accesses the SD card, you would add the following attribute to the AndroidManifest.xml file:

```
android:permissionGroup=" android.permission-group.STORAGE"
```

One thing to note is that your application will need to be installed on the device before any other dependent application. This is usually the case; but during development, it bears remembering because you may run into difficulties if the application is not installed first.

Protection Levels

When creating your own permissions, you have the option of categorizing the permission according to the level of protection you want the operating system to offer. In our preceding example, we defined the protectionLevel of our permission to purge the database as "dangerous". The "dangerous" protection level indicates that, by granting this permission, the end user will enable an application to modify private user data in a way that could adversely affect him.

A permission marked with protectionLevel "dangerous" or higher will automatically trigger the operating system to prompt or notify the end user. This behavior exists to let the end user know that the application being executed has the potential to cause harm. It also offers the user a chance to either signify trust or mistrust in the application by granting or denying permission to the requested API call. Descriptions of the permission protection levels are provided in Table 3-2.

Table 3-2. Permission Protection Levels

Constant	Value	Description
normal	0	A somewhat low-risk permission that gives an application access to isolated application-level features, with minimal risk to other applications, the system, or the user. The system automatically grants this type of permission to a requesting application at installation, without asking for the user's explicit approval (though the user always has the option to review these permissions before installing).
dangerous	1	A higher risk permission that gives a requesting application access to private user data or control over the device in a way that can negatively impact the user. Because this type of permission introduces potential risk, the system may not automatically grant it to the requesting application. Any dangerous permissions requested by an application may be displayed to the user and require confirmation before proceeding, or some other approach may be taken so the user can avoid automatically allowing the use of such facilities.
signature	2	The system will grant this permission only if the requesting application is signed with the same certificate as the application that declared the permission. If the certificates match, the system automatically grants the permission without notifying the user or asking for the user's explicit approval.
signatureOrSystem	3	The system grants this permission only to packages in the Android system image or that are signed with the same certificates. Please avoid using this option because the signature protection level should be sufficient for most needs, and it works regardless of exactly where applications are installed. This permission is used for certain special situations where multiple vendors have applications built into a system image, and these applications need to share specific features explicitly because they are being built together.

Sample Code for Custom Permissions

The sample code in this section provides concrete examples of how to implement custom permissions in an Android application. The project package and class structure is depicted in Figure 3-4.

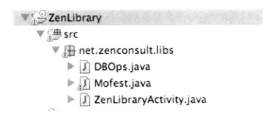

Figure 3-4. The structure and classes of the example

The `Mofest.java` file contains a nested class called permissions that holds the permission string constants that will be invoked by calling applications. The source code is in Listing 3-1.

Listing 3-1. The Mofest Class

```java
package net.zenconsult.libs;

public class Mofest {
            public Mofest(){

            }

            public class permission {
                        public permission(){
                                    final String PURGE_DATABASE =↵
    "net.zenconsult.libs.Mofest.permission.PURGE_DATABASE";
                        }
            }
}
```

At this point, the `DBOps.java` file is of no consequence because it contains no code. The `ZenLibraryActivity.java` file contains our application's entry point. Its source code is given in Listing 3-2.

Listing 3-2. The ZenLibraryActivity Class

```java
package net.zenconsult.libs;

import android.app.Activity;
import android.os.Bundle;

public class ZenLibraryActivity extends Activity {
        /** Called when the activity is first created. */
    @Override
    public void onCreate(Bundle savedInstanceState) {
        super.onCreate(savedInstanceState);
        setContentView(R.layout.main);

    }
}
```

Again, this class does nothing remarkable; it starts up the main activity of this application. The real changes lie in the `AndroidManifest.xml` file of this project, which is shown in Listing 3-3. This is where the permissions are defined and used.

Listing 3-3. The Project's AndroidManifest.xml File

```xml
<?xml version="1.0" encoding="utf-8"?>
<manifest xmlns:android="http://schemas.android.com/apk/res/android"
     package="net.zenconsult.libs"
     android:versionCode="1"
     android:versionName="1.0">
    <uses-sdk android:minSdkVersion="10" />
    <permission android:name="net.zenconsult.libs.Mofest.permission.PURGE_DATABASE"
           android:protectionLevel="dangerous"
           android:label="@string/label_purgeDatabase"
           android:description="@string/description_purgeDatabase"
           android:permissionGroup="android.permission-group.COST_MONEY"/>
    <uses-permission android:name="net.zenconsult.libs.Mofest.permission↵
.PURGE_DATABASE" />
    <uses-permission android:name="android.permission.SET_WALLPAPER" />

    <application android:icon="@drawable/icon" android:label="@string/app_name">
        <activity android:name=".ZenLibraryActivity"
          android:permission="net.zenconsult.libs.Mofest.permission↵
.PURGE_DATABASE"
           android:label="@string/app_name"


        >
          <intent-filter>
           <action android:name="android.intent.action.MAIN" />
           <category android:name="android.intent.category.LAUNCHER" />
          </intent-filter>
        </activity>
    </application>
</manifest>
```

As you can see, we both declare and use the PURGE_DATABASE permission in this application. The code that is in bold all pertains to our custom permission implementation for this application.

To ensure that the installer will prompt for a permission request screen, you have to build the project as an .apk file and sign it. Next, upload the .apk file to a web server or copy it to the device. Clicking this file will start the installation process; and at that time, the device will display the request for permissions screen to the end user. Figure 3-5 shows what this screen looks like.

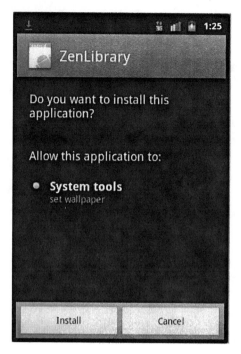

Figure 3-5. The permissions request screen

Summary

In this chapter, we looked at Android permissions, both built-in and custom. We also examined intents, content providers, and how to check permissions in more detail. The key points discussed were as follows:

- Android has a core set of mechanisms that handle application isolation and security.

- Each application will run in its own isolated space with unique user and group identifiers.

- Applications are not allowed to exchange data unless they explicitly request permissions from the user.

- Content providers store and allow access to data. They behave similar to databases.

- Intents are messages sent between applications or the system process to invoke or shut down another service or application.

▨ Access to specific APIs is controlled using permissions. Permissions are divided into four categories, and category 1, 2, and 3 permissions will always notify or prompt the end user. Since these permissions have the ability to adversely affect user data and experience, they are handed over to the user for final confirmation.

Custom permissions can be created to protect your individual applications. An application that wishes to use your application will need to explicitly request your ermission to do so by using the `<uses-permission>` tag in the `AndroidManifest.xml` file.

4

Concepts in Action – Part 1

In this chapter, we will merge together all the topics we discussed in the previous chapters. If you recall, we discussed the Proxim application, through which we looked at data encryption. We will analyze its source code in detail here. We will also work through some examples of applications that require and use permissions.

The Proxim Application

The Proxim project should have a structure similar to that depicted in Figure 4-1

Let's start with the Activity, which is where your programs usually will start (see Listing 4-1). In the Activity, we are creating a new `Contact` object with some information inside.

Listing 4-1. The Main Activity

```
package net.zenconsult.android;

import net.zenconsult.android.controller.SaveController;
import net.zenconsult.android.model.Contact;
import android.app.Activity;
import android.os.Bundle;
import android.view.View;
import android.view.View.OnClickListener;
import android.widget.Button;

public class ProximActivity extends Activity {
    /** Called when the activity is first created. */
    @Override
    public void onCreate(Bundle savedInstanceState) {
        super.onCreate(savedInstanceState);
        setContentView(R.layout.main);
```

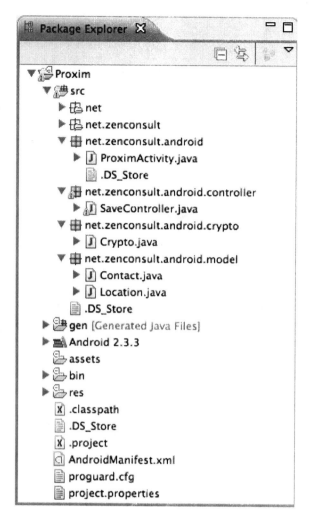

Figure 4-1. The Proxim Application structure

```
        final Contact contact = new Contact();
        contact.setFirstName("Sheran");
        contact.setLastName("Gunasekera");
        contact.setAddress1("");
        contact.setAddress2("");
        contact.setEmail("sheran@zenconsult.net");
        contact.setPhone("12120031337");
    final Button button = (Button) findViewById(R.id.button1);
        button.setOnClickListener(new OnClickListener() {
            public void onClick(View v) {
                SaveController.saveContact(getApplicationContext(), contact);
            }
        });
    }
}
```

It is this line that creates a **Contact** object:

```
Contact contact = new Contact();
```

Subsequent lines that have set in the start of the method name simply add the relevant pieces of data into the Contact object. To understand what the Contact object looks like, take a look at Listing 4-2. As you can see, the object itself is very simple. It has a collection of *getters* and *setters* that will retrieve and insert data, respectively. Consider the firstName variable. To add a person's first name to this object, you call the setFirstName() method and pass in a value like Sheran (as shown in the main Activity).

Listing 4-2. The Proxim Application's Contact Object

```
package net.zenconsult.android.model;

public class Contact {
    private String firstName;
    private String lastName;
    private String address1;
    private String address2;
    private String email;
    private String phone;

    public Contact() {

    }

    public String getFirstName() {
        return firstName;
    }

    public void setFirstName(String firstName) {
        this.firstName = firstName;
    }

    public String getLastName() {
        return lastName;
    }

    public void setLastName(String lastName) {
        this.lastName = lastName;
    }

    public String getAddress1() {
        return address1;
    }

    public void setAddress1(String address1) {
        this.address1 = address1;
    }

    public String getAddress2() {
        return address2;
    }

    public void setAddress2(String address2) {
        this.address2 = address2;
    }
```

```java
    public String getEmail() {
        return email;
    }

    public void setEmail(String email) {
        this.email = email;
    }

    public String getPhone() {
        return phone;
    }

    public void setPhone(String phone) {
        this.phone = phone;
    }

    public String toString() {
        StringBuilder ret = new StringBuilder();
        ret.append(getFirstName()+"|");
        ret.append(getLastName()+"|");
        ret.append(getAddress1()+"|");
        ret.append(getAddress2()+"|");
        ret.append(getEmail()+"|");
        ret.append(getPhone()+"|");
        return ret.toString();
    }

    public byte[] getBytes() {
        return toString().getBytes();
    }
}
```

Since we're covering the data storage objects (or the *Model* in *Model-View-Controller* programming concepts), let's also look at our `Location` object in Listing 4-3. This is, once again, your average, everyday, straightforward `Location` object with getters and setters.

Listing 4-3. The Location Object

```java
package net.zenconsult.android.model;

public class Location {
    private String identifier;
    private double latitude;
    private double longitude;

    public Location() {

    }

    public double getLatitude() {
        return latitude;
    }
```

```java
    public void setLatitude(double latitude) {
        this.latitude = latitude;
    }

    public double getLongitude() {
        return longitude;
    }

    public void setLongitude(double longitude) {
        this.longitude = longitude;
    }

    public void setIdentifier(String identifier) {
        this.identifier = identifier;
    }

    public String getIdentifier() {
        return identifier;
    }

    public String toString() {
        StringBuilder ret = new StringBuilder();
        ret.append(getIdentifier());
        ret.append(String.valueOf(getLatitude()));
        ret.append(String.valueOf(getLongitude()));
        return ret.toString();
    }

    public byte[] getBytes() {
        return toString().getBytes();
    }
}
```

Excellent! We've got that out of the way, so now let's look more closely at our save controller and our cryptography routines. We can see these in Listings 4-4 and 4-5, respectively.

Listing 4-4. The Save Controller

```java
package net.zenconsult.android.controller;

import java.io.File;
import java.io.FileNotFoundException;
import java.io.FileOutputStream;
import java.io.IOException;
import java.security.InvalidKeyException;
import java.security.NoSuchAlgorithmException;

import javax.crypto.BadPaddingException;
import javax.crypto.Cipher;
import javax.crypto.IllegalBlockSizeException;
import javax.crypto.NoSuchPaddingException;
import javax.crypto.spec.SecretKeySpec;

import net.zenconsult.android.crypto.Crypto;
import net.zenconsult.android.model.Contact;
import net.zenconsult.android.model.Location;
```

```java
import android.content.Context;
import android.os.Environment;
import android.util.Log;

public class SaveController {
    private static final String TAG = "SaveController";

    public static void saveContact(Context context, Contact contact) {
        if (isReadWrite()) {
            try {
                File outputFile = new File(context.getExternalFilesDir(null),contact.
getFirstName());
                FileOutputStream outputStream = new FileOutputStream(outputFile);
                byte[] key = Crypto.generateKey("randomtext".getBytes());
                outputStream.write(encrypt(key,contact.getBytes()));
                outputStream.close();

            } catch (FileNotFoundException e) {
                Log.e(TAG,"File not found");
            } catch (IOException e) {
                Log.e(TAG,"IO Exception");
            }

        } else {
            Log.e(TAG,"Error opening media card in read/write mode!");
        }
    }

    public static void saveLocation(Context context, Location location) {
        if (isReadWrite()) {
            try {
                File outputFile = new File(context.getExternalFilesDir(null),location.
getIdentifier());
                FileOutputStream outputStream = new FileOutputStream(outputFile);
                byte[] key = Crypto.generateKey("randomtext".getBytes());
                outputStream.write(encrypt(key,location.getBytes()));
                outputStream.close();

            } catch (FileNotFoundException e) {
                Log.e(TAG,"File not found");
            } catch (IOException e) {
                Log.e(TAG,"IO Exception");
            }

        } else {
            Log.e(TAG,"Error opening media card in read/write mode!");
        }
    }

    private static boolean isReadOnly() {
        Log.e(TAG,Environment
                .getExternalStorageState());
        return Environment.MEDIA_MOUNTED_READ_ONLY.equals(Environment
                .getExternalStorageState());
    }
```

```java
    private static boolean isReadWrite() {
        Log.e(TAG,Environment
                .getExternalStorageState());

        return Environment.MEDIA_MOUNTED.equals(Environment
                .getExternalStorageState());
    }

    private static byte[] encrypt(byte[] key, byte[] data){
        SecretKeySpec sKeySpec = new SecretKeySpec(key,"AES");
        Cipher cipher;
        byte[] ciphertext = null;
        try {
            cipher = Cipher.getInstance("AES");
            cipher.init(Cipher.ENCRYPT_MODE, sKeySpec);
            ciphertext = cipher.doFinal(data);
        } catch (NoSuchAlgorithmException e) {
            Log.e(TAG,"NoSuchAlgorithmException");
        } catch (NoSuchPaddingException e) {
            Log.e(TAG,"NoSuchPaddingException");
        } catch (IllegalBlockSizeException e) {
            Log.e(TAG,"IllegalBlockSizeException");
        } catch (BadPaddingException e) {
            Log.e(TAG,"BadPaddingException");
        } catch (InvalidKeyException e) {
            Log.e(TAG,"InvalidKeyException");
        }
        return ciphertext;

    }
}
```

Listing 4-5. The Cryptography routine

```java
package net.zenconsult.android.crypto;

import java.security.NoSuchAlgorithmException;
import java.security.SecureRandom;

import javax.crypto.KeyGenerator;
import javax.crypto.SecretKey;

import android.util.Log;

public class Crypto {
    private static final String TAG = "Crypto";

    public Crypto() {
    }

    public static byte[] generateKey(byte[] randomNumberSeed) {
        SecretKey sKey = null;
        try {
            KeyGenerator keyGen = KeyGenerator.getInstance("AES");
            SecureRandom random = SecureRandom.getInstance("SHA1PRNG");
            random.setSeed(randomNumberSeed);
            keyGen.init(256,random);
```

```
            sKey = keyGen.generateKey();
        } catch (NoSuchAlgorithmException e) {
            Log.e(TAG,"No such algorithm exception");
        }
        return sKey.getEncoded();
    }
}
```

Summary

In this chapter, we've looked at two key concepts that we covered in prior chapters: encrypting data before storing it and using permissions in your application. Specifically, we looked at two applications that incorporate these concepts and studied the various outcomes of running each application with different parameters. The concept of data encryption may be fairly straightforward to grasp, but the topic of Android application permissions may not be immediately apparent. In most cases, the permissions you require have to do with accessing various features on the device itself. An example of this is in connectivity. If your app needs to communicate with the Internet, then you need the Internet permission. Our example application deals more with creating and using custom application permissions. Let's now move on to addressing encryption of data in transit and talking to web applications.

## Chapter 5

Data Storage
and Cryptography

We touched on cryptography very briefly in Chapter 4. This chapter will focus more on the importance of using cryptography to obfuscate and secure user data that you will either store or transport. First, we will cover the basics of cryptography and how they apply to us in the context of application development. Next, we will look at the various mechanisms of storing data on the Android platform. Along the way, I will give examples of how to store and retrieve data from different mechanisms and outline what function each store is ideally suited to perform.

One very important point to keep in mind is you should *never* attempt to write your own cryptographic routines unless you are familiar with cryptographic topics. I have seen many developers try to do this and end up with vulnerable applications both on mobile devices and in web applications. Cryptography is a vast subject by itself; and, in my opinion, I think it is best left to the folks who dedicate their lives to the subject. As an application developer, you will only be interested in a specific subset of topics in cryptography.

I won't cover the history of cryptography. You only need to keep one thing in mind: make your sensitive user data unreadable to unauthorized users. If an attacker compromises your application using either an indirect or direct attack, then your additional layer (see Figure 5-1) of cryptography will not make it trivial for him to steal the sensitive user data. Instead, he has an additional layer that he has to attack. This principle is similar to the Information Assurance principle of Defense in Depth that the US National Security Agency developed.

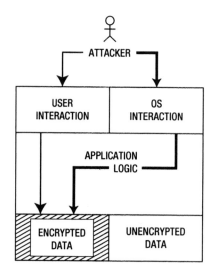

Figure 5-1. An example of the Defense in Depth principle

Public Key Infrastructure

Since we're on the subject of cryptography, it is worthwhile learning a bit about Public Key Infrastructure (PKI). PKI is based on the principle of identity and trust verification based on a trusted third party. Let's examine a scenario that illustrates the principles involved. Bear in mind that this example has nothing to do with application development *for the moment*. We will look at that subject in depth soon enough.

Mr. Krabs owns Krusty Krab, one of the most popular fast food restaurants in the city. He credits his famous Krabby Patty (a wonderfully moist, delicious burger) with the reason for its popularity. No one except Mr. Krabs knows the Krabby Patty's super-secret recipe. Given his popularity, he recently started selling franchises to his restaurant. As most of the new branches under his franchise will be geographically distant, Mr. Krabs decides to dispatch his secret recipe to the owners via courier. The only problem with this approach is that Mr. Krabs's rival, Sheldon James Plankton, has attempted to steal his secret recipe before, and it is likely that he will try again.

I love food, especially burgers, so I decide to open a Krusty Krab franchise in my city. I contact Mr. Krabs; and along with the relevant paperwork, he attaches a document on how I should receive and safeguard his secret Krabby Patty recipe. I'll spare you the countless pages of details and legalese, and instead list only the most salient points. The instructions state that I am to do the following:

1.   Register myself at the nearest police department under the KK program through the IV department.

2.   Receive one padlock with one key that opens the padlock from the police department's IV department.

3.   Give the padlock to my police department.

4.   Guard the key with my life.

5.   Receive and open the steel box that will be sent to me via courier.

Sure enough, after I complete these steps, a package arrives in the mail. Oddly, the outer cardboard packaging seems tampered with, but not the padlock or the solid steel box inside. The key opens the padlock easily and viola! I have the secret Krabby Patty recipe. Later, I hear from Mr. Krabs that Plankton had attempted to hijack and open the steel box, but failed. This explains the outer package tampering that I noticed.

To spare you from more of my idiocy, I'm going to correlate characters and objects in this story to elements associated with PKI (see Table 5-1).

Table 5-1. *The Relationship Between the Story and PKI*

Story Element	PKI Element
Mr. Krabs	The message sender
Me	The message receiver
Plankton	The attacker
The secret recipe	The message/sensitive data
The steel box	The encrypted message
My padlock	My public key
The key to my padlock	My private key
The police department	The Certificate Authority (CA)
The KK program	The CA domain
The IV department	The Registration Authority (RA)

When you look at Table 5-1, it is immediately evident that the setup and running of a PKI is quite complex. All of the elements are essential, however, and serve a very specific purpose to ensure the exchange of messages *and* keys in a secure and trustworthy manner. Let's analyze each element.

- *Mr. Krabs and I:* These are the sender and receiver, respectively. We need to exchange sensitive data (the secret recipe) and follow PKI policies and procedures to do so.

- *Plankton:* He is the attacker. He wants access to the sensitive data and decides to attack it in transit.

- *Secret recipe:* This is the sensitive data. We want to exchange this recipe and keep it private.

- *The steel box:* This is the encrypted message. The sender will encrypt it or lock it so that only the key holder can open it. The key holder (me) is the receiver.

- *My padlock:* This is my public key. When you consider the story, you might wonder how a padlock can also be a key, but look at it from a metaphorical sense. My padlock is something anyone can use to lock or encrypt a message. I am not afraid to give anyone my padlock or public key because only I can open the message. I can have an unlimited number of padlocks to give out to anyone who wants to send me a message securely.

- *The key to my padlock:* This is my private key. It is private because no one else has a copy. Only I am able to open my padlocks with this key. I have to safeguard this key at all times because if an attacker gains access to this key, then he can open all the steel boxes locked with my padlock, thereby gaining access to the sensitive data.

- *The police department:* This is the Certificate Authority (CA). One of the fundamental components of a PKI, the CA is the equivalent of a trusted third party. Both Mr. Krabs and I trust our local police departments, and thus they make good candidates for the CA. We rely on them to uphold the law and act with integrity. Therefore, even if somebody who I don't know or have never met wants to send me a secure message, I don't have to worry about trusting the person. I only have to trust the authority that tells me the person is who he says he is.

- *The KK program:* For our story, this is the CA domain. For instance, the police department or CA may be able to act as the trusted third party for many different scenarios. The CA domain will ensure that all transactions occur within the same context. The KK program therefore exists only to deal with Mr. Krabs's franchise.

- *The IV department:* This is our Registration Authority (RA). If a person wants to send or receive secure messages, he first has to register himself with the RA. The RA will require that you prove your identity with an officially issued document, such as a national identification card or a passport. The RA will determine the authenticity of this document and may possibly use other means to decide if the person is who he says he is. On satisfactorily meeting the RA's registration requirements, the person is registered and given a public and private key.

One question that you might have is this: how do two police departments in two separate cities, or even countries, trust each other? We will assume that all police departments establish trust through an internal mechanism to a degree in which many departments can act as one entity.

So to summarize, both Mr. Krabs and I will use a trusted third party to make sure we avoid sending or receiving messages to impostors. So what about attacking this system? There are two key ways to attack this system: 1) The attacker can try to trick the registration process and hijack the identity of a legitimate user, and 2) the attacker can try to conduct a physical attack of the encrypted message while in transit.

The benefit of this infrastructure is that if Plankton tries to impersonate Mr. Krabs or me, he has to do so by tricking the registration process of the CA. In many cases, this is very difficult to accomplish because of the proof of identity stage. To mitigate physical attacks of the message in transit, the system employs strong, unbreakable locks. These locks are the cryptographic encryption algorithms that are used.

Terms Used in Cryptography

I would like to acknowledge Bruce Schneier and his book *Applied Cryptography* (John Wiley & Sons, 1996) in this chapter. I have referred to it on many occasions, including when writing this book. It provides an excellent grounding in the subject of cryptography and is very comprehensive. If you want to gain a more in-depth understanding of cryptography, then I highly recommend this book.

It is essential to learn the correct terminology in cryptography. Without learning the correct terminology, you can still master cryptography, but probably at a slower pace. Table 5-2 lists the terms used in cryptography in the context of writing and securing your own applications.

Table 5-2. Terms Used in Cryptography

Term	Description
Plaintext/cleartext	This is your message. It is the text file you write, the user data you store, or the raw message that you wish to protect from prying eyes. It is generally readable by everyone.
Encryption	This process is used to take plaintext and render it unreadable or obfuscated.
Ciphertext	This is the result of encrypting plaintext. This is the encrypted message.
Decryption	This is the reverse of encryption. It is the process by which you turn obfuscated ciphertext back into readable plaintext.
Cryptographic algorithm/ algorithm/cipher	This is the specific type of mathematical function that is used to encrypt and decrypt plaintext.
Key	This value will uniquely affect the encryption or decryption algorithm in use. There can be separate keys for encryption or decryption. Most commonly used algorithms depend on a key to work.
Shared key/Symmetric key	This is one key that both encrypts and decrypts data. The sender and receiver both have this key; hence, it is defined as a shared key.
Asymmetric key	This is when there is one key for encryption and another for decryption. You can use this type of key to encrypt data to a specific person. All you need to do is encrypt the data using the person's public key and he can then decrypt it using his private key. Therefore, there is a one key for encryption (public key) and another for decryption (private key).
Cryptanalysis	This refers to the study of breaking ciphertext without having prior knowledge of the key or algorithm.

Cryptography in Mobile Applications

Implementing PKI for general, every day applications seems like overkill, especially when you consider the amount of work and complexity involved. When you consider mobile applications, you're faced with an even tougher task due to the limited resources available. It is possible to do, however, and a paper detailing the theory of Lightweight PKI in mobile environments (LPKI) was presented at the 11th IEEE Singapore International Conference held at Singapore in 2008 (http://ieeexplore.ieee.org/xpl/freeabs_all.jsp?arnumber=4737164).

But we will not be using PKI or LPKI in any of our applications. Instead, we will try to strike a balance and use techniques from cryptography in a manner that suits the limited resources of a mobile computing environment. So let's examine how we want cryptography to fit in with our application. As I've mentioned in previous chapters, protecting your user data is critical. If you look back at the example in Chapter 2 with the Contact Object encryption, can you identify what type of key we used? We used the *Advanced Encryption Standard* (AES) algorithm. This is a symmetric key algorithm because there is only one key for both encryption and decryption. If you look closely, you will begin to question my sanity for using a random 256-bit key. One question you might ask is, how do we decrypt data if we just used a random key to encrypt the data in the first place? I'm hoping you answered this question in the exercise at the end of Chapter 2. If you haven't, then let's go ahead and tackle that now.

Symmetric Key Algorithms

AES is a symmetric key algorithm or block cipher. As we saw, this means that there is only one key used in encryption and decryption. Algorithms work to encrypt or decrypt data. How this data is processed gives rise to a further division of symmetric algorithms. For instance, we can process a fixed number of data bits at a time, known as a block of data; or we can process data one bit at a time, known as a stream. This distinction gives us block ciphers and stream ciphers. Generally, AES is considered a block cipher that operates on groups of data 128 bits long. A block of plaintext 128 bits long will have a resulting block of ciphertext of the same length. AES allows for a key size from 0 to 256 bits. In our example, we used the maximum key size. For this book, I will use of the AES block cipher. I've included some other notable block ciphers in Table 5-3 that come packaged with Android. The principle for generating keys for the other block ciphers remains the same as in Listing 5-1, shown in the next section. Simply substitute the algorithm name in the KeyGenerator.getInstance() method from AES to one of the block ciphers listed in the table.

Table 5-3. Block Ciphers that Can Be Used in Android 2.3.3

Block Cipher	Block Size	Key Size (in bits)
AES	128 bit	0–256
Camellia	128 bit	128, 192, 256
Blowfish	64 bit	0–448
Twofish	128 bit	128, 192, 256

Key Generation

A key is an integral part of cryptography. Most modern cryptographic algorithms require a key to work correctly. In our example in Chapter 2, I used a pseudo-random number generator (PRNG) to generate our encryption key (see Listing 5-1). A good rule of thumb that I use is to always pick the maximum key size of an algorithm. If I find that my application is severely lagging when I test it, then I reduce my key size to the next smaller one. In cryptography, you will always want to use the largest possible key size for your algorithm. The reason for this is to make it harder to perform brute-force attacks on your key.

To illustrate, let's suppose you picked a key size of 16 bits. This means an attacker has to try a combination of 1s and 0s a total of 2^{16} or 65,536 times. If, however, you picked the full 256-bit key size, then the attacker has to make 2^{256} or 11.6^{77} (1.16e77) attempts to crack your key, which will take him several years to achieve. Of course, this duration can be reduced with the progression of computing power, but this is true in all areas of cryptanalysis. Thus, the large key sizes and strong algorithms ensure that an attacker cannot easily compromise your ciphertext.

In most cases, encrypted data acts as a deterrent to attackers who are after the low-hanging fruit. Rather than spending time breaking your cryptography, they will move onto the next easy-to-attack application–assuming, of course, that the value of your data does not exceed the value of time, effort, and resources your attacker is willing to invest in breaking your cryptography.

> **Note**   A brute-force attack on a key or password occurs when an attacker keeps trying to guess the correct password by sequentially creating and trying passwords based on combinations of different character sets such as A–Z, a–z, 0–9, and special characters. Eventually, in the course of trying all possible combinations, she is likely to guess the correct password.

I know a few developers who still believe that an encryption key is equivalent to a password. It is not. Well, not strictly. In our key generation example, we use a random 256-bit key. Generally, these encryption routines all take place behind the scenes; and although user passwords can be turned into keys, I don't advise doing this. One reason to avoid doing this is that user passwords are almost always no greater than 10 to 12 bytes, and this does not even cover half the key length (256 / 8 = 32 bytes). Given what we know about brute-force attacks, it is better to pick the maximum allowable key length.

Listing 5-1. A Key Generation Algorithm

```java
public static byte[] generateKey(byte[] randomNumberSeed) {
            SecretKey sKey = null;
            try {
                    KeyGenerator keyGen = KeyGenerator.getInstance("AES");
                    SecureRandom random = SecureRandom.getInstance("SHA1PRNG");
                    random.setSeed(randomNumberSeed);
                    keyGen.init(256, random);
                    sKey = keyGen.generateKey();
            } catch (NoSuchAlgorithmException e) {
                    Log.e(TAG, "No such algorithm exception");
            }
            return sKey.getEncoded();
    }
```

Data Padding

So far, I've talked about symmetric algorithms processing a fixed block size of data. However, what about the situation that occurs when your data is less than the input block size required by the algorithm? Consider the case in Figure 5-2. Here, we have two blocks of data, but only one of them contains the full block size (we will use an 8-byte block size to simplify things); the second one contains only 4 bits. If we ran this last block through our AES algorithm, it would fail. To counter situations like this, there are several different padding options available.

```
Offset  | 00 01 02 03 04 05 06 07 | 00 01 02 03 04 05 06 07 |
Data    | 41 42 43 44 45 46 47 48 | 49 50 51 52             |
```

Figure 5-2. *Two blocks of data without proper alignment*

Possibly one of your first thoughts when you encounter the situation in Figure 5-2 is to pad the remaining 4 bits with zeros. This is possible and is known as *Zero Padding*. Other different padding options exist. I won't go into too much detail at this point, but you will need to keep in mind that you can't simply take plaintext and run it through a block cipher. Block ciphers always work with a fixed input block size and will always have a fixed output block size. Figures 5-3 and 5-4 show examples of Zero Padding and PKCS5/7 Padding.

```
Offset  | 00 01 02 03 04 05 06 07 | 00 01 02 03 04 05 06 07 |
Data    | 41 42 43 44 45 46 47 48 | 49 50 51 52 00 00 00 00 |
```

Figure 5-3. *Two blocks of data with Zero Padding. Padding is in bold.*

```
Offset  | 00 01 02 03 04 05 06 07 | 00 01 02 03 04 05 06 07 |
Data    | 41 42 43 44 45 46 47 48 | 49 50 51 52 04 04 04 04 |
```

Figure 5-4. *Two blocks of data with PKCS5/7 Padding. Padding is in bold.*

> **Note** *PKCS5/7 Padding* is when you take the length of the remaining bits you need to pad and use that as the pad bit. For example, if there are 10 bits left to pad the block to the correct size, then the pad bit is 0A (which is 10 in hexadecimal). Similarly, if there were 28 bits to pad, then the padding bit would be 1C.

My example in Chapter 2 does not specify any padding. By default, Android will use PKCS5 Padding.

Modes of Operation for Block Ciphers

Block ciphers have various mechanisms of encryption and decryption. The simplest form of encryption is when one block of plaintext is encrypted to provide one block of ciphertext. The next block of plaintext is then encrypted to give the next block of ciphertext, and so on. This is known as the Electronic Code Book (ECB) mode. Figure 5-5 shows a visual representation of ECB encryption.

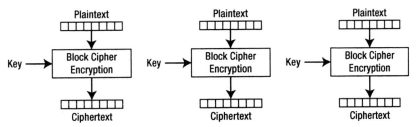

Electronic Codebook (ECB) mode encryption

Figure 5-5. *ECB encryption (courtesy Wikipedia)*

Although simple, ECB mode offers no protection against a pattern recognition cryptanalysis. This means that if the message text contains two identical plaintext blocks, then there will also be two corresponding ciphertext blocks. When conducting a cryptanalysis, one of the techniques used is to identify and locate patterns within ciphertext. After patterns are identified, it can be significantly easier to deduce that ECB encryption is used and, thus, an attacker only needs to focus on decrypting a specific block of the ciphertext. He need not decrypt the entire message.

To prevent this, there are several other modes of operation for block ciphers: *1)* cipher-block chaining (CBC), *2)* propagating cipher-block chaining (PCBC), *3)* cipher feedback (CFB), and *4)* output feedback (OFB). I cover only the encryption routines in this section (simply reverse the steps in the encryption mode to get the decryption routines):

▪ *CBC mode:* Cipher-block chaining mode (see Figure 5-6) uses an additional value known as an *initialization vector* (IV) that is used to perform a XOR operation on the first block of plaintext. After this, each resulting ciphertext block is XORd with the next plaintext block, and so on. This type of mode ensures that each resulting ciphertext block is dependent on the previous plaintext block.

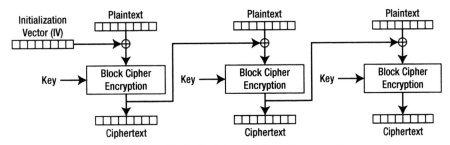

Cipher Block Chaining (CBC) mode encryption

Figure 5-6. *CBC encryption (courtesy Wikipedia)*

- *PCBC mode:* Propagating cipher-block chaining mode (see Figure 5-7) is very similar to CBC mode. The difference is that, instead of only XORing the IV for the first block and the ciphertext for subsequent blocks, PCBC mode XORs the IV *and* the ciphertext for the first block and then plaintext *and* ciphertext for additional blocks. The design of this mode is such that a small change in the ciphertext propagates throughout the encryption or decryption process.

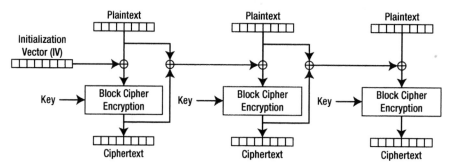

Propagating Cipher Block Chaining (PCBC) mode encryption

Figure 5-7. PCBC encryption (courtesy Wikipedia)

- *CFB mode:* Cipher feedback mode (see Figure 5-8) switches places between the IV and plaintext in CBC mode. Therefore, instead of XORing the plaintext and encrypting it, and subsequently XORing the ciphertext with the plaintext; CFB mode will encrypt the IV first, then XOR it with the plaintext to receive the ciphertext. Then, for subsequent blocks, the ciphertext is again encrypted and XORd with the plaintext to give the next block of ciphertext.

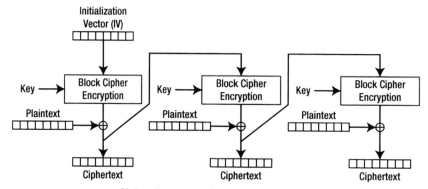

Cipher Feedback (CFB) mode encryption

Figure 5-8. CFB encryption (courtesy Wikipedia)

■ *OFB mode:* Output feedback mode (see Figure 5-9) is very similar to CFB mode. The difference is that, instead of using the XORd IV and ciphertext, it is used before the XORing takes place. So, for the first block, the IV is encrypted with the key and this is used as input for the next block. The ciphertext from the first block is then XORd with the first block of plaintext. Subsequent encryptions take place with the ciphertext from the previous block before XORing.

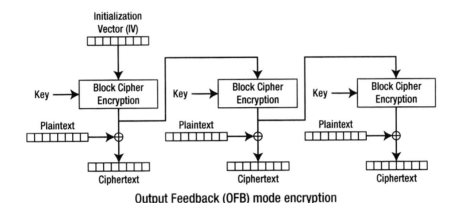

Output Feedback (OFB) mode encryption

Figure 5-9. OFB encryption (courtesy Wikipedia)

Note   XOR (denoted by the symbol ∧) is the standard abbreviation for the logical operation *exclusive or* (also known as *exclusive disjunction*). Its truth table is as follows:

0 ∧ 0 = 0

0 ∧ 1 = 1

1 ∧ 0 = 1

1 ∧ 1 = 0

If you look at my original example, you will see that I am not using a specific encryption mode. By default, Android will use the ECB mode to perform its encryption or decryption. It is up to you as the developer to select a more complex encryption mode, such as CBC or CFB.

Now that you are more aware of the inner workings of the AES symmetric algorithm, I will show how you can change the padding and mode of operation when encrypting. Going back to our original example, change the code to read the same as Listing 5-2. Note the line of bold code. We have only made a couple changes. First, we changed AES to AES/CBC/PKCS5Padding; second, we have added the initialization vector (IV) to our init() method. As I mentioned before, the default mode that Android will use when you specify just AES encoding is AES/ECB/PKCS5Padding. You can verify this by running the program twice, once with AES and once with AES/ECB/PKC5Padding. Both will give you the same ciphertext.

Listing 5-2. Reworked Encryption Routine with CBC Encryption Mode

```
private static byte[] encrypt(byte[] key, byte[] data, byte[] iv){
            SecretKeySpec sKeySpec = new SecretKeySpec(key,"AES");
            Cipher cipher;
            byte[] ciphertext = null;
            try {
                    cipher = Cipher.getInstance("AES/CBC/PKCS5Padding");
                    IvParameterSpec ivspec = new IvParameterSpec(iv);
                    cipher.init(Cipher.ENCRYPT_MODE, sKeySpec, ivspec);
                    ciphertext = cipher.doFinal(data);
            } catch (NoSuchAlgorithmException e) {
                    Log.e(TAG,"NoSuchAlgorithmException");
            } catch (NoSuchPaddingException e) {
                    Log.e(TAG,"NoSuchPaddingException");
            } catch (IllegalBlockSizeException e) {
                    Log.e(TAG,"IllegalBlockSizeException");
            } catch (BadPaddingException e) {
                    Log.e(TAG,"BadPaddingException");
            } catch (InvalidKeyException e) {
                    Log.e(TAG,"InvalidKeyException");
            }
            return ciphertext;
    }
```

Assume you were to select the secret key of your choice. Instead of using the random number generator to generate your secret key, you could write a routine similar to that shown in Listing 5-3. In this listing, `stringKey` is the key you want to encrypt your data.

Listing 5-3. Reworked Key Generation Example with Fixed Key Value

```
public static byte [] generateKey(String stringKey) {
            try {
                    SecretKeySpec sks = new
                    SecretKeySpec(stringKey.getBytes(),"AES");

            } catch (NoSuchAlgorithmException e) {
                    Log.e(TAG,"No such algorithm exception");
            }
            return sks.getEncoded();
    }
```

Data Storage in Android

I wanted to cover the topic of cryptography and data storage in one chapter because I believe you can link the two to provide a more secure application. Android runs applications in separate security contexts. This means that each application will run with its own UID and GID; when one application writes data, other applications will not be able to read that data. If you want to share data between applications, then you will need to explicitly enable this sharing by using a content provider. I can see your question forming now: "Why cover all the crypto topics if Android already protects data?" As I alluded to at the start of this chapter, we can build another layer of security over the Android security layer, just for those unforeseen times when a vulnerability, virus, or Trojan rears its ugly head.

Android allows you to store data using five different options (see Table 5-4). Obviously, you will need to decide where to store your application-specific data based on your requirements.

Table 5-4. *Mechanisms of Data Storage on Android*

Storage Method	Description	Data Privacy
Shared preferences	Allows you to store primitive data types (e.g., int, Boolean, float, long, and String) that will persist across the device session. Even if your application is not running, your data will persist until the device is restarted.	Can set four modes of privacy: MODE_PRIVATE, MODE_WORLD_READABLE, MODE_WORLD_WRITABLE, and MODE_MULTI_PROCESS. Default mode is MODE_PRIVATE
Internal storage	Allows you to store your data in the device's internal memory. Generally, this data is not accessible by other applications or even the end user. This is a private data storage area. Data stored here will persist even after a device restarts. When the end user removes your application, Android will also delete your data.	Can set three modes of privacy: MODE_PRIVATE, MODE_WORLD_READABLE, and MODE_WORLD_WRITABLE. Default mode is MODE_PRIVATE.
External storage	Data stored here is world-readable. The device user and other applications can read, modify, and delete this data. The external storage is associated with SD Cards or device internal storage (which is nonremovable).	Data is world readable by default.
SQLite databases	If you need to create a database for your application to take advantage of SQLite's searching and data management capabilities, use the SQLite database storage mechanism.	Databases that you create are accessible by any class within your application. Outside applications have no access to this database.
Network connection	You can store and retrieve data remotely through web services. You can read more about this in Chapter 6.	Based on your web service settings.

Which mechanism you choose to store your data largely depends on your requirements. Looking at our Proxim application in Chapter 2, we can also consider storing our data in a SQLite database because this will save us from unnecessarily deciding to enforce a data structure. Let's look at a few examples of how to store and retrieve data using each of these mechanisms.

Shared Preferences

Shared preferences are mostly useful for storing application settings that will be valid until a device reboot takes place. As the name states, the storage mechanism is best suited to holding user preferences for an application. Let's say we have to store information about an e-mail server that our application needs to retrieve data from. We need to store the mail server hostname, port, and whether the mail server uses SSL. I've given basic code to store (see Listing 5-4) and retrieve (see Listing 5-5) data into the shared preferences. The StorageExample1 class puts it all together (see Listing 5-6), and the accompanying output is shown in Figure 5-10.

Listing 5-4. Code that Stores Data to the SharedPreferences

```
package net.zenconsult.android;

import java.util.Hashtable;

import android.content.Context;
import android.content.SharedPreferences;
import android.content.SharedPreferences.Editor;
import android.preference.PreferenceManager;

public class StoreData {

        public static boolean storeData(Hashtable data, Context ctx) {
                SharedPreferences prefs = PreferenceManager
                                .getDefaultSharedPreferences(ctx);
                String hostname = (String) data.get("hostname");
                int port = (Integer) data.get("port");
                boolean useSSL = (Boolean) data.get("ssl");
                Editor ed = prefs.edit();
                ed.putString("hostname", hostname);
                ed.putInt("port", port);
                ed.putBoolean("ssl", useSSL);
                return ed.commit();
        }
}
```

Listing 5-5. Code that Retrieves Data from the SharedPreferences

```
package net.zenconsult.android;

import java.util.Hashtable;

import android.content.Context;
import android.content.SharedPreferences;
import android.preference.PreferenceManager;

public class RetrieveData {
        public static Hashtable get(Context ctx) {
                String hostname = "hostname";
                String port = "port";
                String ssl = "ssl";
```

```
                   Hashtable data = new Hashtable();
                   SharedPreferences prefs = PreferenceManager
                                   .getDefaultSharedPreferences(ctx);
                   data.put(hostname, prefs.getString(hostname, null));
                   data.put(port, prefs.getInt(port, 0));
                   data.put(ssl, prefs.getBoolean(ssl, true));
                   return data;
            }
}
```

Listing 5-6. StorageExample1, the Main Class

```
package net.zenconsult.android;

import java.util.Hashtable;

import android.app.Activity;
import android.content.Context;
import android.os.Bundle;
import android.util.Log;
import android.widget.EditText;

public class StorageExample1Activity extends Activity {
        /** Called when the activity is first created. */
        @Override
        public void onCreate(Bundle savedInstanceState) {
                super.onCreate(savedInstanceState);
                setContentView(R.layout.main);
                Context cntxt = getApplicationContext();

                Hashtable data = new Hashtable();
                data.put("hostname", "smtp.gmail.com");
                data.put("port", 587);
                data.put("ssl", true);

                if (StoreData.storeData(data, cntxt))
                        Log.i("SE", "Successfully wrote data");
                else
                        Log.e("SE", "Failed to write data to Shared Prefs");

                EditText ed = (EditText) findViewById(R.id.editText1);
                ed.setText(RetrieveData.get(cntxt).toString());
        }
}
```

Figure 5-10. The output of the StorageExample1 application

Internal Storage

As we saw, `SharedPreferences` is ideally suited to key-value pair data types. This is somewhat similar to a `Hashtable` or even the standard Java `Properties` object. The limitation with the `SharedPreferences` mechanism is that you are limited to storing only primitive data types. You wouldn't be able to store more complex types such as `Vectors` or `Hashtables`. If you want to store data other than primitive types, you can look to the internal storage. The internal storage mechanism will allow you to write your data via an `OutputStream`. Thus, any object that can be serialized into a string of bytes can be written to the internal storage. Let's begin by creating our `StorageExample2` class (see Listing 5-7). As before, I've shown the storage and retrieval modules in separate listings (see Listings 5-8 and 5-9, respectively). Figure 5-11 shows the output.

Listing 5-7. StorageExample2, the Main Class

```
package net.zenconsult.android;

import android.app.Activity;
import android.content.Context;
import android.os.Bundle;
import android.widget.EditText;

public class StorageExample2Activity extends Activity {
        /** Called when the activity is first created. */
        @Override
```

```
        public void onCreate(Bundle savedInstanceState) {
                super.onCreate(savedInstanceState);
                setContentView(R.layout.main);

                Context ctx=getApplicationContext();

                // Store data
                Contact contact=new Contact();
                contact.setFirstName("Sheran");
                contact.setLastName("Gunasekera");
                contact.setEmail("sheran@zenconsult.net");
                contact.setPhone("+12120031337");

                StoreData.storeData(contact.getBytes(), ctx);

                // Retrieve data

                EditText ed=(EditText) findViewById(R.id.editText1);
                ed.setText(new String(RetrieveData.get(ctx)));

        }
}
```

Listing 5-8. Use StoreData.java to Store Data in the Internal Storage

```
package net.zenconsult.android;

import java.io.FileNotFoundException;
import java.io.FileOutputStream;
import java.io.IOException;

import android.content.Context;
import android.util.Log;

public class StoreData {
        public static final String file="contacts";

        public static void storeData(byte[] data, Context ctx) {

                try {
                        FileOutputStream fos=ctx.openFileOutput(file, ctx.MODE_PRIVATE);
                        fos.write(data);
                        fos.close();
                } catch (FileNotFoundException e) {
                        Log.e("SE2", "Exception: "+e.getMessage());
                } catch (IOException e) {
                        Log.e("SE2", "Exception: "+e.getMessage());
                }
        }
}
```

Listing 5-9. Use RetrieveData.java to Retrieve Data from the Internal Storage

```
package net.zenconsult.android;

import java.io.ByteArrayOutputStream;
import java.io.FileInputStream;
import java.io.FileNotFoundException;
```

```java
import java.io.IOException;

import android.content.Context;
import android.util.Log;

public class RetrieveData {
        public static final String file="contacts";

        public static byte[] get(Context ctx) {
                byte[] data=null;
                try {
                        int bytesRead=0;
                        FileInputStream fis=ctx.openFileInput(file);
                        ByteArrayOutputStream bos=new ByteArrayOutputStream();
                        byte[] b=new byte[1024];
                        while ((bytesRead=fis.read(b)) !=-1) {
                                bos.write(b, 0, bytesRead);
                        }
                        data=bos.toByteArray();

                } catch (FileNotFoundException e) {
                        Log.e("SE2", "Exception: "+e.getMessage());
                } catch (IOException e) {
                        Log.e("SE2", "Exception: "+e.getMessage());
                }
                return data;
        }
}
```

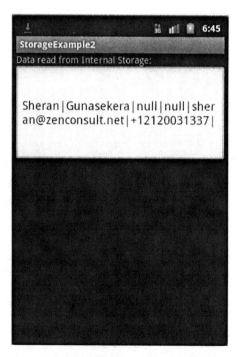

Figure 5-11. The output of the StorageExample2 application

Notice that Listing 5-7 uses the old Contact object from the Proxim example to store the data.

SQLite Databases

I'm going to skip the external storage examples because you already know how to store data externally (e.g., take a look at the source code for the Proxim application). It stores all its data on the external store. Instead, let's focus on how to create, store, and retrieve data using Android's SQLite database object. I will create a database table that we can use to store `Contact` objects from our Proxim application. Table 5-5 shows the layout of the table. I have taken the easy way out and designated all columns as TEXT. When you're creating your own table, make sure to specify columns that are numbers, dates, or times based on your data types.

Table 5-5. The Contacts Table Inside the ContactsDB SQLite Database

Column Name	Column Data Type
FIRSTNAME	TEXT
LASTNAME	TEXT
EMAIL	TEXT
PHONE	TEXT
ADDRESS1	TEXT
ADDRESS2	TEXT

Create a new project called StorageExample3 in your development environment with the structure shown in Figure 5-12. If you need the `Contact` object, copy it from the Proxim example.

Figure 5-12. The StorageExample3 project structure

The `StorageExample3` class shows the main class for working with a SQLite database, creating a `Contact` object with data in it (see Listing 5-10). Listing 5-11 shows a helper class that you can use to manipulate a SQLite database, while Listing 5-12 shows how to use a class to write data from the `Contact` object into the database. Finally, Figure 5-13 shows you how to fetch data from a SQLite database and return a contact object. One you've had a chance to peruse these listings, we'll take a closer look at what each piece of this code does and how it does it.

Listing 5-10. The StorageExample3

```
package net.zenconsult.android;

import android.app.Activity;
import android.os.Bundle;
import android.util.Log;
import android.widget.EditText;

public class StorageExample3Activity extends Activity {
        /** Called when the activity is first created. */
        @Override
        public void onCreate(Bundle savedInstanceState) {
                super.onCreate(savedInstanceState);
                setContentView(R.layout.main);

                // Store data
                Contact contact=new Contact();
                contact.setFirstName("Sheran");
                contact.setLastName("Gunasekera");
                contact.setEmail("sheran@zenconsult.net");
                contact.setPhone("+12120031337");

                ContactsDb db=new
                ContactsDb(getApplicationContext(),"ContactsDb",null,1);
                Log.i("SE3",String.valueOf(StoreData.store(db, contact)));

                Contact c=RetrieveData.get(db);

                db.close();

                EditText ed=(EditText)findViewById(R.id.editText1);
                ed.setText(c.toString());

        }
}
```

Listing 5-11. The ContactsDB Helper Class Handles Our SQLite Database

```
package net.zenconsult.android;

import android.content.Context;
import android.database.sqlite.SQLiteDatabase;
import android.database.sqlite.SQLiteOpenHelper;
import android.database.sqlite.SQLiteDatabase.CursorFactory;

public class ContactsDb extends SQLiteOpenHelper {
        public static final String tblName="Contacts";

        public ContactsDb(Context context, String name, CursorFactory factory,
                        int version) {
                super(context, name, factory, version);
        }
```

```
        @Override
        public void onCreate(SQLiteDatabase db) {
                String createSQL = "CREATE TABLE "+tblName
                                    + " ( FIRSTNAME TEXT, LASTNAME TEXT, EMAIL TEXT,"
                                    + " PHONE TEXT, ADDRESS1 TEXT, ADDRESS2 TEXT);";
                db.execSQL(createSQL);
        }

        @Override
        public void onUpgrade(SQLiteDatabase db, int oldVersion, int newVersion) {
                // Use this to handle upgraded versions of your database
        }

}
```

Listing 5-12. The StoreData Class Writes Data from the Contact Object into the Database

```
package net.zenconsult.android;

import android.content.ContentValues;
import android.database.sqlite.SQLiteDatabase;

public class StoreData {
        public static long store(ContactsDb db, Contact contact) {
                // Prepare values
                ContentValues values = new ContentValues();
                values.put("FIRSTNAME", contact.getFirstName());
                values.put("LASTNAME", contact.getLastName());
                values.put("EMAIL", contact.getEmail());
                values.put("PHONE", contact.getPhone());
                values.put("ADDRESS1", contact.getAddress1());
                values.put("ADDRESS2", contact.getAddress2());

                SQLiteDatabase wdb = db.getWritableDatabase();
                return wdb.insert(db.tblName, null, values);
        }
}
```

Listing 5-13. The RetrieveData class Fetches Data from the SQLite Database and Returns a Contact Object

```
package net.zenconsult.android;

import android.database.Cursor;
import android.database.sqlite.SQLiteDatabase;

public class RetrieveData {
        public static Contact get(ContactsDb db) {
                SQLiteDatabase rdb = db.getReadableDatabase();
                String[] cols = { "FIRSTNAME", "LASTNAME", "EMAIL", "PHONE" };
                Cursor results = rdb.query(db.tblName, cols, "", null, "", "", "");

                Contact c = new Contact();
                results.moveToLast();
                c.setFirstName(results.getString(0));
                c.setLastName(results.getString(1));
```

```
                c.setEmail(results.getString(2));
                c.setPhone(results.getString(3));
                return c;
         }
}
```

In my experience, it is very rare that I've had to use a flat file to store my data. Unless I work with pure binary data (e.g., photos, videos, or music), most of the data that I store is done either as a key-value pair or stored inside a SQLite database. Therefore, I can use Android's SharedPreferences or SQLiteDatabase to do this. Both mechanisms offer very good manageability and that is the biggest draw for me. If you haven't worked with SQLite databases before, then you might want to consider looking into it a bit more. Indeed, most modern mobile operating systems, including Apple's iOS and RIM's BlackBerry Smartphone OS, offer native support for SQLite databases. The good part is that SQLite databases are very portable, and you can create, read, and modify a SQLite database on just about any major operating system, including Mac OS X, Linux, and Windows.

Let's analyze the source from our StorageExample3 project. Listing 5-10 is the main class, and it creates a Contact object with data in it:

```
Contact contact = new Contact();
contact.setFirstName("Sheran");
contact.setLastName("Gunasekera");
contact.setEmail("sheran@zenconsult.net");
contact.setPhone("+12120031337");
```

Next, it uses the ContactsDb class (Listing 5-11) that subclasses the SQLiteOpenHelper class:

```
ContactsDb db = new ContactsDb(getApplicationContext(),"ContactsDb",null,1);
```

If you want to create your own database, then subclassing SQLiteOpenHelper is the way to go. The code then uses the StoreData class's (Listing 5-12) store() method to save the just created Contact object. We call the store() method and pass our newly created SQLite database and our Contact object. StoreData will then break down the Contact object into a ContentValues object:

```
ContentValues values = new ContentValues();
values.put("FIRSTNAME", contact.getFirstName());
values.put("LASTNAME", contact.getLastName());
values.put("EMAIL", contact.getEmail());
values.put("PHONE", contact.getPhone());
values.put("ADDRESS1", contact.getAddress1());
values.put("ADDRESS2", contact.getAddress2());
```

Tip   If you are creating your own data objects and you know you are going to use the SQLite database mechanism to store your data, you might want to consider extending ContentValues for your data object. This makes it a lot easier to pass to when storing and retrieving data.

Next, we write the values to our database table. The SQLiteOpenHelper object can retrieve a WritableDatabase or a ReadableDatabase. We use the most appropriate one when inserting or querying data from our table:

```
SQLiteDatabase wdb=db.getWritableDatabase();
return wdb.insert(db.tblName, null, values);
```

The RetrieveData class handles data retrieval from the database. Here, we are only interested in the last row of values inserted. In a production application, we would iterate over our Cursor to fetch each row:

```
SQLiteDatabase rdb=db.getReadableDatabase();
String[] cols={ "FIRSTNAME", "LASTNAME", "EMAIL", "PHONE" };
Cursor results=rdb.query(db.tblName, cols, "", null, "", "", "");
```

After fetching the data from the table, we re-create a Contact object that we return:

```
Contact c=new Contact();
results.moveToLast();
c.setFirstName(results.getString(0));
c.setLastName(results.getString(1));
c.setEmail(results.getString(2));
c.setPhone(results.getString(3));
return c;
```

The output (see Figure 5-13) looks predictably the same from the previous example.

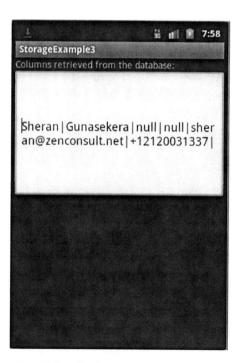

Figure 5-13. The output of the StorageExample3 application

Combining Data Storage with Encryption

We covered two very important points in this chapter, but we did so separately. If you attempted the exercises in Chapter 2, then you already have a fair idea of what we need to do next. We can clearly see that whatever data we store is placed in the clear inside whichever storage mechanism we select. We can rely on Android to ensure that our data is not read by unauthorized applications, but what if a brand new virus is released into the wild next week? This virus affects only Android phones and is able to bypass the SQLite database permissions to read all databases present on the device. Now your only hope of keeping your data private has been compromised and all your data is vulnerable to being copied off your device.

We discussed such attacks in previous chapters and classified them as indirect attacks. They are indirect because the virus does not go after your application directly. Instead, it goes after the Android OS. The aim is to copy all SQLite databases in the hopes that the virus author can copy any sensitive information stored there. If you had added another layer of protection, however, then all the virus author would see is garbled data. Let's build a more permanent cryptographic library that we can reuse in all our applications. Let's start by creating a brief set of specifications:

- *Uses symmetric algorithms:* Our library will use a symmetric algorithm, or block cipher, to encrypt and decrypt our data. We will settle on AES, although we should be able to modify this at a later date.

- *Uses a fixed key:* We need to be able to include a key that we can store on the device that will be used to encrypt and decrypt data.

- *Key stored on device:* The key will reside on the device. While this is a risk to our application from the perspective of direct attacks, it should suffice in protecting us against indirect attacks.

Let's start with our key management module (see Listing 5-14). Because we plan to use a fixed key, we won't need to generate a random one as we did in the past examples. The KeyManager will therefore perform the following tasks:

1. Accept a key as a parameter (the setId(byte[] data) method)

2. Accept an initialization vector as a parameter (the setIv(byte[] data) method)

3. Store the key inside a file in the internal store

4. Retrieve the key from a file in the internal store (the getId(byte[] data) method)

5. Retrieve the IV from a file in the internal store (the getIv(byte[] data) method)

Listing 5-14. The KeyManager Module

```
package net.zenconsult.android.crypto;

import java.io.ByteArrayOutputStream;
import java.io.FileInputStream;
```

```java
import java.io.FileNotFoundException;
import java.io.FileOutputStream;
import java.io.IOException;

import android.content.Context;
import android.util.Log;

public class KeyManager {
        private static final String TAG="KeyManager";
        private static final String file1="id_value";
        private static final String file2="iv_value";

        private static Context ctx;

        public KeyManager(Context cntx) {
                ctx=cntx;
        }

        public void setId(byte[] data) {
                writer(data, file1);
        }

        public void setIv(byte[] data) {
                writer(data, file2);
        }

        public byte[] getId() {
                return reader(file1);
        }

        public byte[] getIv() {
                return reader(file2);
        }

        public byte[] reader(String file) {
                byte[] data=null;
                try {
                        int bytesRead=0;
                        FileInputStream fis=ctx.openFileInput(file);
                        ByteArrayOutputStream bos=new ByteArrayOutputStream();
                        byte[] b=new byte[1024];
                        while ((bytesRead=fis.read(b)) !=-1) {
                                bos.write(b, 0, bytesRead);
                        }
                        data=bos.toByteArray();
                } catch (FileNotFoundException e) {
                        Log.e(TAG, "File not found in getId()");
                } catch (IOException e) {
                        Log.e(TAG, "IOException in setId(): "+e.getMessage());
                }
                return data;
        }

        public void writer(byte[] data, String file) {
                try {
                        FileOutputStream fos=ctx.openFileOutput(file,
                                        Context.MODE_PRIVATE);
                        fos.write(data);
```

```
                                fos.flush();
                                fos.close();
                        } catch (FileNotFoundException e) {
                                Log.e(TAG, "File not found in setId()");
                        } catch (IOException e) {
                                Log.e(TAG, "IOException in setId(): "+e.getMessage());
                        }
                }

        }
```

Next, we do the Crypto module (see Listing 5-15). This module takes care of the encryption and decryption. I have added an armorEncrypt() and armorDecrypt() method to the module to make it easier to convert the byte array data into printable Base64 data and vice versa.

Listing 5-15. The Cryptographic Module

```java
package net.zenconsult.android.crypto;

import java.security.InvalidAlgorithmParameterException;
import java.security.InvalidKeyException;
import java.security.NoSuchAlgorithmException;

import javax.crypto.BadPaddingException;
import javax.crypto.Cipher;
import javax.crypto.IllegalBlockSizeException;
import javax.crypto.NoSuchPaddingException;
import javax.crypto.spec.IvParameterSpec;
import javax.crypto.spec.SecretKeySpec;

import android.content.Context;
import android.util.Base64;

public class Crypto {
        private static final String engine="AES";
        private static final String crypto="AES/CBC/PKCS5Padding";
        private static Context ctx;

        public Crypto(Context cntx) {
                ctx=cntx;
        }

        public byte[] cipher(byte[] data, int mode)
                        throws NoSuchAlgorithmException, NoSuchPaddingException,
                        InvalidKeyException, IllegalBlockSizeException,
                        BadPaddingException, InvalidAlgorithmParameterException {
                KeyManager km=new KeyManager(ctx);
                SecretKeySpec sks=new SecretKeySpec(km.getId(), engine);
                IvParameterSpec iv=new IvParameterSpec(km.getIv());
                Cipher c=Cipher.getInstance(crypto);
                c.init(mode, sks, iv);
                return c.doFinal(data);
        }
```

```
        public byte[] encrypt(byte[] data) throws InvalidKeyException,
                        NoSuchAlgorithmException, NoSuchPaddingException,
                        IllegalBlockSizeException, BadPaddingException,
                        InvalidAlgorithmParameterException {
                return cipher(data, Cipher.ENCRYPT_MODE);
        }

        public byte[] decrypt(byte[] data) throws InvalidKeyException,
                        NoSuchAlgorithmException, NoSuchPaddingException,
                        IllegalBlockSizeException, BadPaddingException,
                        InvalidAlgorithmParameterException {
                return cipher(data, Cipher.DECRYPT_MODE);
        }

        public String armorEncrypt(byte[] data) throws InvalidKeyException,
                        NoSuchAlgorithmException, NoSuchPaddingException,
                        IllegalBlockSizeException, BadPaddingException,
                        InvalidAlgorithmParameterException {
                return Base64.encodeToString(encrypt(data), Base64.DEFAULT);
        }

        public String armorDecrypt(String data) throws InvalidKeyException,
                        NoSuchAlgorithmException, NoSuchPaddingException,
                        IllegalBlockSizeException, BadPaddingException,
                        InvalidAlgorithmParameterException {
                return new String(decrypt(Base64.decode(data, Base64.DEFAULT)));
        }

}
```

You can include these two files in any of your applications that require data storage to be encrypted. First, make sure that you have a value for your key and initialization vector, then call any one of the encrypt or decrypt methods on your data before you store it. Listing 5-16 shows the changes required to the StorageExample3 class. Additionally, Listings 5-17 and 5-18 show the changes required to the StoreData and RetrieveData files, respectively.

Listing 5-16. The New StorageExample3 with Encryption

```
package net.zenconsult.android;

import net.zenconsult.android.crypto.Crypto;
import net.zenconsult.android.crypto.KeyManager;
import android.app.Activity;
import android.os.Bundle;
import android.util.Log;
import android.widget.EditText;

public class StorageExample3Activity extends Activity {
        /** Called when the activity is first created. */
        @Override
        public void onCreate(Bundle savedInstanceState) {
                super.onCreate(savedInstanceState);
                setContentView(R.layout.main);

                String key = "12345678909876543212345678909876";
                String iv = "1234567890987654";
```

```
                    KeyManager km=new KeyManager(getApplicationContext());
                    km.setIv(iv.getBytes());
                    km.setId(key.getBytes());

                    // Store data
                    Contact contact=new Contact();
                    contact.setFirstName("Sheran");
                    contact.setLastName("Gunasekera");
                    contact.setEmail("sheran@zenconsult.net");
                    contact.setPhone("+12120031337");

                    ContactsDb db=new ContactsDb(getApplicationContext(), "ContactsDb",
                                null, 1);
                    Log.i("SE3", String.valueOf(StoreData.store(new Crypto(
                                getApplicationContext()), db, contact)));

                    Contact c=RetrieveData.get(new Crypto(getApplicationContext()), db);

                    db.close();

                    EditText ed=(EditText) findViewById(R.id.editText1);
                    ed.setText(c.toString());

        }
}
```

Listing 5-17. The Modified StoreData Class

```
package net.zenconsult.android;

import java.security.InvalidAlgorithmParameterException;
import java.security.InvalidKeyException;
import java.security.NoSuchAlgorithmException;

import javax.crypto.BadPaddingException;
import javax.crypto.IllegalBlockSizeException;
import javax.crypto.NoSuchPaddingException;

import net.zenconsult.android.crypto.Crypto;
import android.content.ContentValues;
import android.database.sqlite.SQLiteDatabase;
import android.util.Log;

public class StoreData {
        public static long store(Crypto crypto, ContactsDb db, Contact contact) {
                // Prepare values
                ContentValues values=new ContentValues();
                try {
                        values.put("FIRSTNAME", crypto.armorEncrypt(contact.getFirstName()
                                        .getBytes()));
                        values.put("LASTNAME", crypto.armorEncrypt(contact.getLastName()
                                        .getBytes()));
                        values.put("EMAIL", crypto.armorEncrypt(contact.getEmail()
                                        .getBytes()));
                        values.put("PHONE", crypto.armorEncrypt(contact.getPhone()
                                        .getBytes()));
```

```
                        values.put("ADDRESS1", contact.getAddress1());
                        values.put("ADDRESS2", contact.getAddress2());
                } catch (InvalidKeyException e) {
                        Log.e("SE3", "Exception in StoreData: "+e.getMessage());
                } catch (NoSuchAlgorithmException e) {
                        Log.e("SE3", "Exception in StoreData: "+e.getMessage());
                } catch (NoSuchPaddingException e) {
                        Log.e("SE3", "Exception in StoreData: "+e.getMessage());
                } catch (IllegalBlockSizeException e) {
                        Log.e("SE3", "Exception in StoreData: "+e.getMessage());
                } catch (BadPaddingException e) {
                        Log.e("SE3", "Exception in StoreData: "+e.getMessage());
                } catch (InvalidAlgorithmParameterException e) {
                        Log.e("SE3", "Exception in StoreData: "+e.getMessage());
                }
                SQLiteDatabase wdb=db.getWritableDatabase();
                return wdb.insert(ContactsDb.tblName, null, values);
        }
}
```

Listing 5-18. The Modified RetrieveData Class

```
package net.zenconsult.android;

import java.security.InvalidAlgorithmParameterException;
import java.security.InvalidKeyException;
import java.security.NoSuchAlgorithmException;

import javax.crypto.BadPaddingException;
import javax.crypto.IllegalBlockSizeException;
import javax.crypto.NoSuchPaddingException;

import net.zenconsult.android.crypto.Crypto;
import android.database.Cursor;
import android.database.sqlite.SQLiteDatabase;
import android.util.Log;

public class RetrieveData {
        public static Contact get(Crypto crypto, ContactsDb db) {
                SQLiteDatabase rdb=db.getReadableDatabase();
                String[] cols={ "FIRSTNAME", "LASTNAME", "EMAIL", "PHONE" };
                Cursor results=rdb.query(ContactsDb.tblName, cols, "", null, "", "",
                            "");

                Contact c=new Contact();
                results.moveToLast();

                try {
                        c.setFirstName(crypto.armorDecrypt(results.getString(0)));
                        c.setLastName(crypto.armorDecrypt(results.getString(1)));
                        c.setEmail(crypto.armorDecrypt(results.getString(2)));
                        c.setPhone(crypto.armorDecrypt(results.getString(3)));
                } catch (InvalidKeyException e) {
                        Log.e("SE3", "Exception in RetrieveData: "+e.getMessage());
```

```
        } catch (NoSuchAlgorithmException e) {
                Log.e("SE3", "Exception in RetrieveData: "+e.getMessage());
        } catch (NoSuchPaddingException e) {
                Log.e("SE3", "Exception in RetrieveData: "+e.getMessage());
        } catch (IllegalBlockSizeException e) {
                Log.e("SE3", "Exception in RetrieveData: "+e.getMessage());
        } catch (BadPaddingException e) {
                Log.e("SE3", "Exception in RetrieveData: "+e.getMessage());
        } catch (InvalidAlgorithmParameterException e) {
                Log.e("SE3", "Exception in RetrieveData: "+e.getMessage());
        }

        return c;
    }
}
```

Figure 5-14 shows what it would look like for anyone accessing the SQLite database without decrypting the information. To replicate this, I didn't have the RetrieveData class decrypt any of the data.

Figure 5-14. What the data would look like without decryption

Summary

In this chapter, we covered the basics of cryptography. We examined how PKI and trusted third parties work, as well as how, for our purposes, PKI or even LPKI would be overkill. We then looked at simple mechanisms of encrypting data and learned the terminology. We saw that encryption was not as straightforward as picking a symmetric algorithm, and that you must consider the different aspects such as padding and modes of operation.

We then looked at the various mechanisms of storing data on Android. We covered examples of each of these and settled on SQLite databases and SharedPreferences to enable us to store application data. We then looked at how we could obfuscate our data using encryption, and we built a general-purpose library to perform encryption and decryption. This library can be included in any of our future programs where we need to store data in a secure manner.

Talking to Web Apps

At some point, you will have to interface with a web application. Whether you're talking to a RESTful API from a third party or exchanging data with your own back-end web application, your mobile app needs to be open to the idea of interaction with other applications. Naturally, as a responsible developer, it is your job to ensure that the data exchange is done so that attackers cannot access or alter private data belonging to the end user. We spent time exploring "data at rest" in previous chapters, when we looked at data storage and encryption. In this chapter, we will cover "data in transit."

Originally, I was not planning to spend a lot of time discussing the merits of encrypting your data in transit. Usually, SSL or TLS will handle the secure components of the data in transit. Lately, however, the intrusion into the Certificate Authority called DigiNotar in the Netherlands has led me to reconsider this option (see `http://en.wikipedia.org/wiki/DigiNotar` for more information). In the end, I'll leave it up to you as the developer to decide how to secure your transport data; but clearly, this recent attack has made me think that even trusting SSL is not always the best option. Thus, I will cover some topics related to web application security and how your mobile application should interact with such web applications. I will briefly cover the Open Web Application Security Project (OWASP), as well; it is a very good resource with which to secure your web applications.

Consider how secure the source code in Listing 6-1 is. Now ask yourself what would you do to make it more secure? (Check at the end of the chapter for the solution and compare your own notes to see if you were on the right track.)

Listing 6-1. The Client Login

```
package net.zenconsult.android.examples;

import java.io.IOException;
import java.io.UnsupportedEncodingException;
import java.util.ArrayList;
import java.util.List;

import org.apache.http.HttpResponse;
import org.apache.http.NameValuePair;
```

```java
import org.apache.http.client.ClientProtocolException;
import org.apache.http.client.HttpClient;
import org.apache.http.client.entity.UrlEncodedFormEntity;
import org.apache.http.client.methods.HttpPost;
import org.apache.http.impl.client.DefaultHttpClient;
import org.apache.http.message.BasicNameValuePair;

import android.util.Log;

public class Login {
    private final String TAG = "HttpPost";

    public Login() {

    }

    public HttpResponse execute() {
        HttpClient client = new DefaultHttpClient();
        HttpPost post = new HttpPost("http://logindemo1.appspot.com/logindemo");
        HttpResponse response = null;

        // Post data with number of parameters
        List<NameValuePair> nvPairs = new ArrayList<NameValuePair>(2);
        nvPairs.add(new BasicNameValuePair("username", "sheran"));
        nvPairs.add(new BasicNameValuePair("password", "s3kretc0dez"));

        // Add post data to http post
        try {
            UrlEncodedFormEntity params = new UrlEncodedFormEntity(nvPairs);
            post.setEntity(params);
            response = client.execute(post);

        } catch (UnsupportedEncodingException e) {
            Log.e(TAG, "Unsupported Encoding used");
        } catch (ClientProtocolException e) {
            Log.e(TAG, "Client Protocol Exception");
        } catch (IOException e) {
            Log.e(TAG, "IOException in HttpPost");
        }
        return response;
    }

}
```

Preparing Our Environment

Let's begin by setting up our testing environment. We obviously will need a ready-made web application-hosting infrastructure. I usually rely on Google App Engine when I need to deploy or test a web application fast. It saves me a lot of time, and I don't have to worry about setting up the hardware, web server, and application server. With Google App Engine, I can start coding with minimal setup overhead.

Let's first sign up for an account on Google App Engine (if you already have a Google account for Gmail, then you can skip the following steps and use that):

1. Navigate to `http://code.google.com/appengine/` (see Figure 6-1).

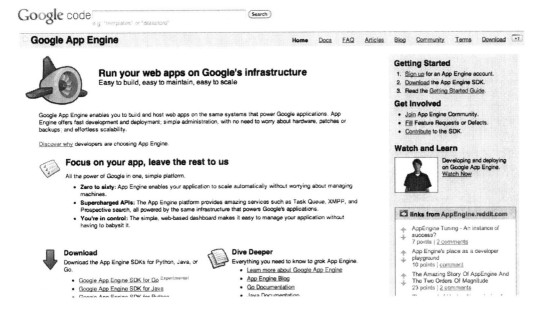

Figure 6-1. The Google App Engine home page

2. Click the `Sign Up` link. When prompted, sign in with your Gmail account. You will then be taken to your Applications list (see Figure 6-2).

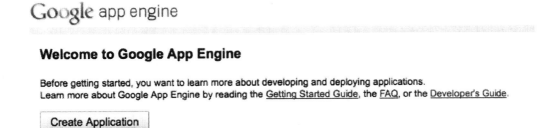

Figure 6-2. The applications list

3. Click the Create Application button. The next page allows you to select details about your application. (see Figure 6-3). Since your application will be publicly visible, Google provides you with a subdomain for `.appspot.com`. This subdomain pool is shared among the entire user base of App Engine developers; so, in some cases, you may not receive the application name you are after. For instance, you're unlikely to receive the `logindemo1` subdomain because I have already registered it. You can check the availability of the subdomain by clicking the Check Availability button.

Figure 6-3. Giving your application a name

4. Fill in the subdomain of the application you want; it should be something like *<your name>*login demo1.appspot.com (see Figure 6-3). Give your application a title, say Login Demo 1. Leave the rest of the options as they are and click Create Application.

5. If all went well, you will see a page similar to Figure 6-4 telling you that your application was created successfully. Next, you can explore the status of your application by clicking the "dashboard" link. Your application hasn't done anything yet, so the statistics will still be empty (see Figure 6-5).

Google app engine

sheran.g@gmail.com | My Account | Help | Sign out

Application Registered Successfully

The application will use **joelogindemo1** as an identifier. This identifier belongs in your application's configuration as well. Note that this identifier cannot be changed. Learn more

The application uses the **High Replication** storage scheme. Learn more

If you use Google authentication for your application, **Login Demo 1** will be displayed on Sign In pages when users access your application.

Choose an option below:

• View the dashboard for Login Demo 1.
• Use appcfg to upload and deploy your application code.
• Add administrators to collaborate on this application.

© 2008 Google | Terms of Service | Privacy Policy | Blog | Discussion Forums

Figure 6-4. Successful app creation

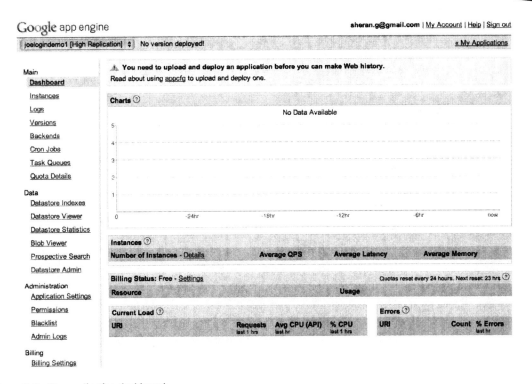

Figure 6-5. *The application dashboard*

Next, you have to download the SDK for Google App Engine, so that you can write, run, and debug your applications on your local computer before you publish them to the Google App Engine servers. I use Eclipse for most of my development, and I will outline the steps required to download the SDK and integrate it directly with Eclipse. Also, since we're covering Android, we will stick to the Java SDK for App Engine.

You will find detailed instructions on how to install the Google Apps plugin for Eclipse at the following URL: `http://code.google.com/eclipse/docs/getting_started.html`. Even if the final URL changes, you should always be able to reach the documentation section by navigating to the base URL, which is `http://code.google.com/eclipse`.

We're not going to write any back-end code yet. First, let's write a stub application that we can start with and build onto. In your Eclipse IDE, create a new Google App Engine Project by going to File ➤ New ➤ Web Application Project. Fill in the Project Name as LoginDemo and the package as net.zenconsult.gapps.logindemo. Uncheck the box next to Use Google Web Toolkit (see Figure 6-6). When you're done, click Finish. You will end up with a project named LoginDemo; and inside the named package, you will find one file called `LoginDemoServlet`. The file contains the code shown in Listing 6-2. For the moment, it does nothing special. The code waits for an HTTP GET request and then responds with the plain text: "Hello, world."

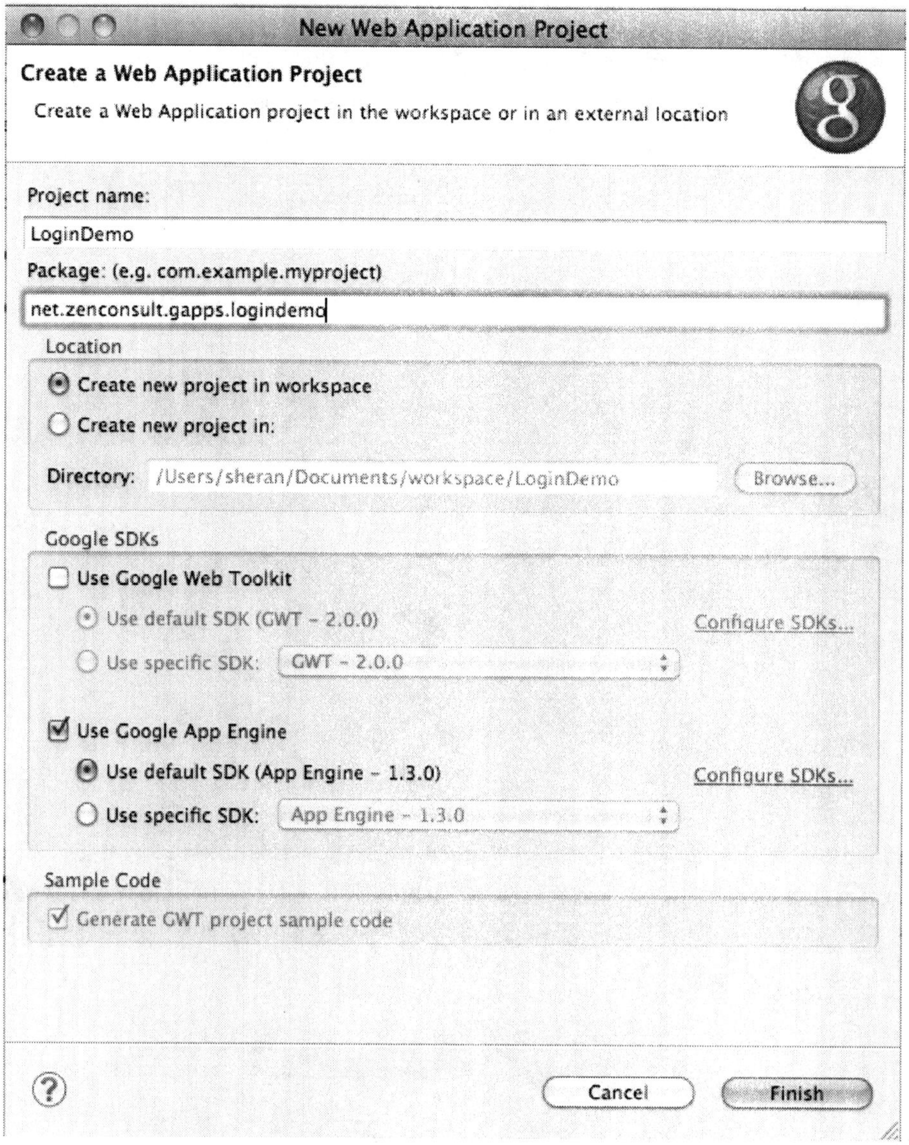

Figure 6-6. *Creating a new Google App Engine project*

Listing 6-2. *The default stub application package, net.zenconsult.gapps.logindemo*

```
import java.io.IOException;
import javax.servlet.http.*;

@SuppressWarnings("serial")
public class LoginDemoServlet extends HttpServlet {
    public void doGet(HttpServletRequest req, HttpServletResponse resp)
            throws IOException {
```

```
        resp.setContentType("text/plain");
        resp.getWriter().println("Hello, world");
    }

}
```

Let's deploy this application to Google App Engine and see if we can reach it through our web browser. To deploy the application, right-click it in the Eclipse Package Manager and click Google ➤ Deploy to App Engine.

You're then prompted to choose the name of the remote application that you created on the Google website. Enter the name you created in the `Application ID` field (see Figure 6-7) and click OK. In the next window, click Deploy to upload your application to Google (see Figure 6-8).

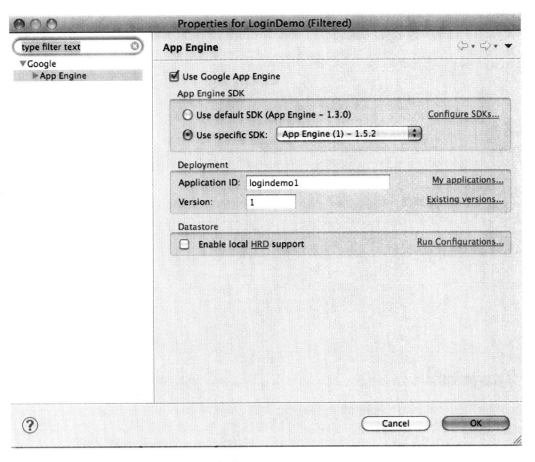

Figure 6-7. Selecting the name of the remote application

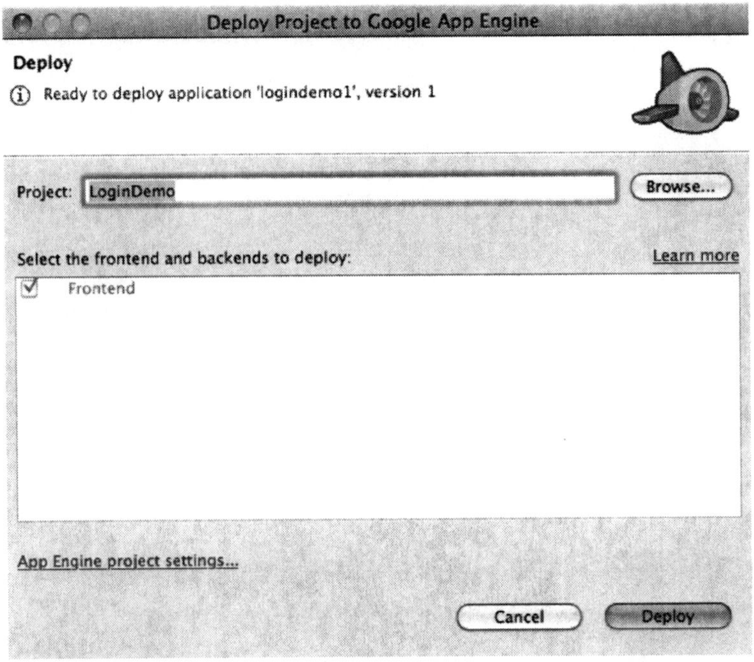

Figure 6-8. Deploying the application to Google

Once you have successfully deployed your app, you can check it by navigating to the URL that you selected when you created your application (http://<*your name* > logindemo1.appspot.com). In my case, when I navigate to http://logindemo1.appspot.com, I see the "Hello, world" response message (see Figure 6-9).

Hello, world

Figure 6-9. Accessing the login servlet

We now have our very own working web application that we can use for whatever we choose. You may have noticed how convenient it was to set up a Google App Engine application. It certainly saves us the time and effort of building a server, installing an operating system, installing server software, and configuring it. Let's look at a bit of theory related to web applications.

HTML, Web Applications, and Web Services

Any web developer will know what HTML is. It is one of the fundamental building blocks of any modern website. HTML (Hyper Text Markup Language) started its life as a draft write up in 1991; it was a very simple language that could be leveraged to create basic web pages. Fast-forward to 2008, when the draft for HTML version 5 was released. Pure HTML pages are referred to as *static* pages. In other words, they render on an end user's browser and remain there until the user navigates to another page.

A *web application* is a piece of software that end users access over a network—just like HTML pages. A web application, however, consists of more dynamic elements than plain vanilla HTML. For instance, modern web applications have a lot of *server-side* languages. These languages (e.g., PHP, JSP, and ASP) generate static HTML on the fly at runtime, based on an end user's input. The web application is installed on a web server and is hosted on hardware that can be accessed by end users over a network such as the Internet. The server-side application framework takes care of rendering the user interface, any application logic (e.g., search, calculation, or any other process), and data storage or retrieval functions. All the end user has to do is show up to the party with his favorite web browser. In other words, because all the complex processing takes place at the back end or server side, the thinner, lighter web browser is nothing more than a mechanism of interacting with the user interface.

Web applications offer developers a number of advantages and are a ubiquitous part of online life today. One of their biggest advantages is the ability to roll out updates or patches to the server and not have to worry about updating hundreds or thousands of clients. Another big advantage of web applications is that end users only require a thin client—a web browser—and that's it. Thus, you can reach not only a large number of users from the personal computing crowd, but also the mobile computing crowd.

A *web service* is similar to a web application in that it can be accessed remotely over a network. It is also similar in that it also runs some sort of server software. The primary difference, however, is that users do not access the service interactively. In most cases, web services interact with other client or server applications. A web service is, in most cases, capable of describing the services it offers and how other applications can access them. It uses a Web Services Description Language (WSDL) file to do this. Other applications can understand how to work with the web service by processing the WSDL file that is published. Generally, web services use a specific XML format to exchange information. One of the popular protocols is SOAP (Simple Object Access Protocol). SOAP is made up of various XML payloads based on the specific application. An example of a SOAP message is shown in Listing 6-3.

Listing 6-3. An Example of a SOAP Message (courtesy of Wikipedia)

```
POST /InStock HTTP/1.1
Host: www.example.org
Content-Type: application/soap+xml; charset = utf-8
Content-Length: 299
SOAPAction: "http://www.w3.org/2003/05/soap-envelope"

<?xml version="1.0"?>
<soap:Envelope xmlns:soap="http://www.w3.org/2003/05/soap-envelope">
<soap:Body>
    <m:GetStockPrice xmlns:m="http://www.example.org/stock">
      <m:StockName>IBM</m:StockName>
    </m:GetStockPrice>
  </soap:Body>
</soap:Envelope>
```

Another way web services can work is by exposing a RESTful API. REST, or Representational State Transfer, is an architecture that uses an underlying, stateless, client-server protocol to expose end-points of web services. The premise of REST is to use a much simpler medium of access (like HTTP) with separate URIs for each resource, rather than relying on more complex protocols like SOAP (which works with a single URI and multiple parameters).

You can read more about REST in Roy Fielding's dissertation at `www.ics.uci.edu/~fielding/ pubs/dissertation/rest_arch_style.htm` or on Wikipedia at `http://en.wikipedia.org/wiki/ Representational_state_transfer`. Although using a RESTful web service is simple, it can still perform the same tasks as a web service that uses SOAP. Take our SOAP example in Listing 6-3. If our web service exposed this to us as a RESTful API, then we would do something like this:

```
http://www.example.com/stocks/price/IBM
```

Note that this is the extent of the request. It can be sent as a simple HTTP GET request to the server, which can then respond. Sometimes, servers can return data in several different representations. For example, if we were to request the server for XML output, we could add an extension of `xml`. If we wanted it in JSON format instead, we could append a `json` extension, as shown here:

```
http://www.example.com/stocks/price/IBM.xml
http://www.example.com/stocks/price/IBM.json
```

Now is a great time to talk a bit about HTTP (HyperText Transfer Protocol). HTTP is the protocol that drives the web. While HyperText originally referred to plain old HTML, it can now be expanded to include XML (Extensible Markup Language). XML follows the rules of HTTP, but it includes custom HTML tags (or keywords) that can be used. HTTP functions as a request-and-response protocol. The request-response cycle takes place between two parties, known as the client and server. The client, or *user-agent* (a web browser), makes a request to a web server that sends back a response of either HTML or XML. Most veteran web developers will also sometimes expect comparable formats to XML, such as JSON (JavaScript Object Notation).

HTTP requests are further broken down into request types, or *methods*. While there are several methods, the most popularly used ones are GET and POST. GET requests are used to retrieve data, and POST requests are used to submit data. If you're filling in a registration form, clicking the Submit button prompts the browser to POST your data to the server. If you look back at Listing 6-1 at the beginning of the chapter, you will see this line:

```
HttpPost post = new HttpPost("http://logindemo1.appspot.com/logindemo");
```

This is the creation of an HTTP POST request to a specific URL. As you're probably aware, a URL (Uniform Resource Locator) is a type of address that tells user-agents where to retrieve a specific resource from. Resources can be files, documents, or objects stored on servers remotely. HTTP requests and responses both have similar structures. Both contain headers and content areas. You can find lots of additional information regarding HTTP at `www.w3.org`.

Components in a Web Application

Web applications are composed of various layers, or tiers. Typical web applications will have three tiers (see Figure 6-10): the Presentation tier, the Logic tier, and the Data tier. Based on the requirements and complexity of an application, the number of tiers can increase. There are

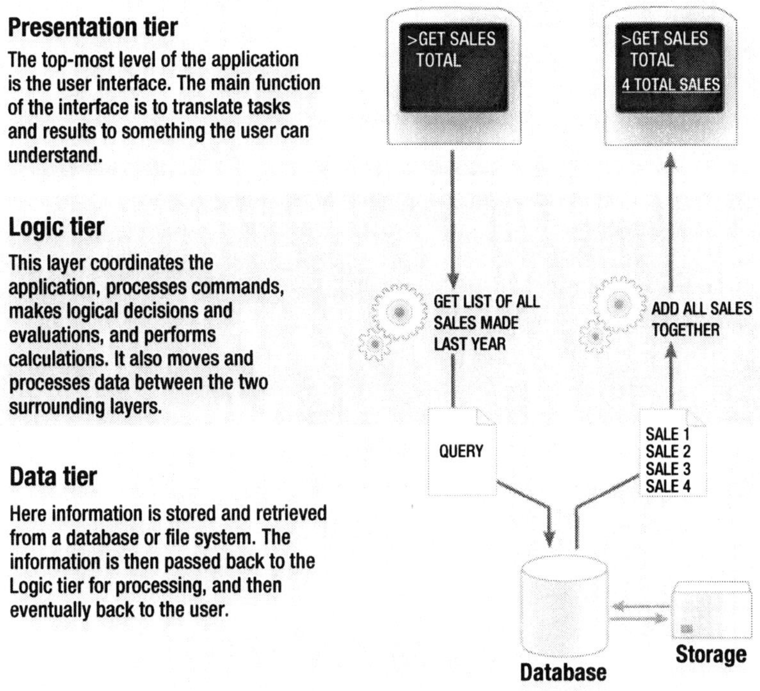

Presentation tier

The top-most level of the application is the user interface. The main function of the interface is to translate tasks and results to something the user can understand.

Logic tier

This layer coordinates the application, processes commands, makes logical decisions and evaluations, and performs calculations. It also moves and processes data between the two surrounding layers.

Data tier

Here information is stored and retrieved from a database or file system. The information is then passed back to the Logic tier for processing, and then eventually back to the user.

>GET SALES
TOTAL

>GET SALES
TOTAL
4 TOTAL SALES

GET LIST OF ALL
SALES MADE
LAST YEAR

ADD ALL SALES
TOGETHER

QUERY

SALE 1
SALE 2
SALE 3
SALE 4

Database   **Storage**

Figure 6-10. A three-tiered web application (courtesy of Wikipedia)

many advantages to having multi-tiered applications: one of them is that system owners can replace or scale hardware or server configurations independently of the other tiers. Consider the scenario where a company needs to increase its amount of data storage; the IT department can upgrade this tier without making significant changes in the other tiers. The next advantage is that the security teams can have control that is more granular at each tier. Each tier has a different function, and thus a different set of requirements and related security controls. Multi-tiered applications allow owners to have more locked-down controls at individual tiers rather than leaving gaps because all three tiers are on one system.

Therefore, based on the three-tier architecture, a web application will contain a web server to present its data, an application server to handle all requests for exchanging data, and a database server that stores and retrieves data.

Let's look at how each tier is involved by considering an example.

Login Process

A standard user-authentication session that a client makes with a server will look something like this:

1. The client requests the Login page from the web server **[Web Server/ Presentation Tier]**.

2. The client sends credentials to the web server **[Web Server/ Presentation Tier]**.

3. The application server receives the data and checks whether it conforms to validation rules **[Application Server/Logic Tier]**.

4. If the data is good, the application server queries the database server to find out whether matching credentials exist **[Application Server/Logic Tier]**.

5. The database server responds to the application server with success or failure **[Database Server/Data Tier]**.

6. The application server tells the web server to give the client its portal (if the credentials were correct) or an error message (if the credentials didn't match) **[Application Server/Logic Tier]**.

7. Web Server displays message from Application Server **[Web Server/ Presentation Tier]**.

While this is a simplified example, it does illustrate how the process flow moves from the outside to the inside–and back again.

Web App Technology

There are multiple technologies that you can use for each tier of a web application. You can choose from many web servers, application frameworks, application servers, server-side scripting languages, and database servers. Your selection criteria depend on factors such as application requirements, budget, and availability of support for the technology you choose.

Since Android development is predominantly done on Java, I've decided to stick with Java for our web application, as well. Apart from Java, you can use other server-side technologies. Some of them are listed here:

- PHP: www.php.net
- Python: www.python.org
- Django: www.djangoproject.com
- Perl: www.perl.org (less common but still sometimes used)
- Cold Fusion: www.adobe.com/product/coldfusion-family.html
- ASP.NET: www.asp.net
- Ruby on Rails: www.rubyonrails.org

Similarly, you can use many popular databases for your application for the data tier, depending on your requirements. Many free and commercial databases exist. This is one more decision that you or your application architect will have to make initially. Here's a short list of popular databases and a URL indicating where you can learn more about them:

- Oracle: www.oracle.com

- Microsoft SQL Server: www.microsoft.com/sqlserver

- MySQL: www.mysql.com

- PostgreSQL: www.postgresql.org

- CouchDB: http://couchdb.apache.org

- MongoDB: www.mongodb.org

Let's take a few minutes now to complete our web application, so that it supports rudimentary password checks. Note that I have deliberately made the example very simple. Authentication routines for actual web applications will be more complex. Check Listing 6-4 for the code.

Listing 6-4. The New Credential Verification Code

```java
package net.zenconsult.gapps.logindemo;

import java.io.IOException;
import javax.servlet.http.*;

@SuppressWarnings("serial")
public class LoginDemoServlet extends HttpServlet {
    private String username = "sheran";
    private String password = "s3kr3tc0dez"; // Hardcoded here intended to
                                              // simulate a database fetch

    public void doGet(HttpServletRequest req, HttpServletResponse resp)
            throws IOException {
        resp.setContentType("text/plain");
        resp.getWriter().println("Hello, world");
    }

    public void doPost(HttpServletRequest req, HttpServletResponse resp)
            throws IOException {
        String user = req.getParameter("username"); // No user input validation
                                                     // here!
        String pass = req.getParameter("password"); // No user input validation
                                                     // here!

        resp.setContentType("text/plain");
        if (user.equals(username) && pass.equals(password)) {
            resp.getWriter().println("Login success!!");
        } else {
            resp.getWriter().println("Login failed!!");
        }

    }

}
```

The next step is to publish your code, just as you did when you first set up your Google App Engine account, and then create a new Android project that handles authentication (see Figure 6-11 for the project structure). Listings 6-5, 6-6, 6-7, and 6-8 contain the source code for the `Login`, `LoginDemoClient1Activity`, `strings.xml`, and `main.xml` files, respectively. Make sure to add this line to your `AndroidManifest.xml` file, as you will need to access the Internet to reach your Google App Engine application:

```
<uses-permission android:name = "android.permission.INTERNET"></uses-permission>
```

Figure 6-11. The project structure

Listing 6-5. The Login Class

```java
package net.zenconsult.android.examples;

import java.io.IOException;
import java.io.UnsupportedEncodingException;
import java.util.ArrayList;
import java.util.List;

import org.apache.http.HttpResponse;
import org.apache.http.NameValuePair;
import org.apache.http.client.ClientProtocolException;
import org.apache.http.client.HttpClient;
import org.apache.http.client.entity.UrlEncodedFormEntity;
import org.apache.http.client.methods.HttpPost;
import org.apache.http.impl.client.DefaultHttpClient;
import org.apache.http.message.BasicNameValuePair;

import android.util.Log;

public class Login {
    private final String TAG = "HttpPost";
    private String username;
    private String password;
```

```
    public Login(String user, String pass) {
        username = user;
        password = pass;
    }

    public HttpResponse execute() {
        Log.i(TAG, "Execute Called");
        HttpClient client = new DefaultHttpClient();
        HttpPost post = new HttpPost("http://logindemo1.appspot.com/logindemo");
        HttpResponse response = null;

        // Post data with number of parameters
        List<NameValuePair>nvPairs = new ArrayList<NameValuePair>(2);
        nvPairs.add(new BasicNameValuePair("username", username));
        nvPairs.add(new BasicNameValuePair("password", password));

        // Add post data to http post
        try {
            UrlEncodedFormEntity params = new UrlEncodedFormEntity(nvPairs);
            post.setEntity(params);
            response = client.execute(post);
            Log.i(TAG, "After client.execute()");

        } catch (UnsupportedEncodingException e) {
            Log.e(TAG, "Unsupported Encoding used");
        } catch (ClientProtocolException e) {
            Log.e(TAG, "Client Protocol Exception");
        } catch (IOException e) {
            Log.e(TAG, "IOException in HttpPost");
        }
        return response;
    }

}
```

The code listing in 6-5 contains the login routine. The class constructor, Login, takes two parameters, which are username and password. The execute() method will use these parameters to make an HTTP POST request to the server.

Listing 6-6. The LoginDemoClient1Activity Class

```
package net.zenconsult.android.examples;

import java.io.BufferedReader;
import java.io.IOException;
import java.io.InputStreamReader;

import org.apache.http.HttpResponse;
import org.apache.http.HttpStatus;

import android.app.Activity;
import android.os.Bundle;
import android.util.Log;
import android.view.View;
import android.view.View.OnClickListener;
import android.widget.Button;
import android.widget.EditText;
```

```java
public class LoginDemoClient1Activity extends Activity implements
        OnClickListener {
    private final String TAG = "LoginDemo1";
    private HttpResponse response;
    private Login login;

    /** Called when the activity is first created. */
    @Override
    protected void onCreate(Bundle savedInstanceState) {
        super.onCreate(savedInstanceState);
        setContentView(R.layout.main);

        Button button = (Button) findViewById(R.id.login);
        button.setOnClickListener(this);

    }

    @Override
    public void onClick(View v) {
        String u = ((EditText) findViewById(R.id.username)).toString();
        String p = ((EditText) findViewById(R.id.password)).toString();

        login = new Login(u, p);

        String msg = "";
        EditText text = (EditText) findViewById(R.id.editText1);
        text.setText(msg);

        response = login.execute();
        Log.i(TAG, "After login.execute()");

        if (response ! = null) {
            if (response.getStatusLine().getStatusCode() == HttpStatus.SC_OK) {
                try {
                    BufferedReader reader = new BufferedReader(
                            new InputStreamReader(response.getEntity()
                                    .getContent()));
                    StringBuilder sb = new StringBuilder();
                    String line;
                    while ((line = reader.readLine()) ! = null) {
                        sb.append(line);
                    }
                    msg = sb.toString();
                } catch (IOException e) {
                    Log.e(TAG, "IO Exception in reading from stream.");
                }
            } else {
                msg = "Status code other than HTTP 200 received";
            }
        } else {
            msg = "Response is null";
        }
        text.setText(msg);
    }
}
```

The code listing in 6-6 is a standard Android activity. This can be considered the application's entry, or start point.

Listing 6-7. The strings.xml File

```xml
<?xml version = "1.0" encoding = "utf-8"?>
<resources>
    <string name = "hello">Web Application response:</string>
    <string name = "app_name">LoginDemoClient1</string>
    <string name = "username">Username</string>
    <string name = "password">Password</string>
    <string name = "login">Login</string>
</resources>
```

Listing 6-8. The main.xml File

```xml
<?xml version = "1.0" encoding = "utf-8"?>
<LinearLayout xmlns:android = "http://schemas.android.com/apk/res/android"
    android:orientation = "vertical"
    android:layout_width = "fill_parent"
    android:layout_height = "fill_parent"
    android:weightSum = "1">
    <TextView android:textAppearance = "?android:attr/textAppearanceLarge"
    android:id = "@+id/textView1" android:layout_height = "wrap_content"
    android:layout_width = "wrap_content" android:text = "@string/username">
    </TextView>
<EditText android:layout_height = "wrap_content"
    android:layout_width = "match_parent" android:id = "@+id/username">
</EditText>
<TextView android:textAppearance = "?android:attr/textAppearanceLarge"
    android:id = "@+id/textView2" android:layout_height = "wrap_content"
    android:layout_width = "wrap_content" android:text = "@string/password">
</TextView>
<EditText android:layout_height = "wrap_content"
    android:layout_width = "match_parent" android:inputType = "textPassword"
    android:id = "@+id/password">
</EditText>
<Button android:text = "@string/login" android:layout_height = "wrap_content"
    android:layout_width = "166dp" android:id = "@+id/login">
</Button>
<TextView android:text = "@string/hello" android:layout_height = "wrap_content"
    android:layout_width = "fill_parent">
</TextView>
<EditText android:id = "@+id/editText1" android:layout_height = "wrap_content"
    android:layout_width = "match_parent" android:inputType = "textMultiLine"
    android:layout_weight = "0.13">
    <requestFocus></requestFocus>
</EditText>
</LinearLayout>
```

The strings.xml and main.xml files contain our set of defined string constants and the graphical layout of the application, respectively.

Run your application and enter different usernames and passwords. You should see two distinct response messages, one for success and another for a failed password (see Figure 6-12). That's it! You're done writing both your mobile login client and server. Next, we'll go over security on the web and the various attacks that you may have to face on your web applications.

Figure 6-12. Logon failure

OWASP and Web Attacks

The Open Web Application Security Project (OWASP) at www.owasp.org is an organization that provides a body of knowledge, techniques, and guidelines for testing and securing web applications. OWASP was founded in December 2001 and attained US not-for-profit charitable status in 2004. It lists, as its core purpose, to "*be the thriving global community that drives visibility and evolution in the safety and security of the world's software.*" It is a great resource for learning about and fixing your web application's security.

The OWASP Top Ten project has been a sub-project of the OWASP foundation since 2004. On a semi-regular basis, the OWASP Top Ten lists the ten most critical application security vulnerabilities. The vulnerabilities are listed as a broad consensus of what project members and security experts globally have experienced in web applications. The Top Ten list is used and adopted by a large number of commercial organizations, and it has become a de facto standard for web application security.

At the time this book was published, the 2010 OWASP Top Ten was still the most recent update to the list. It can be found here: www.owasp.org/index.php/Top_10_2010.

The topics for the 2010 OWASP Top Ten are listed here:

- A1: Injection
- A2: Cross-Site Scripting (XSS)
- A3: Broken Authentication and Session Management
- A4: Insecure Direct Object References
- A5: Cross-Site Request Forgery (CSRF)
- A6: Security Misconfiguration
- A7: Insecure Cryptographic Storage
- A8: Failure to Restrict URL Access
- A9: Insufficient Transport Layer Protection
- A10: Unvalidated Redirects and Forwards

One of the newer OWASP projects is the Mobile Top Ten, which is part of the OWASP Mobile Security Project. The project is still in development, and no finalized lists have been released at the time of writing. There is, however, a list of practical tips on the website that will prove of immense help to you as a mobile developer. Most of the topics covered in this chapter share many techniques and principles with the Mobile Top Ten. Here are the topics covered by the list:

- Identify and protect sensitive data on the mobile device.
- Handle password credentials securely on the device.
- Ensure that sensitive data is protected in transit.
- Implement user authentication/authorization and session management correctly.
- Keep the back-end APIs (services) and the platform (server) secure.
- Perform data integration with third party services/applications securely.
- Pay specific attention to the collection and storage of consent for the collection and use of the user's data.
- Implement controls to prevent unauthorized access to paid-for resources (e.g., wallet, SMS, and phone calls).
- Ensure secure distribution/provisioning of mobile applications.
- Carefully check any runtime interpretation of code for errors.

Authentication Techniques

Let's continue with our topic of securing "data in transit" now. I wanted you to have a fair understanding of what goes on behind the scenes in a web application, and that is why I covered topics related to web applications in this chapter. If you've dedicated your life to being a mobile application developer, then it is interesting to see how your application communicates with the web app you want to talk to. A better understanding of the application can also lead you to make improvements in security and performance. If, like me, you do all your coding from end-to-end, including web application development, then you may already be familiar with the topics I'll discuss. Either way, since you've now had a short refresher on web applications and security, let's move onto the main task at hand.

Authentication is an important feature of mobile applications that need to interact with remote web applications. Almost all present-day applications rely on some form of a username and password or PIN combination to grant access to their data. The username and password are stored on the server, and whenever an end user wishes to authenticate with the application, a comparison is made. If you take a new look at Listing 6-1, you'll see that we are doing exactly that. The following lines contain the username and password for the web application:

```
nvPairs.add(new BasicNameValuePair("username", "sheran"));
nvPairs.add(new BasicNameValuePair("password", "s3kretc0dez"));
```

In this case, the information is hard-coded, but it could just as easily be stored on the device (with encryption, of course!) and retrieved whenever a user wants to log in. But what if our traffic was intercepted while it was in transit? "Aha! But we have SSL!" you say. That's true, but we don't seem to be using it in our example because our POST request goes to a non-SSL/TLS port:

```
HttpPost post = new HttpPost("http://logindemo1.appspot.com/logindemo");
```

OK, that was a cheap shot. But let's seriously consider that our SSL traffic has been breached. The attacker that is eavesdropping on our conversation with the web application now has access to our credentials. All she has to do now is to use them directly on the full web application or on another mobile device. If she does, she will have full control over our user profile. If this were a social networking site, then we might not be too concerned; however, if it were our online banking application, then we would be pretty worried.

Thus far, we know the risks that we face when authenticating remotely. Although our data may traverse a secure channel, it is still vulnerable to attacks. And it doesn't have to be a severe attack like the DigiNotar incident, where an attacker can issue her own certificates. For example, the attack could be as prosaic as an SSL man-in-the-middle attack.

Since I've mentioned DigiNotar and not trusting SSL more than once, I think it is only fair that I outline my reasoning.

You can't always trust SSL. In general, end users think SSL means they are secure. A padlock icon and the address bar on the browser turning green are indicators that tell you that you are browsing a secure site. This need not be necessarily true, however. I'd like to take a moment to go over some of the concepts of SSL.

SSL (Secure Sockets Layer) is a transport protocol that encrypts data in transit between two computers. An eavesdropper cannot intercept encrypted data–at least not without going through some effort. Thus, SSL ensures that data remains private between the client and server computers. SSL is old. Most people refer to encrypted HTTP data transfer between client and server as SSL; but in reality, the newer protocol is TLS (Transport Layer Security). An integral part of SSL and TLS is the X.509 Certificate. X.509 is the standard for Public Key Infrastructure (PKI) that I covered briefly in Chapter 5. Commonly, users will refer to the X.509 server certificate as an SSL certificate. This is a key and very important component of SSL. Figure 6-13 shows a browser setting up an SSL session.

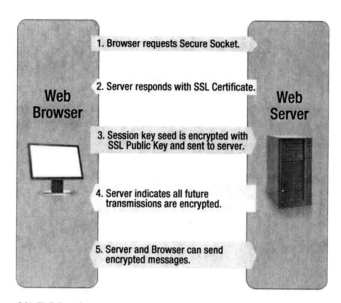

Figure 6-13. Setting up an SSL/TLS Session

TLS and SSL use a combination of cryptographic techniques to ensure data transmission is secure. Let's look at this session setup now. I'm not giving you surgical detail because you will almost never need to write your own TLS negotiation algorithm. Instead, this section will give you an idea of how encryption is set up and what takes place during a TLS session.

First, the client or browser will contact a web server and send it some information. The information contains details of the version of TLS it can support and a list of encryption algorithms. These are called *CipherSuites*, and they contain supported algorithms for various tasks like key exchange, authentication, and bulk ciphers.

Next, the server responds after selecting a specific CipherSuite that it supports and the highest common TLS version that both the client and server support. The server will then also send the client its SSL Certificate.

The client then uses the server's public key to encrypt and exchange a *PreMaster* key, a key that generates a Master key.

Once the PreMaster key is exchanged, the client and server will use random values and the PreMaster key to generate a final Master key. This master key is stored on the client and server.

The server and client then switch to encrypting all data sent back and forth. The selected CipherSuite is used, and the symmetric Master key is used at both ends to encrypt and decrypt data. Figure 6-14 shows what you would see if you were able to capture an encrypted data session between the client and server. Figure 6-15 shows the handshake and other relevant details when viewed using OpenSSL. One look at it will immediately tell you that there is absolutely no usable data for an attacker. What does this mean to you as a developer, then? That you should use SSL and never worry about prying eyes when you exchange sensitive data between the client and server? I won't accept your answer just yet. Let's first look at a few details, and we will come back to your answer later.

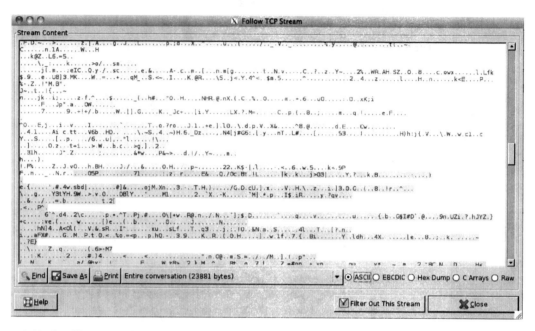

Figure 6-14. A traffic capture of an SSL session

```
azazel:~ sheran$ openssl s_client -connect mail.google.com:443
CONNECTED(00000003)
depth=1 /C=ZA/O=Thawte Consulting (Pty) Ltd./CN=Thawte SGC CA
verify error:num=20:unable to get local issuer certificate
verify return:0
---
Certificate chain
 0 s:/C=US/ST=California/L=Mountain View/O=Google Inc/CN=mail.google.com
   i:/C=ZA/O=Thawte Consulting (Pty) Ltd./CN=Thawte SGC CA
 1 s:/C=ZA/O=Thawte Consulting (Pty) Ltd./CN=Thawte SGC CA
   i:/C=US/O=VeriSign, Inc./OU=Class 3 Public Primary Certification Authority
---
Server certificate
-----BEGIN CERTIFICATE-----
MIIDIjCCAougAwIBAgIQHxn23jXdY6FCkYrVLMCrEjANBgkqhkiG9w0BAQUFADBM
MQswCQYDVQQGEwJaQTElMCMGA1UEChMcVGhhd3RlIENvbnN1bHRpbmcgKFB0eSkg
THRkLjEWMBQGA1UEAxMNVGhhd3RlIFNHQyBDQTAeFw0wOTEyMTgwMDAwMDBaFw0x
MTEyMTgyMzU5NTlaMGkxCzAJBgNVBAYTAlVTMRMwEQYDVQQIEwpDYWxpZm9ybmlh
MRYwFAYDVQQHFA1Nb3VudGFpbiBWaWV3MRMwEQYDVQQKFApHb29nbGUgSW5jMRgw
FgYDVQQDFA9tYWlsLmdvb2dsZS5jb20wgZ8wDQYJKoZIhvcNAQEBBQADgY0AMIGJ
AoGBANknyBHye+RFyUa2Y3WDsXd+F0GJgDjxRSegPNnoqABL2QfQut7t9CymrNwn
E+wMwaaZF0LmjSfSgRSwS4L6ssXQuyBZYiijlrVh9nbBbUbS/brGDz3RyXeaWDP2
BnYyrVFfKV9u+BKLrebFCDmzQOOpW5Ed1+PPUd91WY6NgKtTAgMBAAGjgecwgeQw
DAYDVR0TAQH/BAIwADA2BgNVHR8ELzAtMCugKaAnhiVodHRwOi8vY3JsLnRoYXd0
ZS5jb20vVGhhd3RlU0U0dDQ0EuY3JsMCgGCGCCsGAQUFBwMBBggrBgEF
BQcDAgYJYYIZIAYb4QgQBMHIGCCsGAQUFBwEBBGYwZDAiBggrBgEFBQcwAYYWaHR0
cDovL29jc3AudGhhd3RlLmNvbTA+BggrBgEFBQcwAoYyaHR0cDovL3d3dy50aGF3
dGUuY29tL3JlcG9zaXRvcnkvVGhhd3RlX1NHQ19DQS5jcnQwDQYJKoZIhvcNAQEF
BQADgYEAicju7fexy+yRP2drx57Tcqo+BElR1CiHNZlnhPmS9QSZaudDA8jy25IP
VWvjEgaq13Hro0Hg32ZNVK53qcXwjWtnCAReojvNwj6/x1Ciq5B6D7E6eiYDSfXJ
8/a2vR5IbgY89nq+wuHaA6vspH6vNR848x03z1PQ7BrIjnYQlA0=
-----END CERTIFICATE-----
subject=/C=US/ST=California/L=Mountain View/O=Google Inc/CN=mail.google.com
issuer=/C=ZA/O=Thawte Consulting (Pty) Ltd./CN=Thawte SGC CA
---
No client certificate CA names sent
---
SSL handshake has read 1773 bytes and written 316 bytes
---
New, TLSv1/SSLv3, Cipher is RC4-SHA
Server public key is 1024 bit
Secure Renegotiation IS supported
Compression: NONE
Expansion: NONE
SSL-Session:
    Protocol  : TLSv1
    Cipher    : RC4-SHA
    Session-ID: 66EE866203EE2F764591D20357C4C1556DA9C5CB8476A04A5E4BFC84C3FC10F1
    Session-ID-ctx:
    Master-Key: E08CE3405A61A2F0F53EDCCCC0673F01FAE0E9DB7FE1D5F56156A88C8A35537BA8E8B5C163EB94506D1F1A374E1E2B96
    Key-Arg   : None
    Start Time: 1319528177
    Timeout   : 300 (sec)
    Verify return code: 0 (ok)
---
```

Figure 6-15. An SSL Handshake when viewed using the s_client option of OpenSSL

SSL is all about trust. Well, actually, X.509 is all about trust. An SSL certificate is issued to an individual or company based on certain criteria. The issuing authority, known as the CA or Certificate Authority, is responsible for determining if you are who you say you are. For example, you couldn't just request a www.google.com certificate without proving that you were somehow affiliated with, or had the capacity to act on behalf of, the company. This matters because, if the CA does not check these credentials, then anyone can apply for an SSL certificate and install it on his web server.

By tricking an end user into believing your server is a google.com server, you could conduct a man-in-the-middle (MitM) attack and intercept all his data. We'll look at a man-in-the-middle attack shortly; but first, I want to cover another topic that you may be aware of, the self-signed certificate.

> **Note**   A CA issues SSL certificates to clients. While issuing the certificate, the CA will also sign the SSL certificate with its own Root certificate. This signature indicates that the CA trusts the issued SSL certificate. A browser can verify the SSL certificate by looking at the CA signature first and verifying whether the signature is a match to the Root certificate.
>
> Many well-known Root CAs exist around the world. Generally, the CA Root certificates come packaged inside your web browser. This allows the browser to verify SSL certificates issued by different CAs.
>
> For example, let's say you applied to VeriSign for a certificate for your domain, `example.com`. VeriSign first establishes that you are the correct owner for this domain, and it then issues you a certificate for your web server. It signs this certificate with its own Root certificate. After you receive your SSL certificate, you install it on your web server and set up your website. Now when I visit your website, my browser first looks at your SSL certificate, and then tries to verify whether your certificate is indeed issued by a trusted CA. To do this, my browser will look at its internal store of trusted Root certificates to determine whether the VeriSign Root certificate's signature matches the signature on your certificate. If it does, then I can continue browsing your site. However, if there is difficulty in verifying your certificate, then my browser warns me that it was unable to verify the certificate.
>
> Note that your browser will verify a number of other details about the certificate before giving it the green light.

Self-Signed Certificates

During the development and testing phase of some projects, developers will sometimes use a self-signed certificate on their websites. This type of certificate is identical in all respects to the SSL certificate issued by a CA. The main difference, however, is that the signature on this certificate is not from a trusted CA. Instead, the developer signs the certificate himself. When a browser connects to a site with a self-signed SSL certificate, it has no way of verifying who signed certificate. That is because the person who signed it is not listed in the browser's internal trusted certificate store. The browser will then alert the user with a warning similar to the one shown in Figure 6-16.

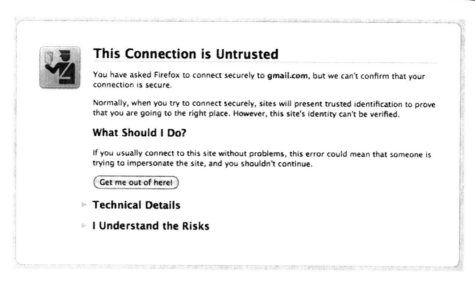

Figure 6-16. A warning for an untrusted or self-signed certificate

This verification phase that takes place on the browser is very important. It exists so that an attacker can't simply issue himself a certificate belonging to `www.google.com` and trick users. The browser will always alert a user if it cannot verify the SSL certificate.

Man-in-the-Middle Attack

A man-in-the-middle (MitM) attack is a method by which an attacker can eavesdrop on network traffic or data flowing between two parties. The attacker positions herself so that he is able to intercept traffic from both the sender and receiver, effectively putting himself in the middle of the two (see Figure 6-17). In this position, he is able to intercept and relay information between the two parties. If executed correctly, the users at either end of the conversation will not know that the attacker is relaying and intercepting their traffic.

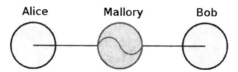

Figure 6-17. Mallory in the middle of Alice and Bob (courtesy of Wikipedia)

What follows is an example of an MitM attack using Figure 6-17 as a reference:

```
Alice "Hi Bob, it's Alice. Give me your key"-->  Mallory      Bob
Alice      Mallory "Hi Bob, it's Alice. Give me your key"-->   Bob
Alice      Mallory  <--[Bob's_key] Bob
Alice   <--[Mallory's_key] Mallory      Bob
Alice "Meet me at the bus stop!"[encrypted with Mallory's key]-->  Mallory      Bob
Alice      Mallory "Meet me in the windowless van at 22nd Ave!"[encrypted with Bob's⏎
 key]-->  Bob
```

Most of the time, the attacks that we see are focused on self-signed certificates or tricking browsers into believing that the attacker possesses a valid certificate. Until recently, attackers knew very little about CA security, and there were far fewer incidents involving CAs. This was true until June 2011, anyway.

In theory, attacking a CA to obtain legitimately signed, trusted SSL certificates is also an option. Not many attackers would consider this because they would obviously expect a high degree of security when it comes to CAs. Right? Wrong! In June 2011, a CA called DigiNotar was attacked. The attacker issued himself over 500 rogue SSL certificates signed by DigiNotar. As a trusted CA, DigiNotar had its Root certificate in all modern browsers. This meant that the attacker had legitimate SSL certificates that he could use to carry out MitM attacks. Since the browsers already trusted the DigiNotar Root certificate, they would always validate these rogue SSL certificates, and an end user would never know that the attacker was intercepting her data.

Why did this happen? DigiNotar had very lax security controls in its infrastructure. The attacker was able to remotely compromise its servers and gain access to the very systems that are responsible for issuing legitimate certificates. After this, it is a relatively simple task for the attacker to keep issuing himself certificates whenever he wants. Some of the more prominent websites that had rogue certificates include:

> `*.google.com` (This means any sub-domain of `google.com`, including `mail.google.com`, `docs.google.com`, `plus.google.com`, and so on)
>
> `*.android.com`
>
> `*.microsoft.com`
>
> `*.mozilla.org`
>
> `*.wordpress.org`
>
> `www.facebook.com`
>
> `www.mossad.gov.il`
>
> `www.sis.gov.uk`

All the web browser developers blacklisted DigiNotar's Root certificate, and DigiNotar began to systematically revoke all the rogue certificates. Unfortunately, by the time all of this took place, DigiNotar had lost the trust of thousands of users worldwide. The company declared bankruptcy in September 2011.

If such a large CA can suffer such a big breach of security, which compromised hundreds of SSL certificates, then can we really just rely on SSL all the time? Actually, yes we can. Events such as DigiNotar occur very infrequently, so I would choose to trust SSL. However, I would also choose to deploy my own layer of data encryption between my mobile app and the server. Then, if the SSL layer is breached in any way, the attacker will have yet another layer of encryption to deal with. In most cases, this additional layer will act as a deterrent, and the attacker may leave your application alone.

Is there a way we can prevent an attacker from snooping on our credentials while traveling over SSL? Yes indeed! Let's look at two ways we can prevent our credentials from being compromised even if our secure transport channels fail. One is OAuth, and the other is Challenge/Response.

OAuth

The OAuth protocol allows third-party sites or applications, known as *consumers*, to use end-user data on a web application called a *service provider*. The end user has ultimate control over the amount of access he can grant to these third parties and will do so without having to divulge or store his existing web application credentials.

Take the example of Picasa Web Albums; the photo editing application Picnik (`www.picnik.com`) allows end users to edit their photographs. Picnik also allows end users to import from other sites like Picasa and Flickr. Before OAuth, a user would have to log in to Picnik and *also* enter his Picasa or Flickr username and password, so that Picnik could begin importing photos from these sites. The problem with this approach is that now the user has saved or used his credentials with Picnik. His level of exposure has increased because he has stored his credentials at Picasa *and* Picnik.

If the same scenario were to be re-enacted with OAuth, then the user would not have to enter his credentials once again on the Picnik site. Instead, Picnik (the consumer) would redirect him to his Picasa (service provider) site (see Figure 6-18) and ask him to grant or deny access to the photographs stored on Picasa (see Figure 6-19). In this way, the user's credentials are safer.

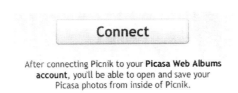

Figure 6-18. Picnik requesting to connect to Picasa, so that it can request an access token

Figure 6-19. Picasa requests authorization for Picnik to look at some photos

OAuth works by using request tokens. Sites that want to access data in a web application need to be granted a token from that same application before they can start accessing this data.

Let's take a look at how OAuth works for the Picasa Web Albums first. As an example, suppose you have written an Android application that lists a user's Picasa albums. Your Android application requires access to a user's Picasa Web Album to do this. In this case, the actors are your Android app (the consumer), Picasa (the service provider), and your end user.

OAuth requires that you first register your consumer application on the site that you are authenticating against. This is necessary because you will receive an application identifier that you will need to use in your code. To register your application, you have to visit `http://code.google.com/apis/console` (see Figure 6-20), create a project, and create an OAuth client ID (see Figures 6-21, 6-22, 6-23, and 6-24).

Figure 6-20. Creating a new project on Google APIs

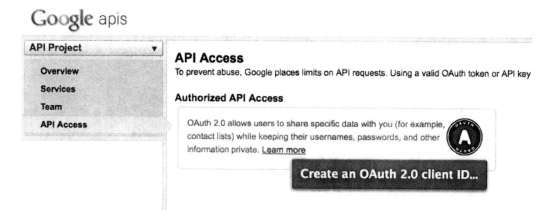

Figure 6-21. Creating a new client ID

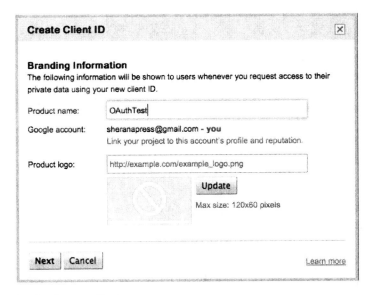

Figure 6-22. Fill in the details of your application

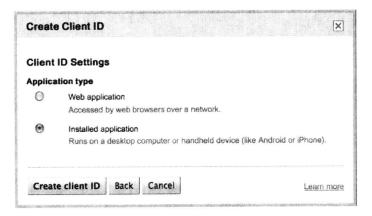

Figure 6-23. Choose your application type

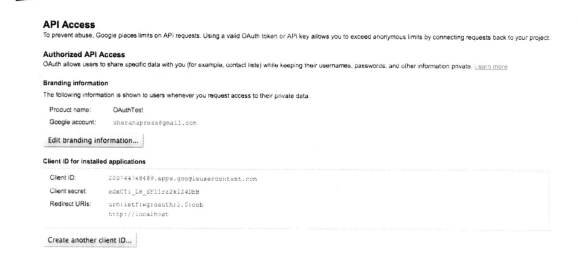

Figure 6-24. *Your Client ID and Client Secret are now created*

Now that you've got your OAuth Client ID, let's take a look at the authentication flow of an OAuth Application (see Figure 6-25)

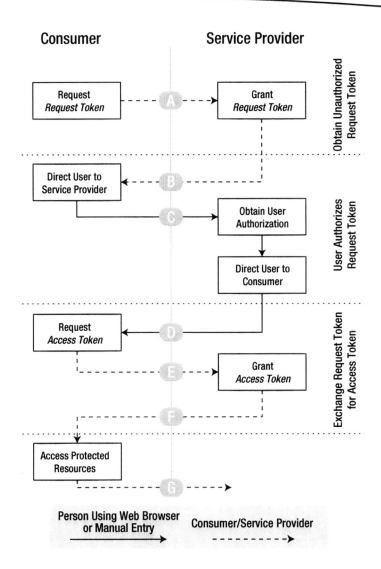

Figure 6-25. OAuth authentication flow (courtesy of Google)

OAuth is a multi-stage process that has three main interacting parties. The consumer is the application that wishes to access data from a service provider, and this can only happen if the user authorizes the consumer explicitly. Let's go over the steps in detail:

The following scenario is initiated when the end user opens your Android app:

1. *Flow A:* The Consumer application (your Android App) asks the Service Provider (Picasa) for a Request Token.

2. *Flow B:* Picasa tells your application to redirect the end user to Picasa's web page. Your app then opens up a browser page that will direct the end user to the specific URL.

3. *Flow C:* The end user enters her credentials in this screen. Remember that she is logging into the service provider (Picasa) website and granting access to your app. She is sending her credentials to the website and not storing them anywhere on the device.

4. *Flow D:* Once Picasa is happy that the end user has entered the correct username and password and has granted access to your app, it replies with a response indicating whether the Request Token has been authorized. At this point, your application has to detect this response and act accordingly. Assuming authorization was granted, your application now has an authorized Request Token.

5. *Flow E:* Using this authorized Request Token, your app makes another request to the service provider.

6. *Flow F:* The service provider then exchanges the Request Token for an Access Token and sends that back in the response.

7. *Flow G:* Your app now uses this Access Token to access any protected resources (in this case, the user's Picasa Albums) until such time that the token expires.

Your app has now successfully gained access to Picasa without needing to store the end user's credentials. If the user's phone is ever compromised and an attacker copies all the application data, he is not going to find the Picasa username and password in your app data. In this way, you've ensured that your app does not unnecessarily leak sensitive data.

I've used Picasa here simply as a frame of reference. Our ultimate goal is to create an OAuth authentication system for our back-end applications, as well. Therefore, instead of Picasa being the service provider, your back-end web application will be the OAuth service provider. Your end user has to log onto your application via a web browser and explicitly authorize it to access resources. Next, your mobile app and back-end web app will communicate using Request and Access tokens. Most importantly, your mobile app will not save the username and password for your web app.

To illustrate these concepts, I have created an example application for Picasa. I will show you how to implement OAuth on your web application in Chapter 8.

Challenge/Response with Cryptography

The second mechanism for protecting your end-user credentials from traversing the Internet is to use the Challenge/Response technique. This technique is similar in many respects to OAuth in that no credentials go across the wire. Instead, one party requests the other party for a challenge. The other party will then encrypt a random piece of information according to a specifically chosen algorithm and cryptographic function. The key used to encrypt this data is the user password. This encrypted data is sent to the challenging party, which then encrypts the same piece of information by using the password stored at its end. The ciphertext is then compared; if it matches, the user is allowed access. The best way to learn about this technique is to work through an actual example. As with OAuth, I have included source code and examples of applications in Chapter 8.

Summary

In this chapter, we focused a lot on how to transport our data securely from mobile application to web application. We also covered how there are mature protocols and mechanisms to secure our data in transit. At the same time, we saw that, in some cases, we are unable to trust the protocols themselves. In cases like this, we looked at options that can help us protect our end user's credentials from being stolen or intercepted.

We also covered topics that involve web application security. Considering that most mobile applications communicate with a web application in some form or another, it is always good to know how that side of technology works. Finally, we looked at some useful resources for helping us secure our web applications, as well as some concrete examples for protecting our user credentials while in transit.

## Chapter 7

Security in the Enterprise

All along, we have been looking at mobile applications from the perspective of individual developers. Although I believe that individual developers or smaller developer firms far outweigh enterprise developers, I think it would be useful to focus a bit on the enterprise developer and the unique challenges he can face. You might be tempted to skip this chapter because you do not fit into the "enterprise developer" category; however, I would urge you to consider this: most enterprises these days look at outsourcing their development work.

It might not make sense for an enterprise or business to have an in-house mobile development team, unless that is the company's core business focus. I have seen numerous businesses outsourcing their development work to individuals or smaller companies, just so they don't need to worry about managing an in-house mobile development team.

If there comes a time when a business hires you to develop a mobile application for it, then you might want to consider a few areas before you jump in and start developing. In most respects, your target base is much smaller than if you were releasing your application to the public.

One important thing, however, is that, in the case of the enterprise, you could be dealing with a lot more than a loss of personal information. For instance, in an enterprise environment, the likelihood that you will deal with confidential information (e.g., trade secrets, corporate financial information, or sensitive server credentials) is much higher than when you're dealing with an application that is released to the general public. Additionally, your application could become more of a target given that, presently, many attackers view the mobile platform as "easy pickings" due to its lower level of security. Let's first look at some of the key differences in enterprise applications when compared with an application released to the public.

Connectivity

Connecting to the enterprise environment from a remote location has become commonplace lately. Telecommuting, remote support, and outsourcing have all led to enterprise technology teams allowing authorized users into their organization's networks. This doesn't mean that the network admin just leaves the firewall wide open for telnet and remote desktops; the inbound connectivity is subject to certain security controls. To ensure the safest route, an organization will usually use a VPN, or virtual private network (see Figure 7-1), to allow remote users to join its network.

Internet VPN

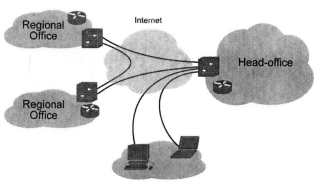

Figure 7-1. A virtual private network (VPN) (courtesy of Wikipedia)

A VPN is typically an additional logical or virtual network that a network administrator will usually create on her border network devices. This network acts as a bridge between a public network, such as the Internet, and the private internal network of an enterprise. Users can connect to the VPN over this public network and use the internal resources of the enterprise (including file servers, internal applications, and so on) just as if they were physically connected to the internal network.

VPNs are gradually making their way into the mobile space, as well. Devices such as the BlackBerry, iPhone, and Android are now able to connect to corporate networks and transfer data securely. Keep this in mind when you design for the enterprise. It's quite likely that an enterprise network administrator will tell you that you need to use the VPN; but in the event that she fails to mention it, you should bring the subject up. Making an enterprise expose more than it should to the Internet is not the goal, here.

If, for some reason, you encounter an organization that does not have or use a VPN, then you might want to spend a bit of time arguing the merits of one. If it is an absolute no-go, then you're going to have to encrypt data between your application and the server. Bear in mind, however, that it is costly to do so, especially if you have significant data exchange. In cases like this, you might also want to consider data compression. I give you an example of data compression later in this chapter. All this adds up to processor usage, though, and you will need to consider that this will, in almost all cases, drain your end user's device battery.

Enterprise Applications

So just what are these enterprise applications I keep talking about? Rest assured, they're not mythical like the unicorn; they do exist. If you've not had much opportunity to work within enterprises, then you might not immediately recognize an enterprise system. There are many different types, but here we will focus on enterprise resource planning (ERP) applications, mainly because they tend to cover a broad spectrum of uses in the enterprise. Your typical ERP applications usually cover one of the following areas:

- Supply chain management

- Customer relationship management

- Manufacturing

- Human resources

- Finance and accounting

- Project management

It is quite likely that the ERP applications you will have to work with are mature and well established. It is also likely that, as the new developer, you will have to write your application to work with the existing systems. This can be a bit frustrating, especially when it means you have to compromise on some form of functionality in your mobile application. One of the best ways around this, in my opinion, is to adopt and use some form of mobile middleware.

Mobile Middleware

Instead of driving yourself insane trying to make your mobile application work with a legacy enterprise application, you might do better if you spend some time developing your own mobile middleware platform. Simply put, the mobile middleware platform acts as the go-between in your mobile app's communication with the enterprise system. The goal is to allow your mobile app to be able to work with the data in the enterprise app without compromising on operating system features or the limited resources available on a mobile device.

I once tested the security of a banking mobile application. The mobile application developer followed the idea of using mobile middleware when integrating with a very proprietary, closed, and inadequately documented application. The developer created a mobile middleware component in the form of a screen translator. Essentially, this was a server-based application that would fetch the website from the banking application, mine or copy all the text on specific pages, and then convert these pages into mobile-formatted text.

Take a look at Figure 7-2. It shows how a mobile application can connect to a middleware system that abstracts the data and user interface of a legacy application. In some cases, the mobile client can access the legacy application directly through the mobile browser, but it would not provide the ideal user experience in this case. Thus, by interfacing with mobile middleware, an application's communications infrastructure can be standardized. Most of the interaction with the legacy application will be done on more powerful hardware.

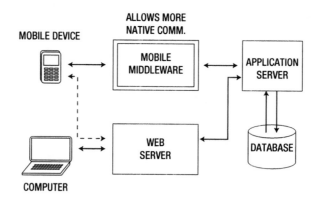

Figure 7-2. Mobile middleware example

With this in mind, we need to identify some of the key scenarios that we will encounter when we decide to develop enterprise mobile applications. In this chapter, I look at two areas that have proven to be a challenge when developing enterprise mobile apps: database access and data representation. These specific areas have proven to be a challenge during mobile enterprise application development. Let's start with database access.

Database Access

Android supports the `javax.sql` and `java.sql` packages that you can use to access a database server. Let's start with a very straightforward, but insecure, example application–just to show you how this approach falls short. Next, we will look at some better techniques. You may wonder why I am wasting your time by looking in some detail at an insecure solution. The point is to see why it is insecure; it is only when you understand how it is insecure that will you fully appreciate the advantages of the correct approach. Feel free to skip forward–at your own peril!

The application will connect to a MySQL database and read the data from the table called `apress`. To execute this correctly, both the Android device and the database server should reside on the same network. I will leave the database setup and creation up to you. Make sure that you set up the database server to listen on the public IP address. You can do this by editing the `my.cnf` file in your MySQL installation. Listing 7-1 contains the database schema. Make sure you create the database named `android` first. After you create the table, enter some test data into it, so that you can retrieve it when you connect to it with your Android app.

Listing 7-1. A MySQL SQL Statement to Create the apress Table

```
CREATE TABLE `apress` (
    `id` int(11) unsigned NOT NULL AUTO_INCREMENT,
    `name` varchar(50) NOT NULL DEFAULT '',
    `email` varchar(50) DEFAULT NULL,
    PRIMARY KEY (`id`)
) ENGINE=MyISAM AUTO_INCREMENT=4 DEFAULT CHARSET=latin1;
```

Let's get started with our app development now. Create a new project called MySQLConnect. In your project folder, create a new folder called lib. Now download the latest version of MySQL Connector/J from www.mysql.com/products/connector/. Next, decompress the archive and copy the .jar file to your lib directory. The file should look something like mysql-connector-java-5.1.15-bin.jar. If you're using Eclipse to develop, then your project layout will look something like the one in Figure 7-3. In my layout, you can see that I have several versions of the MySQL Connector, but I'm using the latest version.

Figure 7-3. The MySQLConnect project structure

In this example, we create a ListView layout. This renders a nice full-screen list of the data we retrieve from our database. Inasmuch as the ListView will contain individual items, we have to tell Android what each item is. To do this, we create a new XML file called list_item.xml containing the text in Listing 7-2, and then save this under the layout folder, as shown in Figure 7-3.

Listing 7-2. The list_item.xml File Contents

```xml
<?xml version="1.0" encoding="utf-8"?>
<TextView xmlns:android="http://schemas.android.com/apk/res/android"
   android:layout_width="fill_parent"
   android:layout_height="fill_parent"
   android:padding="10dp"
   android:textSize="16sp" >
</TextView>
```

This tells Android that each list item is of a text type and gives it some further details about its text padding and font size. Next comes the code for the MySQLConnectActivity.java file (see Listing 7-3). Make a note to change the host IP address, username, and password to what you have created.

Listing 7-3. The MySQLConnectActivity.java Source Code

```java
package net.zenconsult.android;

import java.sql.Connection;
import java.sql.DriverManager;
import java.sql.PreparedStatement;
import java.sql.ResultSet;
import java.sql.SQLException;
import java.util.Enumeration;
import java.util.Hashtable;

import android.app.ListActivity;
import android.os.Bundle;
import android.util.Log;
import android.view.View;
import android.widget.AdapterView;
import android.widget.AdapterView.OnItemClickListener;
import android.widget.ArrayAdapter;
import android.widget.ListView;
import android.widget.TextView;
import android.widget.Toast;

public class MySQLConnectActivity extends ListActivity {
    /** Called when the activity is first created. */
    @Override
    public void onCreate(Bundle savedInstanceState) {
        super.onCreate(savedInstanceState);

        Connection conn = null;
        String host = "192.168.3.105";
        int port = 3306;
        String db = "android";

        String user = "sheran";
        String pass = "P@ssw0rd";
```

```java
String url="jdbc:mysql://"+host+":"+port+"/"+db+"?user="
    + user+"&password="+pass;
String sql="SELECT * FROM apress";

try {
    Class.forName("com.mysql.jdbc.Driver").newInstance();
    conn=DriverManager.getConnection(url);

    PreparedStatement stmt=conn.prepareStatement(sql);
    ResultSet rs=stmt.executeQuery();
    Hashtable<String, String>details=new Hashtable<String, String>();
    while (rs.next()) {
        details.put(rs.getString("name"), rs.getString("email"));
    }
    String[] names=new String[details.keySet().size()];
    int x=0;
    for (Enumeration<String>e=details.keys(); e.hasMoreElements();) {
        names[x]=e.nextElement();
        x++;
    }
    conn.close();
    this.setListAdapter(new ArrayAdapter<String>(this,
        R.layout.list_item, names));

    ListView lv=getListView();
    lv.setTextFilterEnabled(true);

    lv.setOnItemClickListener(new OnItemClickListener() {
        public void onItemClick(AdapterView<?>parent, View view,
        int position, long id) {
            Toast.makeText(getApplicationContext(),
            ((TextView) view).getText(), Toast.LENGTH_SHORT).show();
        }
    });
} catch (ClassNotFoundException e) {
    Log.e("MYSQL", "Class not found!");
} catch (SQLException e) {
    Log.e("MYSQL", "SQL Exception "+e.getMessage());
} catch (InstantiationException e) {
    Log.e("MYSQL", "Instantiation error "+e.getMessage());
} catch (IllegalAccessException e) {
    // TODO Auto-generated catch block
    e.printStackTrace();
}

}
}
```

Because we're accessing the network, you have to make sure that your app has the android.permission.INTERNET permission set in the AndroidManifest.xml file.

Save your project and run it on your Android simulator. Your app should start up, connect to the database, retrieve the data, and display it in a full-screen list view similar to that shown in Figure 7-4.

Figure 7-4. *The output when the app is executed correctly*

As you can see, even though we are able to read data directly from a database, there seems to be a lot of cumbersome code that we need to write, in addition to packaging large JDBC driver libraries with our app.

In some cases, if you have to connect to a database without pure JDBC drivers, then you're stuck. If you look at the security implications, then you need to consider that your database server has to be exposed to the Internet or on the VPN because both the mobile device and the database server should be able to talk to each other. Finally, you can see that the database credentials are stored within the application.

Look at the following section of code:

```
Connection conn = null;
    String host = "192.168.3.105";
    int port = 3306;
    String db = "android";

    String user = "sheran";
    String pass = "P@ssw0rd";
```

```
String url = "jdbc:mysql://"+host+":"+port+"/"+db+"?user = "
    + user+"&password = "+pass;
String sql = "SELECT * FROM apress";
```

The lines starting with `String user` and `String pass` show how the database credentials are hardcoded in the application. If the phone is compromised, an attacker can read the database credentials from your app's data and use them to connect from another computer and attack your database directly.

Therefore, it is not the best approach to use native JDBC connectivity in your Android app. It is better to write a mobile middleware module to allow the app to access the data in a more convenient and secure manner.

How can we improve the database access process? One of the simplest and possibly most mature request/response mechanisms is HTTP. By using HTTP, we can certainly simplify and improve the security of our data access methods. Android already has a very capable HTTP client built in; we have SSL to protect our data; and, if required, we can add an additional layer of encryption to the data going back and forth. You might say it's a no-brainer to use HTTP, so let's do just that.

But how are we supposed to use HTTP to request data from a database? We can use web services to fetch data from our back end. Rather than making very complex web services, we can use REST (representational state transfer) to communicate. Exposing a RESTful API will greatly simplify how our mobile application requests data. Consider this example:

```
https://192.168.3.105/apress/members
```

By making this get request, we can fetch the same set of data that we fetched in our `MySQLConnect` example earlier. It is definitely much simpler to use an HTTP request to fetch the data. Of course, the next step is in retrieving the data. Because we've picked HTTP as our transport mechanism, we have to use a response mechanism that is also HTTP-friendly. This brings us to the problem of data representation. We look at that in the next section.

I hope you're building your own set of libraries for reuse later on. It is a very good practice to get into. I have several different libraries that I create for different tasks when I develop. I have one that handles database connections, one that handles data encoding and decoding, and many other small utility libraries that I use when I build apps. They speed up my development cycles and generally keep everything in a consistent state. I bring this point up now because, if you are going to embark on the journey to build your own custom mobile middleware, then you would be better off if you designed it so that you can plug it into as many deployment scenarios as possible. From there, you can just tweak configuration settings, so you can get up and running quickly.

> **Note**   Custom Libraries
>
> Developing your own libraries as you go is a good practice. For me, writing my own libraries means I will never forget a particular implementation that I did months ago. I can simply call up my shared library function and integrate it with few or no concerns.
>
> Bear in mind, however, that all your external library functions should be extremely simple. These basic functions can later be strung together to perform one complex function. Thus, you can build upon your libraries and completely speed up your development time.
>
> Imagine you spent a lot of time and effort in writing your client an e-commerce application. After your project is completed, there might not be an explicit requirement to keep the source code around. This could matter to you, however, if you meet another customer that wants you to build a similar e-commerce store. Provided you have undisputed ownership of the code you wrote in the earlier application, you can reuse it and, thus, drastically reduce the time required to prepare new applications.

Data Representation

Having got that out of the way, let's talk about data representation. By *data representation*, I'm referring to how your mobile application receives data from the back-end web application. In our case, we're trying to standardize how our mobile app will receive and treat the data. The most common data representation formats available today are XML (eXtensible Markup Language) and JSON (JavaScript Object Notation). So, let's aim to write our mobile application framework to receive and process this type of data. Refer to the appendix for a quick primer on XML and JSON. Another reason to select this type of data representation is that there are many third-party, open source libraries that you can either use or adapt to suit your purpose.

Getting back to our RESTful API request, let's look at the following two potential responses we could have from our mobile middleware:

XML

```
<?xml version = "1.0" encoding = "UTF-8"?>
<apress>
   <users>
    <user name = "Sheran" email = "sheranapress@gmail.com" />
        <user name = "Kevin" email = "kevin@example.com" />
        <user name = "Scott" email = "scottm@example.com" />
   </users>
</apress>
```

JSON

```
{
   users:{
      user:[
```

```
    {
      name:'Sheran',
      email:'sheranapress@gmail.com'
    },
    {
      name:'Kevin',
      email:'kevin@example.com'
    },
    {
      name:'Scott',
      email:'scottm@example.com'
    }
  ]
 }
}
```

The good part is you won't need to write so much code to read the XML and JSON representations. Android includes libraries for parsing both formats. Let's look at some source code. Once again, create a new project and call it RESTFetch. Create the list_item.xml file as you did in the previous example, and then assign the android.permission.INTERNET permission to the app. Listing 7-4 contains the code to the app that will make a request, process the XML response, and render the results in a list. Figure 7-5 contains the output.

Listing 7-4. Fetching Data Using the RESTful API and Processing XML Output

```java
package net.zenconsult.android;

import java.io.BufferedReader;
import java.io.IOException;
import java.io.InputStreamReader;
import java.io.StringReader;
import java.net.URI;
import java.net.URISyntaxException;

import javax.xml.parsers.DocumentBuilder;
import javax.xml.parsers.DocumentBuilderFactory;
import javax.xml.parsers.ParserConfigurationException;

import org.apache.http.HttpResponse;
import org.apache.http.client.HttpClient;
import org.apache.http.client.methods.HttpGet;
import org.apache.http.impl.client.DefaultHttpClient;
import org.w3c.dom.Document;
import org.w3c.dom.NodeList;
import org.xml.sax.InputSource;
import org.xml.sax.SAXException;

import android.app.ListActivity;
import android.os.Bundle;
import android.util.Log;
import android.view.View;
import android.widget.AdapterView;
import android.widget.AdapterView.OnItemClickListener;
```

```java
import android.widget.ArrayAdapter;
import android.widget.ListView;
import android.widget.TextView;
import android.widget.Toast;

public class RESTFetchActivity extends ListActivity {
    @Override
    public void onCreate(Bundle savedInstanceState) {
        super.onCreate(savedInstanceState);
        BufferedReader in = null;

        try {
            HttpClient client = new DefaultHttpClient();
            HttpGet request = new HttpGet();
            request.setURI(new URI("http://192.168.3.105/apress/members"));
            HttpResponse response = client.execute(request);
            in = new BufferedReader(new InputStreamReader(response.getEntity()
                .getContent()));
            StringBuffer sb = new StringBuffer("");
            String line = "";
            String newLine = System.getProperty("line.separator");
            while ((line = in.readLine()) != null) {
                sb.append(line + newLine);
            }
            in.close();

            Document doc = null;

            DocumentBuilderFactory dbf = DocumentBuilderFactory.newInstance();

            DocumentBuilder db = dbf.newDocumentBuilder();

            InputSource is = new InputSource();
            is.setCharacterStream(new StringReader(sb.toString()));
            doc = db.parse(is);

            NodeList nodes = doc.getElementsByTagName("user");
            String[] names = new String[nodes.getLength()];
            for (int k = 0; k < nodes.getLength(); ++k) {
                names[k] = nodes.item(k).getAttributes().getNamedItem("name")
                    .getNodeValue();
            }

            this.setListAdapter(new ArrayAdapter<String>(this,
                R.layout.list_item, names));

            ListView lv = getListView();
            lv.setTextFilterEnabled(true);

            lv.setOnItemClickListener(new OnItemClickListener() {
                public void onItemClick(AdapterView<?> parent, View view,
                    int position, long id) {
                        Toast.makeText(getApplicationContext(),
                        ((TextView) view).getText(), Toast.LENGTH_SHORT)
                        .show();
                }
            });
```

```java
        } catch (IOException e) {
            Log.e("REST", "IOException "+e.getMessage());
        } catch (URISyntaxException e) {
            Log.e("REST", "Incorret URI Syntax "+e.getMessage());
        } catch (ParserConfigurationException e) {
            // TODO Auto-generated catch block
            e.printStackTrace();
        } catch (SAXException e) {
            // TODO Auto-generated catch block
            e.printStackTrace();
        }

    }
}
```

Figure 7-5. The output from the RESTful API query with XML response

For the JSON request/response code and output, take a look at Listing 7-5 and Figure 7-6, respectively.

Listing 7-5. Fetching Data Using the RESTful API and Processing JSON Output

```java
package net.zenconsult.android;

import java.io.BufferedReader;
import java.io.IOException;
import java.io.InputStreamReader;
import java.net.URI;
import java.net.URISyntaxException;
```

```java
import org.apache.http.HttpResponse;
import org.apache.http.client.HttpClient;
import org.apache.http.client.methods.HttpGet;
import org.apache.http.impl.client.DefaultHttpClient;
import org.json.JSONArray;
import org.json.JSONException;
import org.json.JSONObject;

import android.app.ListActivity;
import android.os.Bundle;
import android.util.Log;
import android.view.View;
import android.widget.AdapterView;
import android.widget.AdapterView.OnItemClickListener;
import android.widget.ArrayAdapter;
import android.widget.ListView;
import android.widget.TextView;
import android.widget.Toast;

public class RESTJSONActivity extends ListActivity {
    @Override
    public void onCreate(Bundle savedInstanceState) {
        super.onCreate(savedInstanceState);
        BufferedReader in = null;

        try {
            HttpClient client = new DefaultHttpClient();
            HttpGet request = new HttpGet();
            request.setURI(new URI("http://192.168.3.105/apress/members.json"));
            HttpResponse response = client.execute(request);
            in = new BufferedReader(new InputStreamReader(response.getEntity()
                .getContent()));
            StringBuffer sb = new StringBuffer("");
            String line = "";
            while ((line = in.readLine()) != null) {
                sb.append(line);
            }
            in.close();

            JSONObject users = new JSONObject(sb.toString())
                .getJSONObject("users");
            JSONArray jArray = users.getJSONArray("user");
            String[] names = new String[jArray.length()];
            for (int i = 0; i < jArray.length(); i++) {
                JSONObject jsonObject = jArray.getJSONObject(i);
                names[i] = jsonObject.getString("name");
            }

            this.setListAdapter(new ArrayAdapter<String>(this,
                R.layout.list_item, names));

            ListView lv = getListView();
            lv.setTextFilterEnabled(true);

            lv.setOnItemClickListener(new OnItemClickListener() {
                public void onItemClick(AdapterView<?> parent, View view,
```

```
        int position, long id) {
            Toast.makeText(getApplicationContext(),
            ((TextView) view).getText(), Toast.LENGTH_SHORT)
            .show();
        }
    });
} catch (IOException e) {
    Log.e("RESTJSON", "IOException "+e.getMessage());
} catch (URISyntaxException e) {
    Log.e("RESTJSON", "Incorret URI Syntax "+e.getMessage());
} catch (JSONException e) {
    // TODO Auto-generated catch block
    e.printStackTrace();
}

}
}
```

Figure 7-6. *The output from the RESTful API query with a JSON response*

If required, you can combine both the XML and JSON examples into one class file. To distinguish between the response types, you can usually append a file extension to the members request. Thus, for an XML response, call http://192.168.3.105/apress/members.xml; and, for a JSON response, call http://192.168.3.105/apress/members.json. Again, we can modify our examples so that we analyze the response data to discover the structure automatically. This will free us to extract data based on certain keywords, regardless of where they appear. In most cases, however, it doesn't hurt to define your data structure in your code because, after all, your mobile app will only talk to your mobile middleware.

Speaking of mobile middleware, where exactly is the server-side code to generate the XML and JSON responses? At the present time, such code is beyond the scope of this book. But in order to give you a better understanding of how you can implement this type of mobile middleware, take a look at the appendix for a very basic example that also shares deployment instructions.

Summary

We took a very quick look at two of the problems you would face if asked to develop a mobile application that works with a legacy enterprise system. No doubt, you might come across different challenges when you set foot in the realm of mobile enterprise app development. In almost all cases, you can overcome these problems by building translation or bridge modules in your mobile middleware.

As far as security is concerned, at the beginning of this chapter, we discussed that opening up the enterprise environment to the public is a bad idea. The best approach is to reduce the exposure that enterprise systems have by using middleware. We decided to use HTTP, not only for its simplicity, but also because we don't need to do anything magical to secure it. The same security controls as SSL can be applied without having to change any of our code. Of course, we could also create additional layers of encryption and compression for our data.

## Chapter 8

Concepts in Action: Part 2

In this chapter, as in Chapter 4, we will take a closer look at source code and applications that implement some of the theoretical concepts we've discussed. This will give you a better feeling for how to apply them in practice. This chapter's code examples will focus on secure authentication and safeguarding passwords on the device. Recall that we've discussed two mechanisms of logging in to back-end applications without storing credentials on the device. Here, we will explore more detailed source code related to that.

OAuth

Let's revisit the OAuth login example covered in Chapter 6. We discussed developing an application that will interact with Google Picasa Web Albums to read off a list of albums from a specific user. The code in this chapter will do this. Check this book's page on the Apress web site at `www.apress.com` for the latest code. First, let's look at our project structure in Figure 8-1. You will see several source files. We will go over each source file's key functionality.

Retrieving the Token

You can see the structure of the OAuth example project in Figure 8-1. Let's start with the application's entry point, which is `OAuthPicasaActivity.java`, shown in Listing 8-1.

Figure 8-1. The OAuth example's project structure

You will see that this file is doing several things. First, it instantiates the OAuth class. Next, it retrieves the Token object and tests whether the token is valid to make a request in the isValidForReq() function. It also tests whether the token is expired in the isExpired() function. If the token is valid, then it goes onto instantiate the DataFetcher object that queries Picasa for a list of all albums belonging to the user, sheranapress. This is done in the df.fetchAlbums("sheranapress") line.

Listing 8-1. The Application Entry Point

```
package net.zenconsult.android;

import android.app.ListActivity;
import android.content.Intent;
import android.os.Bundle;
import android.view.View;
import android.widget.AdapterView;
import android.widget.AdapterView.OnItemClickListener;
import android.widget.ArrayAdapter;
```

```java
import android.widget.ListView;
import android.widget.TextView;
import android.widget.Toast;

public class OAuthPicasaActivity extends ListActivity {
        OAuthPicasaActivity act;

        /** Called when the activity is first created. */
        @Override
        public void onCreate(Bundle savedInstanceState) {
                super.onCreate(savedInstanceState);
                act = this;
                OAuth o = new OAuth(this);
                Token t = o.getToken();

                if (!t.isValidForReq()) {
                        Intent intent = new Intent(this, AuthActivity.class);
                        this.startActivity(intent);
                }
                if (t.isExpired()) {
                        o.getRequestToken();
                }

                DataFetcher df = new DataFetcher(t);
                df.fetchAlbums("sheranapress");
                String[] names = new String[] {}; // Add bridge code here to parse XML
                                                  // from DataFetcher and populate
                                                  // your List

                this.setListAdapter(new ArrayAdapter<String>(this, R.layout.list_item,
                                names));

                ListView lv = getListView();
                lv.setTextFilterEnabled(true);

                lv.setOnItemClickListener(new OnItemClickListener() {
                        public void onItemClick(AdapterView<?> parent, View view,
                                        int position, long id) {
                                Toast.makeText(getApplicationContext(),
                                                ((TextView) view).getText(),
Toast.LENGTH_SHORT).show();
                        }
                });
        }
}
```

Obviously, the first time this application is run, there won't be a valid Token object. The application handles this condition by first fetching an authorization code, and then fetching a request token with that authorization code (per Google's OAuth 2 specification). Let's see how this is done next.

Handling Authorization

Listing 8-2 shows the source code for the part of our application that handles authorization. If you look at the doAuth() function, you will see that a request to Google is made, and the application displays the response in a WebView object. A WebView object is a field that displays HTML content. You can think of it like a minimalistic browser. This allows the end user to log into her Google account and grant or deny our application access. The user is presented with the Google login web page and is asked to log in with her credentials. These credentials are not stored anywhere in our application. If he grants our application permission to use her Picasa stream, then Google sends back an authorization code. Our application will store this authorization code in the Token object. This is done in the ClientHandler object (see Listing 8-3).

Listing 8-2. The Auth Activity Gets the Authorization Code.

```java
package net.zenconsult.android;

import java.net.URI;
import java.net.URISyntaxException;

import org.apache.http.message.BasicNameValuePair;

import android.app.Activity;
import android.content.Context;
import android.os.Bundle;
import android.util.Log;
import android.webkit.WebView;

public class AuthActivity extends Activity {
    private BasicNameValuePair clientId = new BasicNameValuePair("client_id",
                "200744748489.apps.googleusercontent.com");
    private BasicNameValuePair clientSecret = new BasicNameValuePair(
                "client_secret", "edxCTl_L8_SFl1rz2klZ4DbB");
    private BasicNameValuePair redirectURI = new BasicNameValuePair(
                "redirect_uri", "urn:ietf:wg:oauth:2.0:oob");
    private String scope = "scope=https://picasaweb.google.com/data/";
    private String oAuth = "https://accounts.google.com/o/oauth2/auth?";
    private String httpReqPost = "https://accounts.google.com/o/oauth2/token";
    private final String FILENAME = ".oauth_settings";
    private URI uri;
    private WebView wv;
    private Context ctx;
    private Token token;

    @Override
    public void onCreate(Bundle savedInstanceState) {
        super.onCreate(savedInstanceState);
        setContentView(R.layout.auth);
        doAuth();
    }

    public void doAuth() {
        try {
            uri = new URI(oAuth + clientId + "&" + redirectURI + "&" + scope
                        + "&response_type = code");
            wv = (WebView) findViewById(R.id.webview);
            wv.setWebChromeClient(new ClientHandler(this));
            wv.setWebViewClient(new MWebClient());
            wv.getSettings().setJavaScriptEnabled(true);
```

```
                    wv.loadUrl(uri.toASCIIString());
                    Log.v("OAUTH", "Calling " + uri.toASCIIString());
            } catch (URISyntaxException e) {
                    e.printStackTrace();
            }
        }
}
```

Think of the ClientHandler as an observer. It watches for a specific string–"Success"–in each HTML web page. If it finds the word, then we've got the correct authorization code, which means that our end user has approved our access.

Listing 8-3. The ClientHandler Writes the Authorization Code to the Token Object.

```java
package net.zenconsult.android;

import android.app.Activity;
import android.util.Log;

import android.webkit.WebChromeClient;
import android.webkit.WebView;
import android.widget.Toast;

public class ClientHandler extends WebChromeClient {
        private Activity activity;
        private OAuth oAuth;

        public ClientHandler(Activity act) {
                activity = act;
                oAuth = new OAuth(activity);
        }

        @Override
        public void onReceivedTitle(WebView view, String title) {
                String code = "";
                if (title.contains("Success")) {
                        code = title.substring(title.indexOf(' = ') + 1, title.length());
                        setAuthCode(code);
                        Log.v("OAUTH", "Code is " + code);
                        oAuth.getRequestToken();
                        oAuth.writeToken(oAuth.getToken());
                        Toast toast = Toast.makeText(activity.getApplicationContext(),
                                        "Authorization Successful", Toast.LENGTH_SHORT);
                        toast.show();
                        activity.finish();
                } else if (title.contains("Denied")) {
                        code = title.substring(title.indexOf(' = ') + 1, title.length());
                        setAuthCode(code);
                        Log.v("OAUTH", "Denied, error was " + code);
                        Toast toast = Toast.makeText(activity.getApplicationContext(),
                                        "Authorization Failed", Toast.LENGTH_SHORT);
                        toast.show();
                        activity.finish();
                }
        }
}
```

```
        public String getAuthCode() {
                return oAuth.getToken().getAuthCode();
        }

        public void setAuthCode(String authCode) {
                oAuth.getToken().setAuthCode(authCode);
        }

        @Override
        public void onProgressChanged(WebView view, int progress) {

        }
}
```

After the authorization code has been written to the internal storage, you will need to fetch a request token. In Oauth, you will need a request token to begin the process of requesting access to any resources. Please refer to Figure 6-25 for the OAuth flow process. If you look at our ClientHandler code once more, you will see the lines oAuth.getRequestToken() and oAuth.writeToken(oAuth.getToken()). These two lines use the instantiated OAuth class (see Listing 8-4) to ask for a request token and then write it to the internal storage. The getRequestToken() function handles that part. It is also worth noting that whenever I mention storage, you should consider using encryption. Please refer to the "Data Storage in Android" section in Chapter 5 for more information on implementing secure data storage.

You might have already noticed that the token is being used as a singleton. It gets written to and read from the device's internal storage. This allows different areas of the application to read and write to it during different phases of the authentication process. Ideally, this should be synchronized to ensure that reads and writes occur exclusively from one class.

Listing 8-4. If Authorization Code Is Valid, OAuth Class Gets Request Tokens from Google.

```
package net.zenconsult.android;

import java.io.BufferedInputStream;
import java.io.BufferedOutputStream;
import java.io.File;
import java.io.FileInputStream;
import java.io.FileNotFoundException;
import java.io.FileOutputStream;
import java.io.IOException;
import java.io.ObjectInputStream;
import java.io.ObjectOutputStream;
import java.io.StreamCorruptedException;
import java.io.UnsupportedEncodingException;
import java.net.URI;
import java.util.ArrayList;
import java.util.List;

import org.apache.http.HttpEntity;
import org.apache.http.HttpResponse;
import org.apache.http.NameValuePair;
import org.apache.http.client.ClientProtocolException;
import org.apache.http.client.HttpClient;
```

```java
import org.apache.http.client.entity.UrlEncodedFormEntity;
import org.apache.http.client.methods.HttpPost;
import org.apache.http.impl.client.DefaultHttpClient;
import org.apache.http.message.BasicNameValuePair;
import org.apache.http.util.EntityUtils;
import org.json.JSONException;
import org.json.JSONObject;

import android.app.Activity;
import android.content.Context;
import android.util.Log;
import android.webkit.WebView;
import android.widget.Toast;

public class OAuth {
        private BasicNameValuePair clientId = new BasicNameValuePair("client_id",
                        "200744748489.apps.googleusercontent.com");
        private BasicNameValuePair clientSecret = new BasicNameValuePair(
                        "client_secret", "edxCTl_L8_SFl1rz2klZ4DbB");
        private BasicNameValuePair redirectURI = new BasicNameValuePair(
                        "redirect_uri", "urn:ietf:wg:oauth:2.0:oob");
        private String scope = "scope=https://picasaweb.google.com/data/";
        private String oAuth = "https://accounts.google.com/o/oauth2/auth?";
        private String httpReqPost = "https://accounts.google.com/o/oauth2/token";
        private final String FILENAME = ".oauth_settings";
        private URI uri;
        private WebView wv;
        private Context ctx;
        private Activity activity;
        private boolean authenticated;
        private Token token;

        public OAuth(Activity act) {
                ctx = act.getApplicationContext();
                activity = act;
                token = readToken();
        }

        public Token readToken() {
                Token token = null;
                FileInputStream fis;
                try {
                        fis = ctx.openFileInput(FILENAME);
                        ObjectInputStream in = new ObjectInputStream(
                                        new BufferedInputStream(fis));
                        token = (Token) in.readObject();
                        if (token == null) {
                                token = new Token();
                                writeToken(token);
                        }
                        in.close();
                        fis.close();
                } catch (FileNotFoundException e) {
```

```
                              writeToken(new Token());
              } catch (StreamCorruptedException e) {
                      // TODO Auto-generated catch block
                      e.printStackTrace();
              } catch (IOException e) {
                      // TODO Auto-generated catch block
                      e.printStackTrace();
              } catch (ClassNotFoundException e) {
                      // TODO Auto-generated catch block
                      e.printStackTrace();
              }
              return token;
      }
      public void writeToken(Token token) {
              try {
                      File f = new File(FILENAME);
                      if (f.exists()) {
                              f.delete();
                      }
                      FileOutputStream fos = ctx.openFileOutput(FILENAME,
                                      Context.MODE_PRIVATE);

                      ObjectOutputStream out = new ObjectOutputStream(
                                      new BufferedOutputStream(fos));
                      out.writeObject(token);
                      out.close();
                      fos.close();
              } catch (FileNotFoundException e1) {
                      Log.e("OAUTH", "Error creating settings file");
              } catch (IOException e2) {
                      // TODO Auto-generated catch block
                      e2.printStackTrace();
              }
      }

      public void getRequestToken() {
              HttpClient httpClient = new DefaultHttpClient();
              HttpPost post = new HttpPost(httpReqPost);
              List<NameValuePair> nvPairs = new ArrayList<NameValuePair>();
              nvPairs.add(clientId);
              nvPairs.add(clientSecret);
              nvPairs.add(new BasicNameValuePair("code", token.getAuthCode()));
              nvPairs.add(redirectURI);
              nvPairs.add(new BasicNameValuePair("grant_type", "authorization_code"));
              try {
                      post.setEntity(new UrlEncodedFormEntity(nvPairs));
                      HttpResponse response = httpClient.execute(post);
                      HttpEntity httpEntity = response.getEntity();
                      String line = EntityUtils.toString(httpEntity);
                      JSONObject jObj = new JSONObject(line);
                      token.buildToken(jObj);
                      writeToken(token);
              } catch (UnsupportedEncodingException e) {
```

```
                              // TODO Auto-generated catch block
                              e.printStackTrace();
                    } catch (ClientProtocolException e) {
                              // TODO Auto-generated catch block
                              e.printStackTrace();
                    } catch (IOException e) {
                              if (e.getMessage().equals("No peer certificate")) {
                                        Toast toast = Toast.makeText↵
(activity.getApplicationContext(),
                                                  "Possible HTC Error for Android 2.3.3",
                                                  Toast.LENGTH_SHORT);
                                        toast.show();
                              }
                              Log.e("OAUTH", "IOException " + e.getMessage());
                    } catch (JSONException e) {
                              // TODO Auto-generated catch block
                              e.printStackTrace();
                    }

          }

          public Token getToken() {
                    return token;
          }

          public void setToken(Token token) {
                    this.token = token;
          }
}
```

I have provided the source code to the Token object in Listing 8-5. The object implements the Serializable interface; therefore, it can be written in its entirety to the internal store. Make sure you run it through your data storage encryptor for added security. The Token object contains little logic apart from checking its own expiry date.

Listing 8-5. The Token Object

```
package net.zenconsult.android;

import java.io.Serializable;
import java.util.Calendar;

import org.json.JSONException;
import org.json.JSONObject;

public class Token implements Serializable {
          /**
           *
           */
          private static final long serialVersionUID = 6534067628631656760L;
          private String refreshToken;
          private String accessToken;
          private Calendar expiryDate;
          private String authCode;
          private String tokenType;
```

```java
        private String name;
        public Token() {
                setExpiryDate(0);
                setTokenType("");
                setAccessToken("");
                setRefreshToken("");
                setName("");
        }

        public Token(JSONObject response) {
                try {
                        setExpiryDate(response.getInt("expires_in"));
                } catch (JSONException e) {
                        setExpiryDate(0);
                }
                try {
                        setTokenType(response.getString("token_type"));
                } catch (JSONException e) {
                        setTokenType("");
                }
                try {
                        setAccessToken(response.getString("access_token"));
                } catch (JSONException e) {
                        setAccessToken("");
                }
                try {
                        setRefreshToken(response.getString("refresh_token"));
                } catch (JSONException e) {
                        setRefreshToken("");
                }
        }

        public void buildToken(JSONObject response) {
                try {
                        setExpiryDate(response.getInt("expires_in"));
                } catch (JSONException e) {
                        setExpiryDate(0);
                }
                try {
                        setTokenType(response.getString("token_type"));
                } catch (JSONException e) {
                        setTokenType("");
                }
                try {
                        setAccessToken(response.getString("access_token"));
                } catch (JSONException e) {
                        setAccessToken("");
                }
                try {
                        setRefreshToken(response.getString("refresh_token"));
                } catch (JSONException e) {
                        setRefreshToken("");
                }
        }
}
```

```java
public boolean isValidForReq() {
        if (getAccessToken() != null && !getAccessToken().equals("")) {
                return true;
        } else {
                return false;
        }
}

public boolean isExpired() {
        Calendar now = Calendar.getInstance();
        if (now.after(getExpiryDate()))
                return true;
        else
                return false;
}

public String getRefreshToken() {
        return refreshToken;
}

public void setRefreshToken(String refreshToken) {
        if (refreshToken == null)
                refreshToken = "";
        this.refreshToken = refreshToken;
}

public String getAccessToken() {
        return accessToken;
}

public void setAccessToken(String accessToken) {
        if (accessToken == null)
                accessToken = "";
        this.accessToken = accessToken;
}

public Calendar getExpiryDate() {
        return expiryDate;
}

public void setExpiryDate(int seconds) {
        Calendar now = Calendar.getInstance();
        now.add(Calendar.SECOND, seconds);
        this.expiryDate = now;
}

public String getAuthCode() {
        return authCode;
}

public void setAuthCode(String authCode) {
        if (authCode == null)
                authCode = "";
        this.authCode = authCode;
}
```

```
        public String getTokenType() {
                return tokenType;
        }

        public void setTokenType(String tokenType) {
                if (tokenType == null)
                        tokenType = "";
                this.tokenType = tokenType;
        }

        public String getName() {
                return name;
        }

        public void setName(String name) {
                this.name = name;
        }
}
```

Finally, there is the DataFetcher class (see Listing 8-6). You use this class to make all protected queries to Picasa. For example, you can use this class to fetch albums and photos or even to upload photos. Picasa sends back all its replies in XML (notice that I have left the XML parsing component out). If you want to know how to write a simple XML parser to read Picasa responses, then look in the book's Appendix.

Listing 8-6. The DataFetcher Class

```
package net.zenconsult.android;

import java.io.IOException;

import org.apache.http.HttpEntity;
import org.apache.http.HttpResponse;
import org.apache.http.client.ClientProtocolException;
import org.apache.http.client.HttpClient;
import org.apache.http.client.methods.HttpGet;
import org.apache.http.impl.client.DefaultHttpClient;
import org.apache.http.util.EntityUtils;

public class DataFetcher {
        private HttpClient httpClient;
        private Token token;

        public DataFetcher(Token t) {
                token = t;
                httpClient = new DefaultHttpClient();
        }

        public void fetchAlbums(String userId) {
                String url = "https://picasaweb.google.com/data/feed/api/user/"
                                + userId;
                try {
```

```
                HttpResponse resp = httpClient.execute(buildGet(
                            token.getAccessToken(), url));
                if (resp.getStatusLine().getStatusCode() == 200) {
                        HttpEntity httpEntity = resp.getEntity();
                        String line = EntityUtils.toString(httpEntity);

                        // Do your XML Parsing here
                }
        } catch (ClientProtocolException e) {
                // TODO Auto-generated catch block
                e.printStackTrace();
        } catch (IOException e) {
                // TODO Auto-generated catch block
                e.printStackTrace();
        }
}

public HttpGet buildGet(String accessToken, String url) {
        HttpGet get = new HttpGet(url);
        get.addHeader("Authorization", "Bearer " + accessToken);
        return get;
}

}
```

Challenge Response

We very briefly discussed challenge response-based authentication in Chapter 6. Let's take a closer look at challenge-response authentication techniques. What follows is a brief overview of the steps required, also shown in Figure 8-2. Bear in mind that this is simply a one-way authentication with the server authenticating the client:

1. Client requests a secure resource.

2. Server sends a challenge string C.

3. Client generates a random string R.

4. Client generates a hash based on C, R, and the user's password.

5. Client sends R and the hash back to the server.

6. Server calculates hash based on the stored user password and R.

7. Server sends back the requested resource if correctly authenticated; otherwise, an error message is sent back.

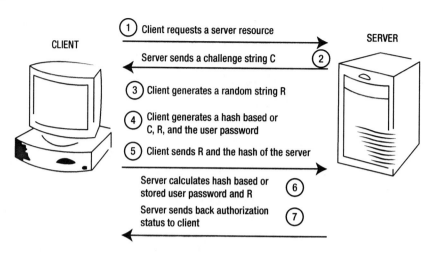

Figure 8-2. *A graphical representation of the data exchange between client and server during a challenge-response session*

> **Note**   You could also have a mutual authentication scenario where the client authenticates the server.

Let's write some simple code that helps us use challenge-response authentication techniques in our applications. You should evolve these sections of code to suit your own needs and then use them them in your applications. They can help reduce the exposure of your end users because you won't be storing any credentials on your device. I've given you examples of both client and server-side code. The server-side code is written in Java, and it can be packaged as a Java Web Archive File (WAR file). To test it, package it as a WAR file and simply drop it in the deployment directory of your servlet container or application server.

Let's start with the server-side code. We will create a Java servlet that will handle the HTTP communications with our client. Figure 8-3 shows the project structure. The structure illustrates that we have a fairly simple project with only four files.

Figure 8-3. Our challenge-response server-side project structure

One of them, the Hex.java file, is a utility class that I use for converting various data types into hexadecimal strings; the other, Constants.java, holds the username and password. These credentials will be used to compare what the client enters.

You will also notice that we are using the Apache Commons Codec library to help with our Base64 encoding and decoding. In this example, we are adapting the CRAM-MD5 authentication approach to use SHA1 hashes instead. (CRAM is the Challenge Response Authentication Mechanism.)

I'll lay out the code first, and then explain what we're trying to do. Let's start with our servlet Login.java, shown in Listing 8-7. This code has two main branches:

- Main Branch 1 handles cases where a request is received without the "challenge" parameter.

- Main Branch 2 handles cases where a request is received with the "challenge" parameter.

Listing 8-7. The Login Class

```
package net.zenconsult.android;

import java.io.IOException;
import javax.servlet.ServletException;
import javax.servlet.annotation.WebServlet;
import javax.servlet.http.HttpServlet;
import javax.servlet.http.HttpServletRequest;
import javax.servlet.http.HttpServletResponse;
import javax.servlet.http.HttpSession;
```

```java
/**
 * Servlet implementation class login
 */
@WebServlet(description = "Login Servlet", urlPatterns = { "/login" })
public class Login extends HttpServlet {
        private static final long serialVersionUID = 1 L;

        /**
         * @see HttpServlet#HttpServlet()
         */
        public Login() {
                super();
                // TODO Auto-generated constructor stub
        }

        /**
         * @see HttpServlet#doGet(HttpServletRequest request, HttpServletResponse
         *       response)
         */
        protected void doGet(HttpServletRequest request,
                        HttpServletResponse response) throws ServletException,
IOException {
                HttpSession session = request.getSession();
                String param = request.getParameter("challenge");
                if (param != null) {
                        CRAM c = (CRAM) session.getAttribute("challenge");
                        if (c == null) {
                                c = new CRAM();
                                session.setAttribute("challenge", c);
                                response.setHeader("Content-Type", "text/xml");
                                response.getWriter().write(c.generate());
                        } else {
                                if (c.verifyChallenge(param.trim())) {
                                        response.setHeader("Content-Type", "text/xml");
                                        response.getWriter().write
(c.generateReply("Authorized"));

                                        session.invalidate();
                                } else {
                                        response.setHeader("Content-Type", "text/xml");
                                        response.getWriter().write
(c.generateReply("Unauthorized"));

                                        session.invalidate();
                                }
                        }
                } else {
                        CRAM c = new CRAM();
                        session.setAttribute("challenge", c);
                        response.setHeader("Content-Type", "text/xml");
                        response.getWriter().write(c.generate());
                }
        }
```

```
/**
 * @see HttpServlet#doPost(HttpServletRequest request, HttpServletResponse
 *        response)
 */
protected void doPost(HttpServletRequest request,
                HttpServletResponse response) throws ServletException, ↵
IOException {
            // TODO Auto-generated method stub

        }
}
```

In each case, we are creating a CRAM object. This object will generate our challenge strings and also do a comparison of the user response. We associate the CRAM object with each HTTP session, so that the same challenge bytes are used for verification.

Now would be a great time to take a protocol-level look at what takes place between client and server (see Figure 8-4). The entire flow had four steps and is quite simple:

1. The client requests a protected resource.

2. The server replies with a challenge.

3. The client uses the end-user credentials to calculate the response and send it back to the server.

4. Finally, the server will calculate the same response, compare it, and decide whether the user is authorized.

All of this is done without sending the user credentials over the Web.

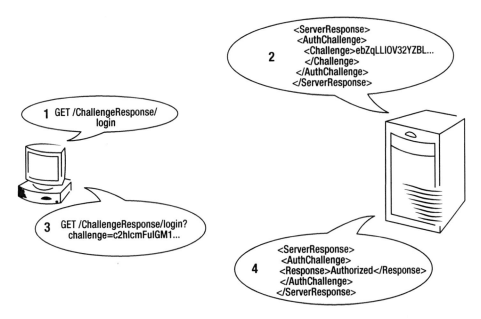

Figure 8-4. The challenge response message flow

The source code for the CRAM object is shown in Listing 8-8.

Listing 8-8. The CRAM Class

```
package net.zenconsult.android;

import java.io.StringWriter;
import java.security.InvalidKeyException;
import java.security.NoSuchAlgorithmException;
import java.security.SecureRandom;

import javax.crypto.Mac;
import javax.crypto.SecretKey;
import javax.crypto.spec.SecretKeySpec;
import javax.xml.parsers.DocumentBuilder;
import javax.xml.parsers.DocumentBuilderFactory;
import javax.xml.parsers.ParserConfigurationException;
import javax.xml.transform.OutputKeys;
import javax.xml.transform.Transformer;
import javax.xml.transform.TransformerConfigurationException;
import javax.xml.transform.TransformerException;
import javax.xml.transform.TransformerFactory;
import javax.xml.transform.dom.DOMSource;
import javax.xml.transform.stream.StreamResult;

import org.apache.commons.codec.binary.Base64;
import org.w3c.dom.Document;
import org.w3c.dom.Element;
import org.w3c.dom.Text;

public class CRAM implements Constants {
        private final byte[] secret = new byte[32];

        public CRAM() {
                SecureRandom sr = new SecureRandom();
                sr.nextBytes(secret);
        }

        public String generate() {
                DocumentBuilderFactory dbFactory = DocumentBuilderFactory.newInstance();
                DocumentBuilder dBuilder = null;
                try {
                        dBuilder = dbFactory.newDocumentBuilder();
                } catch (ParserConfigurationException e) {
                        // TODO Auto-generated catch block
                        e.printStackTrace();
                }
                Document doc = dBuilder.newDocument();

                // Build Root
                Element root = doc.createElement("ServerResponse");
                doc.appendChild(root);

                // Challenge Section
```

```java
        Element authChallenge = doc.createElement("AuthChallenge");
        root.appendChild(authChallenge);

        // The Challenge
        Element challenge = doc.createElement("Challenge");
        Text challengeText = doc.createTextNode(Base64
                        .encodeBase64String(secret));
        challenge.appendChild(challengeText);
        authChallenge.appendChild(challenge);

        TransformerFactory tFactory = TransformerFactory.newInstance();
        Transformer transformer = null;
        try {
                transformer = tFactory.newTransformer();
        } catch (TransformerConfigurationException e) {
                // TODO Auto-generated catch block
                e.printStackTrace();
        }
        transformer.setOutputProperty(OutputKeys.OMIT_XML_DECLARATION, "yes");
        transformer.setOutputProperty(OutputKeys.INDENT, "yes");
        StringWriter sw = new StringWriter();
        StreamResult res = new StreamResult(sw);
        DOMSource source = new DOMSource(doc);
        try {
                transformer.transform(source, res);
        } catch (TransformerException e) {
                // TODO Auto-generated catch block
                e.printStackTrace();
        }
        String xml = sw.toString();
        return xml;
}

public boolean verifyChallenge(String userResponse) {
        String algo = "HmacSHA1";
        Mac mac = null;
        try {
                mac = Mac.getInstance(algo);
        } catch (NoSuchAlgorithmException e) {
                // TODO Auto-generated catch block
                e.printStackTrace();
        }
        SecretKey key = new SecretKeySpec(PASSWORD.getBytes(), algo);

        try {
                mac.init(key);
        } catch (InvalidKeyException e) {
                // TODO Auto-generated catch block
                e.printStackTrace();
        }
        String tmpHash = USERNAME + " " + Hex.toHex(mac.doFinal(secret));
        String hash = Base64.encodeBase64String(tmpHash.getBytes());
        return hash.equals(userResponse);
}
```

```java
public String generateReply(String response) {
        DocumentBuilderFactory dbFactory = DocumentBuilderFactory.newInstance();
        DocumentBuilder dBuilder = null;
        try {
                dBuilder = dbFactory.newDocumentBuilder();
        } catch (ParserConfigurationException e) {
                // TODO Auto-generated catch block
                e.printStackTrace();
        }
        Document doc = dBuilder.newDocument();

        // Build Root
        Element root = doc.createElement("ServerResponse");
        doc.appendChild(root);

        // Challenge Section
        Element authChallenge = doc.createElement("AuthChallenge");
        root.appendChild(authChallenge);

        // Reply
        Element challenge = doc.createElement("Response");
        Text challengeText = doc.createTextNode(response);
        challenge.appendChild(challengeText);
        authChallenge.appendChild(challenge);

        TransformerFactory tFactory = TransformerFactory.newInstance();
        Transformer transformer = null;
        try {
                transformer = tFactory.newTransformer();
        } catch (TransformerConfigurationException e) {
                // TODO Auto-generated catch block
                e.printStackTrace();
        }
        transformer.setOutputProperty(OutputKeys.OMIT_XML_DECLARATION, "yes");
        transformer.setOutputProperty(OutputKeys.INDENT, "yes");
        StringWriter sw = new StringWriter();
        StreamResult res = new StreamResult(sw);
        DOMSource source = new DOMSource(doc);
        try {
                transformer.transform(source, res);
        } catch (TransformerException e) {
                // TODO Auto-generated catch block
                e.printStackTrace();
        }
        String xml = sw.toString();
        return xml;
    }
}
```

At the point when the CRAM object is instantiated, a new 32-byte random number is generated. This is a field, and it is closely associated with the CRAM object. This random string of bytes will be used for further challenge generation and response verification.

Next comes the generate() function, which does nothing more than create a Base64 encoding of the random bytes that we generated. It then creates an XML response, along with this challenge string, and then returns it to the servlet so that it can be sent to the end user.

The next function, verifyChallenge(String userResponse), is an important one. It generates the response that a client should generate if the correct credentials were used. The original random byte sequence is hashed using the HMAC-SHA1 algorithm using the stored user password. The username is then prepended to this hash and Base64 encoded. Next, it is compared to the client response, which should be the same–provided the username and password are correctly entered, of course.

Finally, the generateReply(String response) function will send back the word specified in the response variable as XML text. The servlet calls this function using either of the following words, depending on whether the client response is correct:

- "Authorized"

- "Unauthorized"

You could also have a special authorization cookie set to indicate that the session is authenticated. There are many ways in which this code can be improved and built upon. I've included basic code here, so that you can get a better understanding of how to implement a challenge-response authentication mechanism in your front- and back-end applications.

Now that we've looked at the server-side code, let's write some code for the client side. I've shown the project structure in Figure 8-5. Once again, the skeletal project is fairly simple, with only three files, not counting the hexadecimal functions class. I will take you through the functionality of each file, starting with the entry point, ChallengeResponseClientActivity.java (see Listing 8-9). The code is fairly straightforward with the creation of a Comms object (see Listing 8-10) and a CRAM object (see Listing 8-11). The Comms object handles all network communication between the client and server, while the CRAM object handles the hash generation part. The CRAM object is very similar to the CRAM object on the server side. In this case, there is no verification component because the client does not verify the server. Instead, the CRAM object uses the HMAC-SHA1 to calculate the hash based on the server challenge.

Listing 8-9. The Entry Point and Main Activity

```java
package net.zenconsult.android;

import android.app.Activity;
import android.os.Bundle;
import android.view.View;
import android.widget.Button;
import android.widget.Toast;

public class ChallengeResponseClientActivity extends Activity {
        /** Called when the activity is first created. */
        @Override
        public void onCreate(Bundle savedInstanceState) {
                super.onCreate(savedInstanceState);
                setContentView(R.layout.main);
                final Activity activity = this;

                final Button button = (Button) findViewById(R.id.button1);
                button.setOnClickListener(new View.OnClickListener() {
                        public void onClick(View v) {
                                Comms c = new Comms(activity);
```

```
                                String challenge = c.getChallenge();
                                CRAM cram = new CRAM(activity);
                                String hash = cram.generate(challenge);
                                String reply = c.sendResponse(hash);
                                if (c.authorized(reply)) {
                                        Toast toast = Toast.makeText(
                                                        activity↩
.getApplicationContext(), "Login success",
                                                                Toast.LENGTH_LONG);
                                        toast.show();
                                } else {
                                        Toast toast = Toast.makeText(
                                                        activity↩
.getApplicationContext(), "Login failed",
                                                                Toast.LENGTH_LONG);
                                        toast.show();
                                }
                        }
                });
        }
}
```

Listing 8-10. The Comms Class Handles All HTTP Requests for This App.

```
package net.zenconsult.android;

import java.io.ByteArrayInputStream;
import java.io.IOException;
import java.io.InputStream;
import java.util.ArrayList;
import java.util.List;

import javax.xml.parsers.DocumentBuilder;
import javax.xml.parsers.DocumentBuilderFactory;
import javax.xml.parsers.ParserConfigurationException;

import org.apache.http.HttpResponse;
import org.apache.http.NameValuePair;
import org.apache.http.client.ClientProtocolException;
import org.apache.http.client.methods.HttpGet;
import org.apache.http.client.utils.URLEncodedUtils;
import org.apache.http.impl.client.DefaultHttpClient;
import org.apache.http.message.BasicNameValuePair;
import org.apache.http.util.EntityUtils;
import org.w3c.dom.Document;
import org.w3c.dom.NodeList;
import org.xml.sax.SAXException;

import android.app.Activity;
import android.content.Context;
import android.util.Log;
import android.widget.Toast;
```

```java
public class Comms {
        private final String url = "http://192.168.3.117:8080/ChallengeResponse/login";
        private Context ctx;
        private DefaultHttpClient client;

        public Comms(Activity act) {
                ctx = act.getApplicationContext();
                client = new DefaultHttpClient();
        }

        public String sendResponse(String hash) {
                List<NameValuePair> params = new ArrayList<NameValuePair>();
                params.add(new BasicNameValuePair("challenge", hash));
                String paramString = URLEncodedUtils.format(params, "utf-8");
                String cUrl = url + "?" + paramString;
                return doGetAsString(cUrl);
        }

        public boolean authorized(String response) {
                InputStream is = new ByteArrayInputStream(response.getBytes());
                DocumentBuilderFactory dbFactory = DocumentBuilderFactory.newInstance();
                DocumentBuilder db = null;
                Document doc = null;
                String reply = "";
                try {
                        db = dbFactory.newDocumentBuilder();
                        doc = db.parse(is);
                        NodeList nl = doc.getElementsByTagName("Response");
                        reply = nl.item(0).getTextContent();
                        is.close();
                } catch (ParserConfigurationException e) {
                        // TODO Auto-generated catch block
                        e.printStackTrace();
                } catch (SAXException e) {
                        // TODO Auto-generated catch block
                        e.printStackTrace();
                } catch (IOException e) {
                        // TODO Auto-generated catch block
                        e.printStackTrace();
                }
                return reply.matches("Authorized");
        }

        public String getChallenge() {
                InputStream challengeText = doGetAsInputStream(url);
                DocumentBuilderFactory dbFactory = DocumentBuilderFactory.newInstance();
                DocumentBuilder db = null;
                Document doc = null;
                String challenge = "";
                try {
                        db = dbFactory.newDocumentBuilder();
                        doc = db.parse(challengeText);
                        NodeList nl = doc.getElementsByTagName("Challenge");
                        challenge = nl.item(0).getTextContent();
```

```
                            challengeText.close();
            } catch (SAXException e) {
                    // TODO Auto-generated catch block
                    e.printStackTrace();
            } catch (IOException e) {
                    // TODO Auto-generated catch block
                    e.printStackTrace();
            } catch (ParserConfigurationException e) {
                    // TODO Auto-generated catch block
                    e.printStackTrace();
            }
            return challenge;
    }

    public String doGetAsString(String url) {
            HttpGet request = new HttpGet(url);
            String result = "";
            try {
                    HttpResponse response = client.execute(request);
                    int code = response.getStatusLine().getStatusCode();
                    if (code == 200) {
                            result = EntityUtils.toString(response.getEntity());
                    } else {
                            Toast toast = Toast.makeText(ctx, "Status Code " + code,
                                            Toast.LENGTH_SHORT);
                            toast.show();
                    }
            } catch (ClientProtocolException e) {
                    // TODO Auto-generated catch block
                    e.printStackTrace();
            } catch (IOException e) {
                    // TODO Auto-generated catch block
                    e.printStackTrace();
            }
            return result;
    }

    public InputStream doGetAsInputStream(String url) {
            HttpGet request = new HttpGet(url);
            InputStream result = null;
            try {
                    HttpResponse response = client.execute(request);
                    int code = response.getStatusLine().getStatusCode();
                    if (code == 200) {
                            result = response.getEntity().getContent();
                    } else {
                            Toast toast = Toast.makeText(ctx, "Status Code " + code,
                                            Toast.LENGTH_SHORT);
                            toast.show();
                    }
            } catch (ClientProtocolException e) {
                    // TODO Auto-generated catch block
                    e.printStackTrace();
            } catch (IOException e) {
```

```
                                // TODO Auto-generated catch block
                                e.printStackTrace();
                        }
                        return result;
                }
        }
}
```

Listing 8-11. *The CRAM Class*

```java
package net.zenconsult.android;

import java.security.InvalidKeyException;
import java.security.NoSuchAlgorithmException;

import javax.crypto.Mac;
import javax.crypto.SecretKey;
import javax.crypto.spec.SecretKeySpec;

import android.app.Activity;
import android.util.Base64;
import android.widget.TextView;

public class CRAM {
        private Activity activity;

        public CRAM(Activity act) {
                activity = act;
        }

        public String generate(String serverChallenge) {
                String algo = "HmacSHA1";
                TextView pass = (TextView) activity.findViewById(R.id.editText2);
                byte[] server = Base64.decode(serverChallenge, Base64.DEFAULT);

                Mac mac = null;
                try {
                        mac = Mac.getInstance(algo);
                } catch (NoSuchAlgorithmException e) {
                        // TODO Auto-generated catch block
                        e.printStackTrace();
                }
                String keyText = pass.getText().toString();
                SecretKey key = new SecretKeySpec(keyText.getBytes(), algo);
                try {
                        mac.init(key);
                } catch (InvalidKeyException e) {
                        // TODO Auto-generated catch block
                        e.printStackTrace();
                }
                byte[] tmpHash = mac.doFinal(server);
                TextView user = (TextView) activity.findViewById(R.id.editText1);
                String username = user.getText().toString();
                String concat = username + " " + Hex.toHex(tmpHash);
                String hash = Base64.encodeToString(concat.getBytes(), Base64.URL_SAFE);
                return hash;
        }

}
```

On the client side, if all goes according to plan, your app will greet you with a wonderful "Login success" pop-up message, as shown in Figure 8-5.

Figure 8-5. A successful challenge-response authentication

Summary

I hope these examples give you a better understanding of how to implement alternate authentication mechanisms in your mobile and back-end web applications. By depending less and less on user credential storage, you are improving the security of your app significantly.

Implementing OAuth in your front- and back-end code is not going to be the easiest thing to accomplish. However, it can be rewarding to spend some initial effort and prepare a reusable set of libraries for your future code. The same goes for CRAM. These authentication methods aren't the first thing that many developers will want to consider because of the effort involved. It can, however, ensure your app is more secure than the ones that store and forward user credentials over the wire.

Hopefully, you will consider what you have learned so far useful. My hopes are that you'll be convinced that you haven't been wasting your time on the abbreviation of this new protocol, known as the Challenge Response Authentication Protocol.

Chapter 9

Chapter

Publishing and Selling
Your Apps

You may decide that you want to make some cash by selling the applications that you've spent countless hours developing. With the way the mobile space has evolved lately, it is now easier than ever for an individual developer to market, sell, and earn income from his applications. Apple has the iTunes App Store, BlackBerry has AppWorld, and Android has the Market. The process of selling your apps is simple: sign up as an application seller and publish your app on the online store. Once approved, your app will be instantly available for download by Android users. In this chapter, we will examine this process in a bit more detail, and I'll cover the basics of how you can get your app listed on the Android Market. Along the way, I'll touch on what steps are involved from the time when you've decided your app works well, up until the point you decide to publish it online. I am also going to cover another important point when it comes to selling your apps online: revenue protection. If your app becomes popular on any of the online stores, then it is more than likely that you're going to attract individuals who want to "crack" and pirate your app. Unless you've planned to give out your app for no charge, this could hurt your income. I will spend some time on this topic and explore how you can write good license key and registration routines that will deter piracy. During this section, I will also shed some light on some of the things your app may have to go through if it finds itself in a hostile environment.

Developer Registration

Do you recall the Proxim app that we wrote before? Let's publish that on the Android Market for free. I'll take you through the basics of publishing an app. In this case, I won't enter any specific financial information that would allow me to receive money (e.g., my bank account number) because I'm not planning on selling the app. Also, I don't want to spend too much time telling you how to register yourself as a developer because Google already has a lot of helpful information on that and a comprehensive set of articles on how to get started.

One of the first things you need to do before publishing your app is to sign up as a developer. You can sign up using one of your existing Gmail accounts for this. Navigate to `http://market.android.com/publish` and sign in (see Figure 9-1). At the time of publication, the cost to register a developer is $25. You pay this amount through Google Checkout, and it is a one-time fee for registration (see Figure 9-2). The fee exists to make sure that you are a serious developer. According to Google, it helps to reduce the number of "spammy products" that may make their way onto the market.

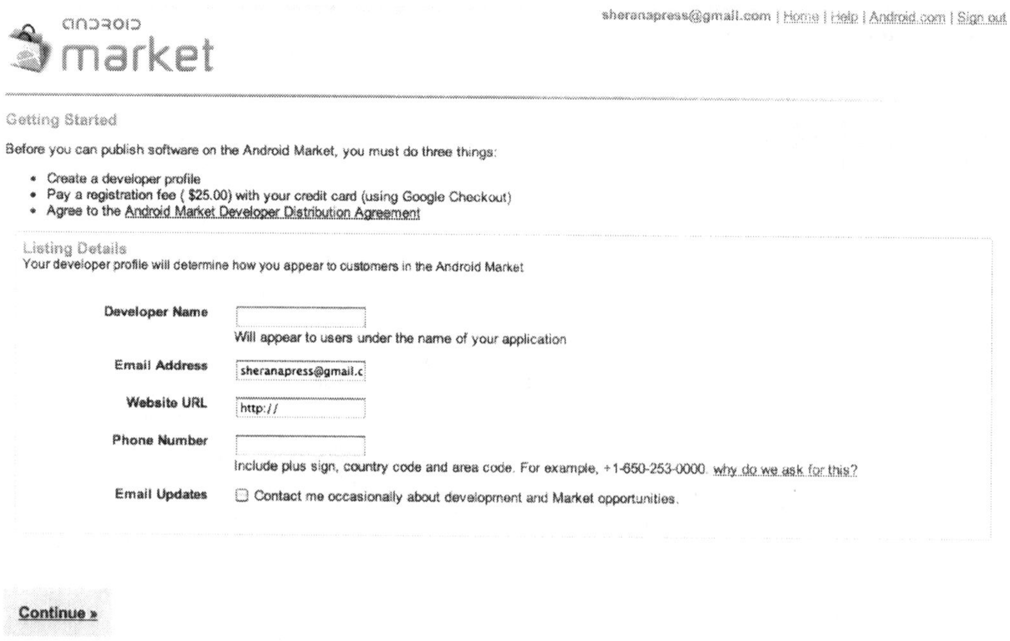

Figure 9-1. Registering to publish your application

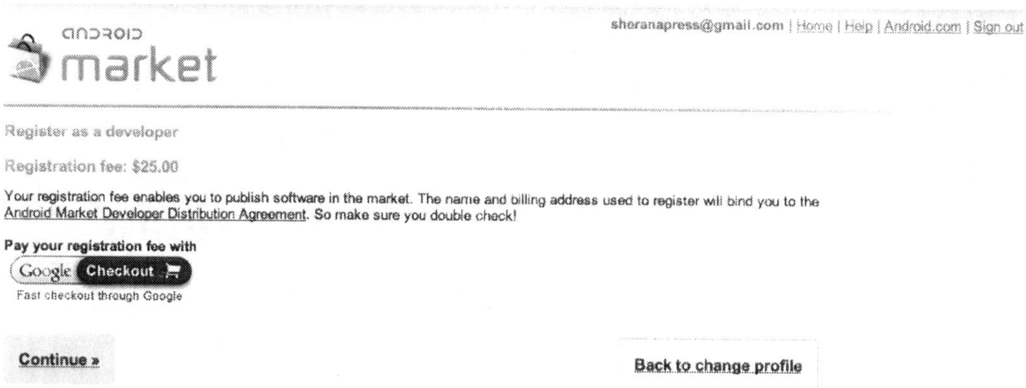

Figure 9-2. The registration fee payment

Your Apps—Exposed

It's a jungle out there. Who knows where your apps will end up? Well, this is probably an exaggeration; but as I mentioned in the beginning of this chapter, any number of people who have access to the Android Market can download your app. It's great if these downloads translate into revenue; unfortunately, in some cases, piracy of your app can make you lose revenue. Piracy is nothing new. It has existed since the desktop computing era began. The formal term for piracy is *copyright infringement of software*; it means copying a piece of software from one device to another without the proper authorization. In most cases, this simply translates into copying software that you haven't purchased and paid for. If a friend buys some software and gives you a copy that you don't pay for, then you are in possession of software that you have not purchased. Growing up, I remember how I would eagerly go into this store where I bought my first 8088 computer (a huge beast of heavy, impregnable metal) and spend my weekly allowance on the latest games. At the time, I never thought that I was engaged in aiding piracy. As far as I knew, I paid cash and received a game in return. I never realized that I was paying about a tenth of what the software cost to buy from the original developer. I was also not aware that my money never reached the original developer; it stayed in the store.

Developers still lose revenue to software piracy. How popular your software is and how you distribute it will play a key role in how much your software is pirated. For instance, if you allow a free trial download of your app that is limited to seven days, but allow full access to all its features, then it is likely that someone will try to circumvent this seven-day trial. If successful, then there is no need for that person to pay for and download the full version of your app. Another insidious form of copyright infringement is code theft. This occurs when someone downloads your software, reverse-engineers it, and copies the code. The person then repackages your code as a new product and puts it on sale, usually for a lower price. The only way to prove this copyright infringement is to download the new and similar app, reverse engineer it and look for coding structures that are identical to your own. If the code is modified though, it will be a tough task to prove and even tougher to fight in court because of high costs involved. As an individual developer, you are probably not going to have many resources to devote to fighting piracy. Therefore it is best to decide if you want to protect your apps from piracy–and if so, how.

In this section, I will discuss some of the topics that you will want to consider in your decision. Then, if you are convinced that you need to secure your apps from piracy, I will give you some examples of how to use Android's License Verification Library (LVL) to deter future pirates from illegally copying and distributing your apps. Let's start with what happens to your app when it is placed on the Android Market.

Available for Download

When your app is available on the Android Market, end-users can download it. If you charge for the app, then obviously the end-user will have to purchase it first before downloading it. Once the app is on a device, you can copy it onto a computer by using the Android Debug Bridge (adb). adb allows you to interact with your Android device in different ways. You can install software, open a Linux shell to explore the device file system, and copy files to and from the device. I've given you a full list of adb features in Listing 9-1. You can find adb in your Android SDK under the `platform-tools` directory. For me, this location is at `/Users/sheran/android-sdk-mac_x86/platform-tools`.

Listing 9-1. Adb Commands and Features

```
Android Debug Bridge version 1.0.29
 -d                            - directs command to the only connected USB device
                                 returns an error if more than one USB device is↵
present.
 -e                            - directs command to the only running emulator.
                                 returns an error if more than one emulator is running.
 -s <serial number>           - directs command to the USB device or emulator with
                                 the given serial number. Overrides ANDROID_SERIAL
                                 environment variable.
 -p <product name or path>    - simple product name like 'sooner', or
                                 a relative/absolute path to a product
                                 out directory like 'out/target/product/sooner'.
                                 If -p is not specified, the ANDROID_PRODUCT_OUT
                                 environment variable is used, which must
                                 be an absolute path.
 devices                       - list all connected devices
 connect <host>[:<port>]       - connect to a device via TCP/IP
                                 Port 5555 is used by default if no port number is↵
specified.
 disconnect [<host>[:<port>]] - disconnect from a TCP/IP device.
                                 Port 5555 is used by default if no port number is↵
specified.

                                 Using this command with no additional arguments
                                 will disconnect from all connected TCP/IP devices.

device commands:
  adb push <local> <remote>    - copy file/dir to device
  adb pull <remote> [<local>]  - copy file/dir from device
  adb sync [ <directory> ]     - copy host->device only if changed
                                 (-l means list but don't copy)
                                 (see 'adb help all')
  adb shell                    - run remote shell interactively
  adb shell <command>          - run remote shell command
  adb emu <command>            - run emulator console command
  adb logcat [ <filter-spec> ] - View device log
  adb forward <local> <remote> - forward socket connections
                                 forward specs are one of:
                                   tcp:<port>
                                   localabstract:<unix domain socket name>
                                   localreserved:<unix domain socket name>
                                   localfilesystem:<unix domain socket name>
                                   dev:<character device name>
                                   jdwp:<process pid> (remote only)
  adb jdwp                     - list PIDs of processes hosting a JDWP transport
 adb install [-l] [-r] [-s] <file>- push this package file to the device and install↵
it
                                 ('-l' means forward-lock the app)
                                 ('-r' means reinstall the app, keeping its data)
                                 ('-s' means install on SD card instead of internal↵
```

```
storage)
  adb uninstall [-k]<package>- remove this app package from the device
                                ('-k' means keep the data and cache directories)
  adb bugreport              -  return all information from the device
                                that should be included in a bug report.

  adb backup [-f<file>] [-apk|-noapk] [-shared|-noshared] [-all] [-system|-nosystem]↵
[<packages...>]
                             -  write an archive of the device's data to<file>.
                                If no -f option is supplied then the data is written
                                to "backup.ab" in the current directory.
                                (-apk|-noapk enable/disable backup of the .apks↵
themselves
                                  in the archive; the default is noapk.)
                                (-shared|-noshared enable/disable backup of the↵
device's
                                  shared storage / SD card contents; the default is↵
noshared.)
                                (-all means to back up all installed applications)
                                (-system|-nosystem toggles whether -all automatically↵
includes
                                  system applications; the default is to include↵
system apps)
                                (<packages...>is the list of applications to be↵
backed up.  If
                                  the -all or -shared flags are passed, then the↵
package
                                  list is optional.  Applications explicitly given↵
on the
                                  command line will be included even if -nosystem↵
would
                                  ordinarily cause them to be omitted.)

  adb restore<file>          - restore device contents from the<file>backup archive

  adb help                   -  show this help message
  adb version                -  show version num
scripting:
  adb wait-for-device        -  block until device is online
  adb start-server           -  ensure that there is a server running
  adb kill-server            -  kill the server if it is running
  adb get-state              -  prints: offline | bootloader | device
  adb get-serialno           -  prints: <serial-number>
  adb status-window          -  continuously print device status for a specified device
  adb remount                -  remounts the /system partition on the device read-write
  adb reboot [bootloader|recovery] - reboots the device, optionally into the↵
bootloader or recovery program
  adb reboot-bootloader      -  reboots the device into the bootloader
  adb root                   -  restarts the adbd daemon with root permissions
  adb usb                    -  restarts the adbd daemon listening on USB
  adb tcpip<port>            -  restarts the adbd daemon listening on TCP on the↵
specified port
networking:
  adb ppp<tty>[parameters]   - Run PPP over USB.
```

```
Note: you should not automatically start a PPP connection.
<tty> refers to the tty for PPP stream. Eg. dev:/dev/omap_csmi_tty1
[parameters] - Eg. defaultroute debug dump local notty usepeerdns
```

```
adb sync notes: adb sync [ <directory> ]
  <localdir> can be interpreted in several ways:
```

```
  - If <directory> is not specified, both /system and /data partitions will be updated.
```

```
  - If it is "system" or "data", only the corresponding partition
    is updated.
```

```
environmental variables:
  ADB_TRACE                      - Print debug information. A comma separated list of⏎
the following values

                                 1 or all, adb, sockets, packets, rwx, usb, sync,⏎
sysdeps, transport, jdwp
  ANDROID_SERIAL                 - The serial number to connect to. -s takes priority⏎
over this if given.
  ANDROID_LOG_TAGS               - When used with the logcat option, only these debug⏎

tags are printed.
```

For someone wishing to copy files to or from the Android device to his computer, the `pull` and `push` commands are useful. Generally, third-party apps are stored in the /data/app directory of the device. First, let's check out the what's in the application directory:

1. Open a shell to your device by typing `adb shell`.

2. Change directories to /data/app by doing `cd /data/app`.

3. List the contents by using `ls`.

You will see something similar to this as your output:

```
$ ./adb shell
# cd /data/app
# ls
net.zenconsult.android.chucknorris-1.apk
test_limits_host
ApiDemos.apk
test_list_host
test_set_host
CubeLiveWallpapers.apk
test_iostream_host
test_iomanip_host
SoftKeyboard.apk
test_iterator_host
test_vector_host
test_algorithm_host
test_uninitialized_host
GestureBuilder.apk
test_sstream_host
test_char_traits_host
test_memory_host
```

```
test_ios_base_host
test_type_traits_host
test_ios_pos_types_host
test_streambuf_host
test_functional_host
test_string_host
```

Let's look at the net.zenconsult.android.chucknorris-1.apk package. We can copy it to have a look at it.

To copy a package from the device, you use the command adb pull. Let's do that. Exit your current adb shell session by typing exit and pressing Return. Next, type in the following:

```
adb pull /data/app/ net.zenconsult.android.chucknorris-1.apk.
```

This will copy the package to your current directory. If you want to copy the file elsewhere on your computer, replace the period with a directory of your choice. You now have a copy of the package file, just as it would have left the developer's computer. We can explore this file further.

Reverse Engineering

The curious sort will not stop with just copying the package file from the device. They will want to take a closer look at the application and code. This is where reverse engineering comes into play. Reverse engineering is the process of taking a compiled binary program and generating equivalent assembly or source code for easier readability. In most cases, obtaining source code is the ideal situation because it is far easier to read source code than it is to read assembly code. The process of reverse engineering a program into assembly code is known as *dis-assembly*, and generating source code from a program is called *de-compiling*. You have to understand that each CPU will have its own assembler and its own assembly language. That is why assembly code on an Intel x86 CPU is different from that on an ARM-based CPU. We don't have to go to such a low level though. Generally, working to the level of the Dalvik VM (DVM) is sufficient.

The DVM also contains an assembler. For the purpose of this explanation, assume that the DVM is the CPU. Therefore, your Java code has to be built to work on the DVM by using this assembler. This is what happens when you build your application using the Android SDK. The resulting executable files that will run on the DVM are called *Dalvik Executable* (DEX) files. You write your code in Java and compile it into a Java class file using the standard Java compiler (javac). Then, to convert this class file into the DEX format, you can use the command called dx. You can find this tool in your platform-tools directory, as well. Once the DEX file is generated, it is packaged into an APK file. You may already be aware that an APK file is nothing more than a ZIP file. If I wanted to examine the files in my APK file, I would extract the file as follows:

```
$ unzip net.zenconsult.android.chucknorris-1.apk
Archive:  net.zenconsult.android.chucknorris-1.apk
  inflating: res/layout/main.xml
  inflating: AndroidManifest.xml
 extracting: resources.arsc
 extracting: res/drawable-hdpi/ic_launcher.png
 extracting: res/drawable-ldpi/ic_launcher.png
 extracting: res/drawable-mdpi/ic_launcher.png
  inflating: classes.dex
  inflating: META-INF/MANIFEST.MF
```

```
inflating: META-INF/CERT.SF
inflating: META-INF/CERT.RSA
$
```

Notice the DEX file.

Fortunately, Eclipse will handle the entire build process and will make sure to insert, align, and package all relevant files within our project. I've shown the entire build process in Figure 9-3.

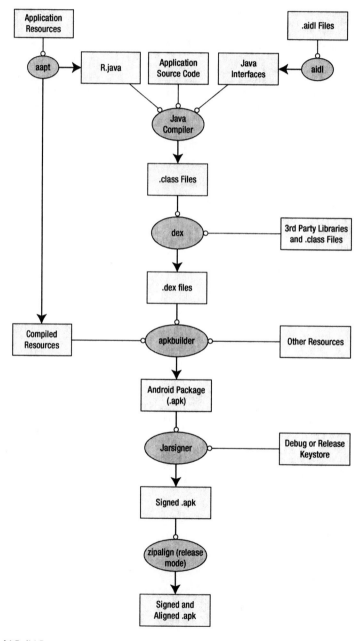

Figure 9-3. *The Android Build Process*

Now that you have a brief idea of how the applications are built, let's see how we can take them apart. As we saw when we extracted the contents of our APK file, we have direct access to the `classes.dex` file. Since we're considering DVM to be our CPU, this is our binary. Just like a Win32 PE-file or a Linux ELF file, this DEX file is our binary because it runs on our CPU (DVM). Google has also provided us with the tool called dexdump (also found in your platform-tools directory). If I were to run dexdump on my extracted `classes.dex` file, I would get a lot of information on how the file was built, including members, calls, and so on. Listing 9-2 shows what a typical dexdump disassembly looks like.

Listing 9-2. Dexdump Output

```
$ dexdump -d classes.dex
...
...
Virtual methods   -
    #0                 : (in Lnet/zenconsult/android/chucknorris/e;)
      name             : 'a'
      type             : '()Ljava/lang/String;'
      access           : 0x0011 (PUBLIC FINAL)
      code             -
      registers        : 16
      ins              : 1
      outs             : 2
      insns size       : 180 16-bit code units
0009d4:                                |[0009d4] net.zenconsult.android↵
.chucknorris.e.a:()Ljava/lang/String;
0009e4: 1202                           |0000: const/4 v2, #int 0 // #0
0009e6: 1a00 5100                      |0001: const-string v0,↵
 "http://www.chucknorrisfacts.com/" // string@0051
0009ea: 7020 2900 0f00                 |0003: invoke-direct {v15, v0},↵
 Lnet/zenconsult/android/chucknorris/e;.a:(Ljava/lang/String;)Ljava/io/InputStream;↵
 // method@0029
0009f0: 0c05                           |0006: move-result-object v5
0009f2: 7100 1600 0000                 |0007: invoke-static {},↵
 Ljavax/xml/parsers/DocumentBuilderFactory;.newInstance:()Ljavax/xml/↵
parsers/DocumentBuilderFactory; // method@0016
0009f8: 0c00                           |000a: move-result-object v0
0009fa: 1a01 0000                      |000b: const-string v1, "" // string@0000
0009fe: 2206 1100                      |000d: new-instance v6,↵
 Ljava/util/Vector; // type@0011
000a02: 7010 1000 0600                 |000f: invoke-direct {v6},↵
 Ljava/util/Vector;.<init>:()V // method@0010
000a08: 6e10 1500 0000                 |0012: invoke-virtual {v0},↵
 Ljavax/xml/parsers/DocumentBuilderFactory;.newDocumentBuilder:()Ljavax/xml↵
/parsers/DocumentBuilder; // method@0015
000a0e: 0c00                           |0015: move-result-object v0
000a10: 6e20 1400 5000                 |0016: invoke-virtual {v0, v5},
...
...
```

I guess you get the idea. Disassembled DEX files are hard to read, just like disassembled code on Linux or Windows. It is not impossible; but for the uninitiated, it can seem overwhelming.

Thanks to some very clever people who also believed disassembled DEX files are hard to read, we now have disassemblers that can generate more readable output. A talented individual known as JesusFreke built a completely new assembler and disassembler for the DEX file format. He called these smali and baksmali, respectively; and he has released them as open source software at http://code.google.com/p/smali/. The beauty of his approach is that you can disassemble a file, modify the disassembly code, and reassemble it into a DEX file. You may wonder what's special about smali and baksmali, so I'll show you some output of the same file disassembled by baksmali:

```
$ java -jar ~/Downloads/baksmali-1.2.8.jar classes.dex
$ cd out/net/zenconsult/android/chucknorris/
$ ls
ChuckNorrisFactsActivity.smali    b.smali               d.smali
a.smali                           c.smali               e.smali
$
```

This disassembles the files into individual ones, and it is far easier to examine. Let's look at the file b.smali. Listing 9-3 shows the disassembled code.

Listing 9-3. Code Disassembled by baksmali

```
.class public final Lnet/zenconsult/android/chucknorris/b;
.super Ljava/lang/Thread;

# instance fields
.field private a:Lnet/zenconsult/android/chucknorris/a;

# direct methods
.method public constructor<init>(Lnet/zenconsult/android/chucknorris/a;)V
    .registers 2

    invoke-direct {p0}, Ljava/lang/Thread;->><init>()V

    iput-object p1, p0, Lnet/zenconsult/android/chucknorris/b;->a:Lnet/zenconsult
/android/chucknorris/a;

    return-void
.end method

# virtual methods
.method public final run()V
    .registers 3

    new-instance v0, Lnet/zenconsult/android/chucknorris/e;

    invoke-direct {v0}, Lnet/zenconsult/android/chucknorris/e;-><init>()V

    iget-object v1, p0, Lnet/zenconsult/android/chucknorris/b;->a:Lnet/zenconsult
/android/chucknorris/a;

    invoke-virtual {v0}, Lnet/zenconsult/android/chucknorris/e;->a()Ljava/lang/String;

    move-result-object v0

    invoke-interface {v1, v0}, Lnet/zenconsult/android/chucknorris/a;->a
(Ljava/lang/String;)V

    return-void
.end method
```

This isn't all that much better, but it is significantly easier to understand and follow. Another tool that allows you to disassemble DEX files is called dedexer, and it was written by Gabor Paller. You can find it at http://dedexer.sourceforge.net/.

A significantly easier tool to use is dex2jar, which you can find at http://code.google.com/p/dex2jar/. This tool helps you deconstruct android .dex files directly into a Java JAR file. After you have the JAR file generated, you can use any standard Java decompiler to retrieve the Java source code. I use JD-, or Java Decompiler, which you can find at http://java.decompiler.free.fr/.

To run dex2jar, simply download and unpack the archive file from the URL given, and then run the .bat or .sh file, as shown in Figure 9-4. This will generate a .jar file with a similar sounding name, except it ends in _dex2jar.jar. If you open this file in JD-GUI, you can look at the reconstructed Java source code. In most cases, the decompiled code can be recompiled in your development environment like Eclipse.

```
○ ○ ○                               4. bash
azazel:dex2jar-0.0.9.7 sheran$ ./dex2jar.sh classes.dex
dex2jar version: translator-0.0.9.7
dex2jar classes.dex -> classes_dex2jar.jar
Done.
azazel:dex2jar-0.0.9.7 sheran$ []
```

Figure 9-4. Running dex2jar on a classes.dex file

Figure 9-5 shows you what the decompiled source code looks like in JD-GUI. JD-GUI has an easy and intuitive interface for browsing the JAR file source code and can even export the source into Java files.

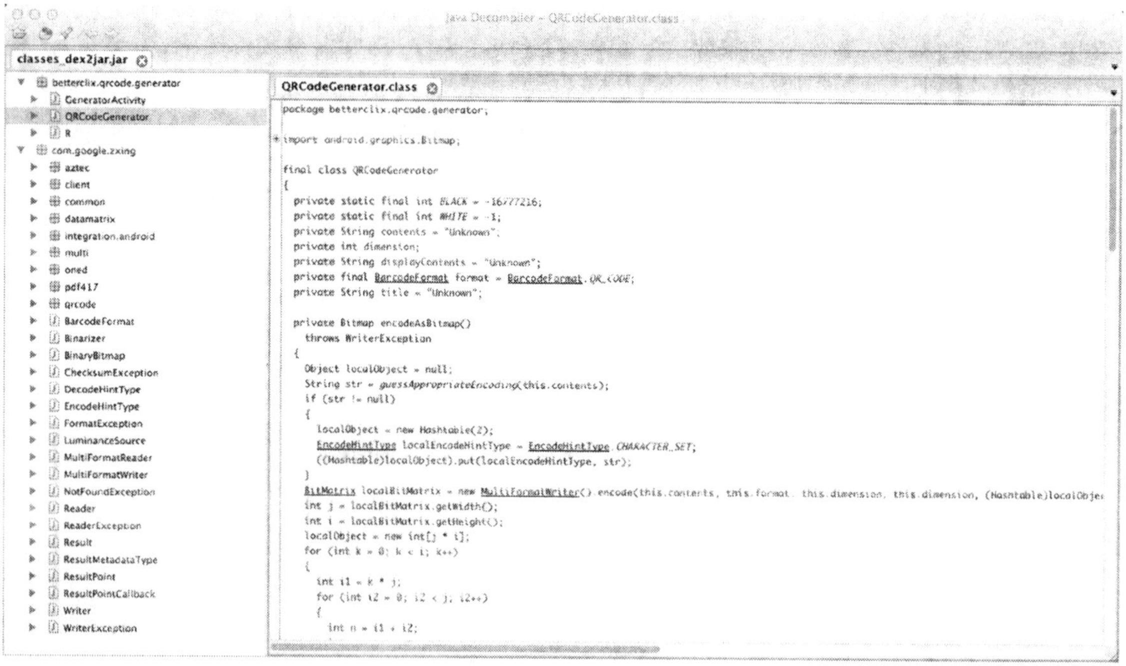

Figure 9-5. *Decompiling the JAR file using JD-GUI*

With evolving tools like this, it is much easier for determined users to download, modify, and repackage your apps. If you plan to write your own protection mechanisms to prevent piracy, then you're off to a good start. But is it something you should consider? I'll talk briefly about that in the next section.

Should You License?

This question is a common one that I see developers asking. Do you really want to spend as much time as you took developing your app just to write a licensing routine? The answer is very subjective, and it really depends on what your app does. If your app has features that are unique or several times more efficient than other apps; or if it demonstrates a sense of uniqueness that can ensure it sells very well, then it might be worth considering to develop a licensing routine. Note, however, that when I say *licensing*, that does not mean the same thing as charging. You can still charge users for your app; it's just that, if your app doesn't have a way of monitoring licenses, then end users will have free rein in copying and distributing the app.

Another reason you might consider developing a licensing routine would be if you plan on developing more apps in the future, and you would want to license them, as well. In that case, you could simply use the one licensing library you've already created. One caveat to this, however, is that you need to vary the algorithms or license check routines for each app slightly. So, if one of your apps is pirated, then the same technique will not work on the other apps.

Android License Verification Library

Google has provided the Android LVL to help developers protect their apps from indiscriminate distribution. You add LVL to your application build path and use APIs from it to check and verify user licenses. LVL interfaces with the Android Market App (see Figure 9-6) that will then check with the Google market server. Based on the response you receive, you can choose whether to permit or deny further application use. The best way to learn about LVL is to use it in an example app, so let's do that. Before you proceed, however, you will need to sign up as an app publisher. You don't need to do that right now, though. Let's begin by writing a very basic app with which to test our licensing routines. Listings 9-4 through 9-7 demonstrate the code for this basic app.

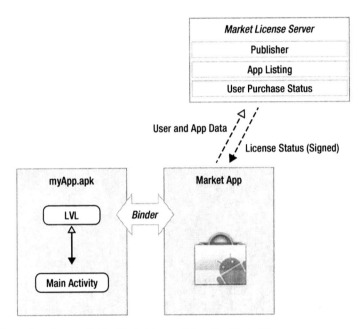

Figure 9-6. *The LVL library interfaces with the Market App and then the Market Server*

The app itself is quite simple. It involves Chuck Norris (as you would have guessed from the previous section of extracting and reverse engineering.) We all know and fear Chuck Norris. His roundhouse kicks are legendary, and people report that they are often the cause of many a natural disaster. To pay my respects to the great man, I will create my app around fetching the latest Chuck Norris fact from a popular site called Chuck Norris Facts (www.chucknorrisfacts.com/). The app will fetch all quotes from this site and display a random one in the text area of our app screen. Simply click the button to fetch another fact. I am relying on the randomness of the quotes from the site to make sure a new quote appears each time. As always, this app is merely an illustration of how and where you will need to add LVL checks. There is little to no error checking, and the functionality of the app is minimal. Having said this, I don't know why I need to defend myself; it's a Chuck Norris app. That alone should be sufficient. You may notice several areas in the app that you can improve. Feel free to do so.

Listing 9-4. The Main Activity—ChuckNorrisFactsActivity.java

```java
package net.zenconsult.android.chucknorris;

import android.app.Activity;
import android.os.Bundle;
import android.view.View;
import android.widget.Button;
import android.widget.TextView;

public class ChuckNorrisFactsActivity extends Activity implements CommsEvent {
        private Activity activity;
        private TextView view;
        private CommsEvent event;

        /** Called when the activity is first created. */
        @Override
        public void onCreate(Bundle savedInstanceState) {
                super.onCreate(savedInstanceState);
                setContentView(R.layout.main);
                activity = this;
                event = this;
                view = (TextView) findViewById(R.id.editText1);

                // Click Button
                final Button button = (Button) findViewById(R.id.button1);
                button.setOnClickListener(new View.OnClickListener() {
                        public void onClick(View v) {
                                view.setText("Fetching fact...");
                                CommsNotifier c = new CommsNotifier(event);
                                c.start();
                        }
                });
        }

        @Override
        public void onTextReceived(final String text) {
                runOnUiThread(new Runnable() {
                        public void run() {
                                view.setText(text);
                        }
                });
        }
}
```

Listing 9-5. The CommsEvent.java file

```java
package net.zenconsult.android.chucknorris;

public interface CommsEvent {
        public void onTextReceived(String text);
}
```

Listing 9-6. The CommsNotifier.java ile

```java
package net.zenconsult.android.chucknorris;

public class CommsNotifier extends Thread {
        private CommsEvent event;

        public CommsNotifier(CommsEvent evt) {
                event = evt;
        }

        public void run() {
                Comms c = new Comms();
                event.onTextReceived(c.get());
        }
}
```

Listing 9-7. The Comms.java File

```java
package net.zenconsult.android.chucknorris;

import java.io.IOException;
import java.io.InputStream;
import java.util.Random;
import java.util.Vector;

import javax.xml.parsers.DocumentBuilder;
import javax.xml.parsers.DocumentBuilderFactory;
import javax.xml.parsers.ParserConfigurationException;

import org.apache.http.HttpResponse;
import org.apache.http.client.ClientProtocolException;
import org.apache.http.client.methods.HttpGet;
import org.apache.http.impl.client.DefaultHttpClient;
import org.apache.http.util.EntityUtils;
import org.w3c.dom.Document;
import org.w3c.dom.NamedNodeMap;
import org.w3c.dom.Node;
import org.w3c.dom.NodeList;
import org.xml.sax.SAXException;

import android.app.Activity;
import android.content.Context;
import android.util.Log;
import android.widget.Toast;

public class Comms {
        private final String url = "http://www.chucknorrisfacts.com/";

        private DefaultHttpClient client;

        public Comms() {
                client = new DefaultHttpClient();
        }
```

```java
public String get() {
        InputStream pageStream = doGetAsInputStream(url);
        DocumentBuilderFactory dbFactory = DocumentBuilderFactory.newInstance();
        DocumentBuilder db = null;
        Document doc = null;
        String pageText = "";
        Vector<String> quotes = new Vector<String>();
        try {
                db = dbFactory.newDocumentBuilder();
                doc = db.parse(pageStream);
                NodeList nl = doc.getElementsByTagName("div");
                for (int x = 0; x < nl.getLength(); ++x) {
                        Node node = nl.item(x);
                        NamedNodeMap attributes = node.getAttributes();
                        for (int y = 0; y<attributes.getLength(); ++y) {
                                if (attributes.getNamedItem("class") ! = null) {
                                        Node attribute =
attributes.getNamedItem("class");

                                        if (attribute.getNodeValue()
                                                        .equals("views-
field-title")) {

                                                NodeList children =
node.getChildNodes();

                                                for (int z = 0; z <
children.getLength(); ++z) {

                                                        Node child =
children.item(z);

                                                        if (child.getNodeName()

.equalsIgnoreCase("span"))

                                                                quotes.add
(child.getTextContent());
                                                }
                                        }
                                }
                        }
                }
                Random r = new Random();
                pageText = quotes.get(r.nextInt(quotes.size() - 1));
                pageStream.close();
        } catch (SAXException e) {
                // TODO Auto-generated catch block
                e.printStackTrace();
        } catch (IOException e) {
                // TODO Auto-generated catch block
                e.printStackTrace();
        } catch (ParserConfigurationException e) {
                // TODO Auto-generated catch block
                e.printStackTrace();
        }
        return pageText;
}
```

```
public String doGetAsString(String url) {
    HttpGet request = new HttpGet(url);
    String result = "";
    try {
        HttpResponse response = client.execute(request);
        int code = response.getStatusLine().getStatusCode();
        if (code == 200) {
            result = EntityUtils.toString(response.getEntity());
        } else {
            Log.e("CN", "Non 200 Status Code "+code);
        }
    } catch (ClientProtocolException e) {
        // TODO Auto-generated catch block
        e.printStackTrace();
    } catch (IOException e) {
        // TODO Auto-generated catch block
        e.printStackTrace();
    }
    return result;
}

public InputStream doGetAsInputStream(String url) {
    HttpGet request = new HttpGet(url);
    InputStream result = null;
    try {
        HttpResponse response = client.execute(request);
        int code = response.getStatusLine().getStatusCode();
        if (code == 200) {
            result = response.getEntity().getContent();
        } else {
            Log.e("CN", "Non 200 Status Code "+code);
        }
    } catch (ClientProtocolException e) {
        // TODO Auto-generated catch block
        e.printStackTrace();
    } catch (IOException e) {
        // TODO Auto-generated catch block
        e.printStackTrace();
    }
    return result;
}

}
```

Starting from the main activity, you can see that there is a button and a text view that we will use for our user interaction. When the user clicks our button, we start our CommNotifier thread. This thread will execute the HTTP get request in our Comms file and return a random quote picked from the list of Chuck Norris facts that it gathers from the website. The CommNotifier then triggers the onTextReceived(String text) function. Our main activity implements the CommEvent interface. Therefore, whenever this method is fired, we need to access the text argument to receive our quote. When we execute the app and click the button, we see something similar to the output shown in Figure 9-7. Chuck Norris is indeed scary.

Figure 9-7. *The Chuck Norris Facts app in action*

Now that we've got our application, let's see what we can do to protect it using LVL.

I'm going to run this demo on an Android simulator. This involves an additional step because the Android simulators do not come pre-packaged with the Android Market app. I will need to download the Google API Add-On platform, which provides a rudimentary background implementation of the Android Market. It implements the Licensing Service that we need to test out LVL. I'm getting ahead of myself, though. Let's start by preparing our development environment. I'm going to make the assumption that you use Eclipse for your development and that you already downloaded and installed the Android SDK with at least API level 8. And off we go!

Download the Google API Add-On

I'm going to describe the steps required to get the Google API Add-On if you use Eclipse. First, open the Android SDK Manager. Select Window ➤ Android SDK Manager. Next, navigate to the API level you plan on using and tick the Google API's by Google Inc. (see Figure 9-8). Before you click the Install button, navigate once more to the Extras folder and tick the Google Market Licensing Package (see Figure 9-9). Now click the Install button. For this app, I use the Android API level 10 for version 2.3.3, so that is what I selected.

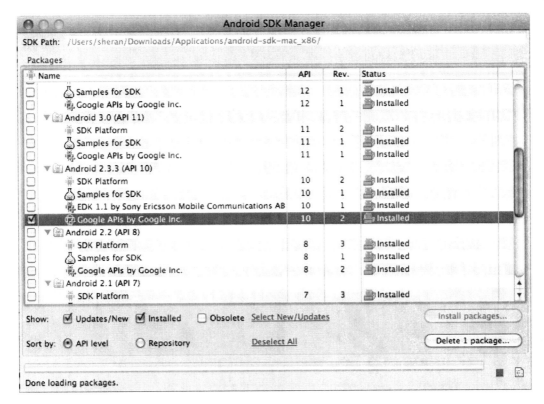

Figure 9-8. Installing the Google APIs for Android Version 2.3.3

Figure 9-9. Installing the Market Licensing Package

That's it. Eclipse will download and install your APIs to your SDK directory. To locate the LVL sources, navigate from your Android SDK directory to /extras/google/market_licensing/ library. Here, you will see a directory structure similar to that shown in Figure 9-10. Let's move onto the next set of steps, which are importing, modifying, and building LVL.

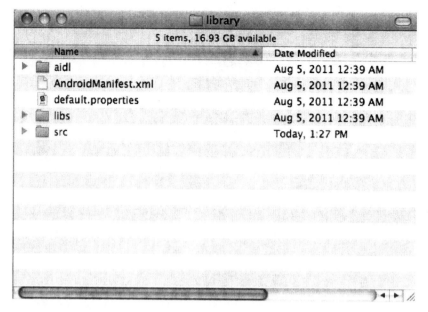

Figure 9-10. The LVL sources

Copy LVL Sources to a Separate Directory

Now that we have the LVL source with us, let's move it to another working directory. The main reason for doing this is because, if we continue to work from the original source directory, whenever we do an update, all our changes are likely going to be overwritten. Therefore, we need to keep our LVL source in a separate directory that will not be overwritten. This is simple enough. Copy the `library` directory and all subdirectories and files into your development directory.

Import LVL Source As a Library Project

We will now build the LVL library. To do this, we have to create a new Eclipse Android project and mark the project as a Library Project. A Library project has no activity and does not interact directly with the end user. Instead, it exists so that other apps can use its functions from within their code. To create a new Eclipse project, select *File ➤ New ➤ Other*, open the Android folder, and choose Android Project (see Figure 9-11). Name your project (see Figure 9-12) and select the correct API version that you plan to develop the project (see Figure 9-13). You will need to name your package the same as the LVL source code, which is `com.android.vending.licensing` (see Figure 9-14).

Figure 9-11. The Android project

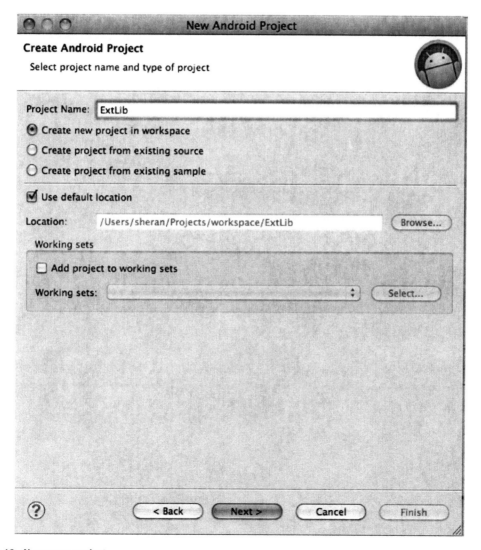

Figure 9-12. Name your project

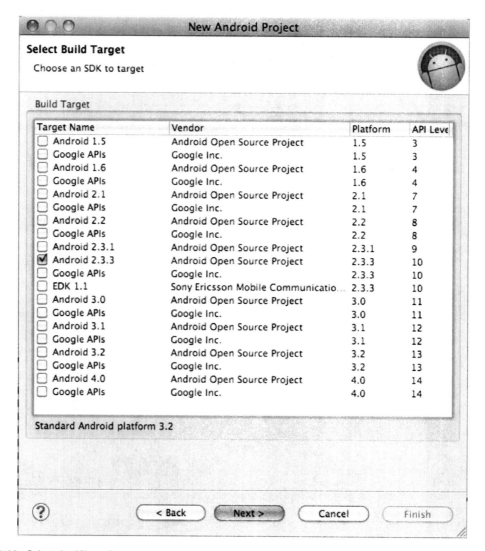

Figure 9-13. Select the API version

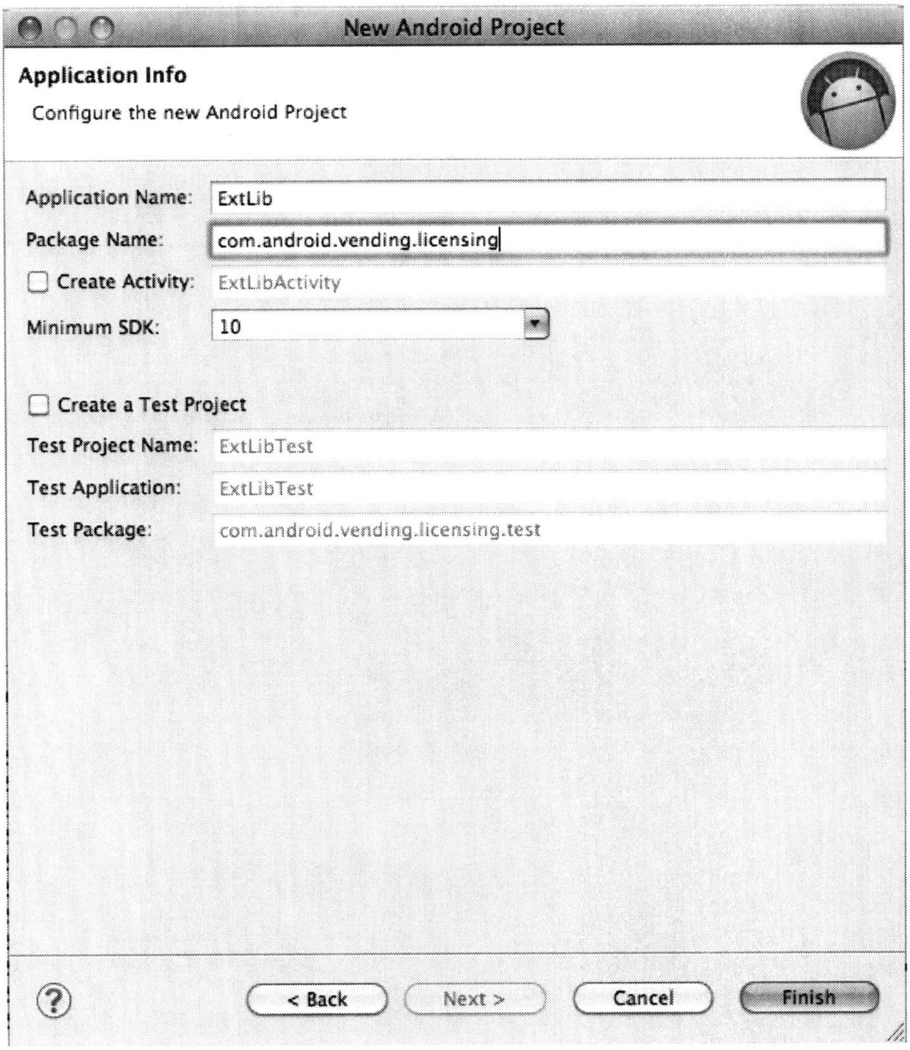

Figure 9-14. Specify the package name. It should be the same as the LVL source package

Once this is done, let's import the LVL source into our project. But before this, let's set the project as a Library project. Right click the project name in your Project Explorer window and select Properties. Select the Android option in the left-hand pane and in the bottom half of the right pane, you will see a tick box marked Is Library. Tick this option and click the OK button (see Figure 9-15).

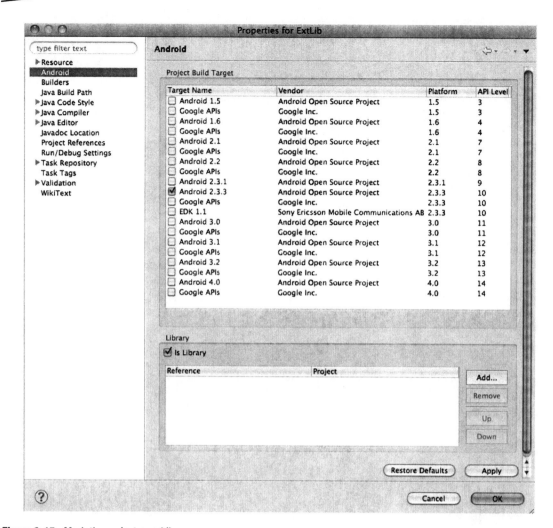

Figure 9-15. Mark the project as a Library

Now we can import our source. Right-click the project name in the Project Explorer window and select Import. In the resulting window, choose File System (see Figure 9-16) and click the Next button. In the next window, click the Browse button and navigate to the library folder that is part of the Android LVL source. On the left-middle window pane, you should then see the directory appear. Tick the library directory and click the Finish button to import the LVL source into your project (see Figure 9-17). If you're asked to overwrite the *AndroidManifest.xml* file, choose Yes. Your LVL source is now part of your project.

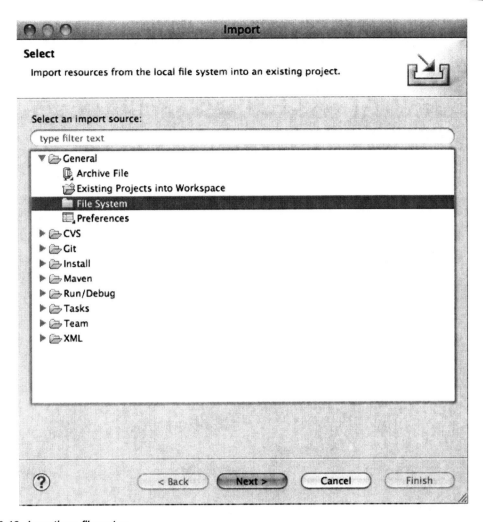

Figure 9-16. Importing a file system

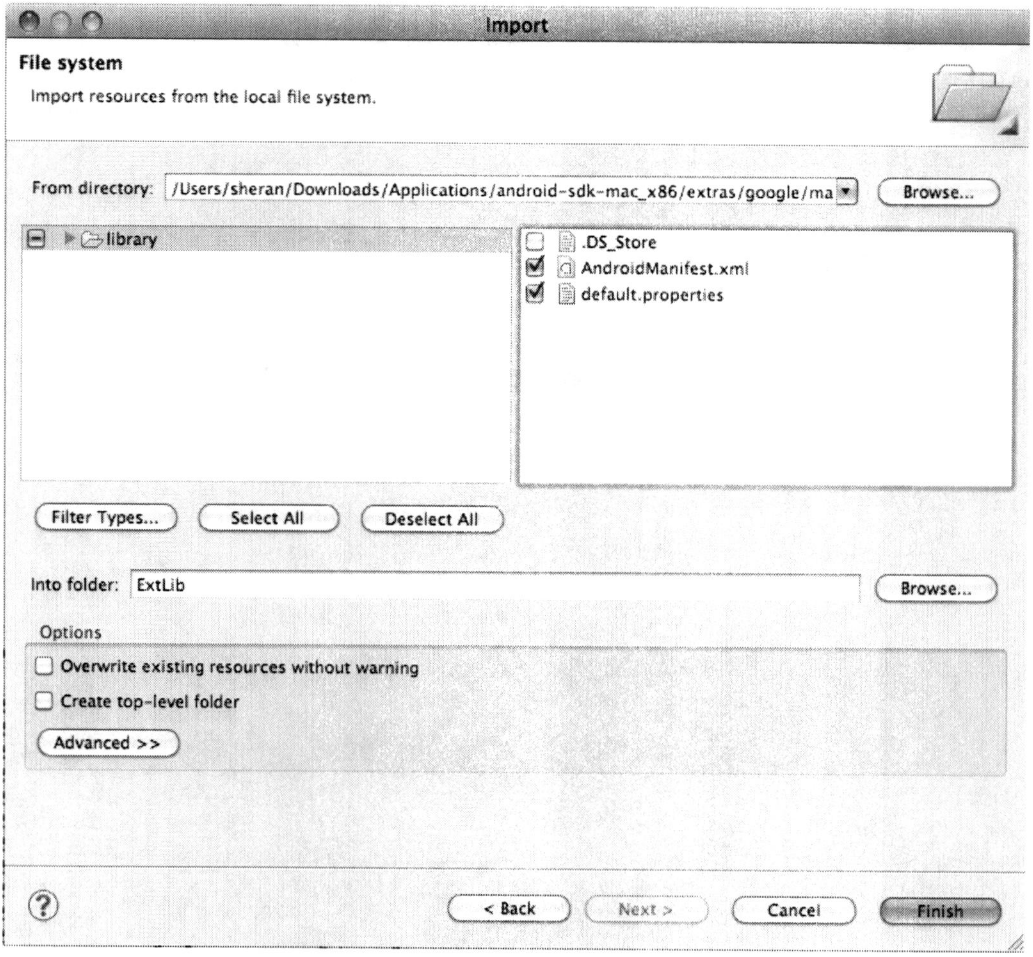

Figure 9-17. Locate and import the source

Building and Including LVL in our app

Let's first integrate the basic version of LVL that Google provides into our app. After this, I will explain some possible areas where you can modify the LVL source to make it your own. I highly recommend this approach because, as I mentioned before, the LVL modified source code you write will not be well known, and thus it will take an attacker longer to break your licensing module.

To include the LVL in your app, navigate to your app name in the Project Explorer view in Eclipse, right click, and select Properties. Select the Android option from the left window pane and, in the bottom-right window page, click the Add button. You're then prompted to select a library project (see Figure 9-18). Choose the Android LVL library project that we just created. After this is done, you will see the library project included in your app's project (see Figure 9-19).

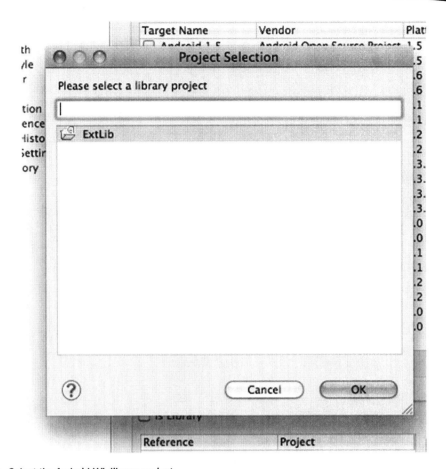

Figure 9-18. Select the Android LVL library project

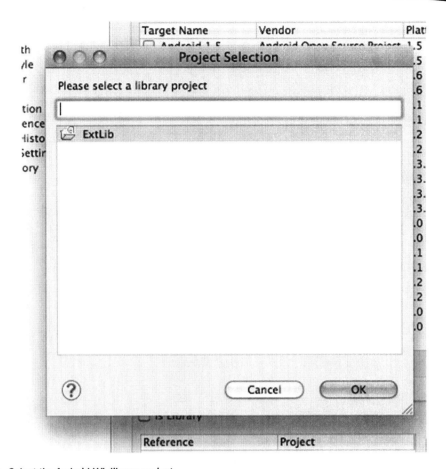

Figure 9-19. The LVL library project is included in the app project

Now let's change our ChuckNorrisFactsActivity.java file to that shown in Listing 9-8. You can see that we have added a new private class called LicCallBack. This implements the LVL's LicenseCheckerCallBack class. This class is called when the license check is complete and when there is either a positive or a negative response from the license server. The allow() or dontAllow() methods are called, respectively.

Listing 9-8. The Modified ChuckNorrisFactsActivity.java File

```java
package net.zenconsult.android.chucknorris;

import java.util.UUID;

import com.android.vending.licensing.AESObfuscator;
import com.android.vending.licensing.LicenseChecker;
import com.android.vending.licensing.LicenseCheckerCallback;
import com.android.vending.licensing.ServerManagedPolicy;

import android.app.Activity;
import android.content.Context;
import android.os.Build;
import android.os.Bundle;
import android.provider.Settings.Secure;
import android.view.View;
import android.view.Window;
import android.widget.Button;
import android.widget.TextView;
import android.widget.Toast;

public class ChuckNorrisFactsActivity extends Activity implements CommsEvent {
        private Button button;
        private TextView view;
        private Activity activity;
        private CommsEvent event;
        private LicCallBack lcb;
        private static final String PUB_KEY = "MIIBI...";// Add your Base64 Public
                                                    // key here
        private static final byte[] SALT = new byte[] { -118, -112, 38, 124, 15,
                    -121, 59, 93, 35, -55, 14, -15, -52, 67, -53, 54, 111, -28,↵
 -87, 12 };

        /** Called when the activity is first created. */
        @Override
        public void onCreate(Bundle savedInstanceState) {
                super.onCreate(savedInstanceState);
                requestWindowFeature(Window.FEATURE_INDETERMINATE_PROGRESS);
                setContentView(R.layout.main);
                event = this;
                activity = this;
                view = (TextView) findViewById(R.id.editText1);

                // Click Button
                button = (Button) findViewById(R.id.button1);
                button.setOnClickListener(new View.OnClickListener() {
                        public void onClick(View v) {
                                // Do License Check before allowing click
```

```
                                // Generate a Unique ID
                                String deviceId = Secure.getString(getContentResolver(),
                                                Secure.ANDROID_ID);
                                String serialId = Build.SERIAL;
                                UUID uuid = new UUID(deviceId.hashCode(),↵
serialId.hashCode());
                                String identity = uuid.toString();
                                Context ctx = activity.getApplicationContext();

                                // Create an Obfuscator and a Policy
                                AESObfuscator obf = new AESObfuscator(SALT,↵
getPackageName(),
                                                identity);
                                ServerManagedPolicy policy = new↵
ServerManagedPolicy(ctx, obf);

                                // Create the LicenseChecker
                                LicenseChecker lCheck = new LicenseChecker(ctx,↵
policy, PUB_KEY);

                                // Do the license check
                                lcb = new LicCallBack();
                                lCheck.checkAccess(lcb);
                    }
                });
        }

        @Override
        public void onTextReceived(final String text) {
                runOnUiThread(new Runnable() {
                        public void run() {
                                setProgressBarIndeterminateVisibility(false);
                                view.setText(text);
                                button.setEnabled(true);
                        }
                });
        }

        public class LicCallBack implements LicenseCheckerCallback {

                @Override
                public void allow() {
                        if (isFinishing()) {
                                return;
                        }
                        Toast toast = Toast.makeText(getApplicationContext(),↵
"Licensed!",
                                        Toast.LENGTH_LONG);
                        toast.show();
                        button.setEnabled(false);
                        setProgressBarIndeterminateVisibility(true);
                        view.setText("Fetching fact...");
                        CommsNotifier c = new CommsNotifier(event);
                        c.start();
                }
```

```java
@Override
public void dontAllow() {
        if (isFinishing()) {
                return;
        }
        Toast toast = Toast.makeText(getApplicationContext(),
                        "Unlicensed!", Toast.LENGTH_LONG);
        toast.show();
}

@Override
public void applicationError(ApplicationErrorCode errorCode) {
        // TODO Auto-generated method stub

}

    }

}
```

The next thing you will notice is that we don't do any activity on our button click. Instead, we do a license check. This means that we move our quote fetching activity into the `allow()` section of the `LicenseCallBack` class. To use the license check from LVL, you have to call the `checkAccess()` method of the `LicenseChecker` class. You have to build the `LicenseChecker` with the following arguments:

1. Application Context

2. A Licensing Policy

3. Your Public Key

For the application context, you can use the current application context. If your `LicenseChecker` is instantiated in another class, then you will need to pass the Application Context object along to this class. Your Base 64 encoded public key will be in your Publisher profile page online. To access it, log into `https://market.android.com/publish/Home`, click Edit Profile, and then scroll down to the section called Licensing & In-App Billing. The text area named Public Key holds your key (see Figure 9-20). Copy and paste this into your app. The licensing policy requires a bit more explanation, so I will describe it in the next section.

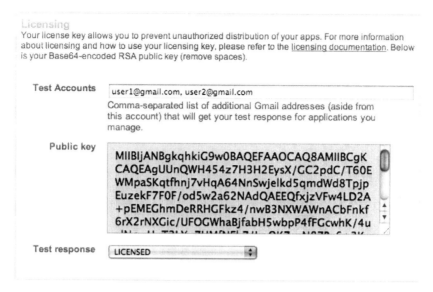

Figure 9-20. *The Base64 encoded public key*

Look at this line code, as well:

```
AESObfuscator obf = new AESObfuscator(SALT, getPackageName(),identity);
```

When your app receives a response from the Android license server, it will need to store information about this response locally, on the device. Leaving the response data in plain text form will only mean that an attacker can read and tamper with this information. To prevent this from happening, LVL allows us to obfuscate the information before storing it on the device. The AESObfuscator class does just this. It requires a salt value (which is just a random 20 bytes) and a unique device identity. The unique identity ensures that the data can only be read from the device with this matching identity. In your own code, you will want to build this identity string from as many sources of information as possible. In this case, I am using the ANDROID_ID and OS Build serial number.

Note also that your app will have to request a new permission. For it to be able to verify licenses through the Android Market, make sure you add the following permission to your AndroidManifest.xml file:

```
<uses-permission android:name = "com.android.vending.CHECK_LICENSE">
```

Your publisher dashboard has a pull-down menu marked Test Response (see Figure 9-20). You can test your app by setting this value to either LICENSED or NOT_LICENSED. The Google API and LVL will contact the Android Market server and present this response to your app. Setting the Test Response value to NOT_LICENSED lets you see how your app behaves if an unlicensed user attempts to use it (see Figure 9-21). Accordingly, you can make changes and either present a message (I present a one word response to indicate whether the app is licensed or not) or redirect the user to the Android Market, so that she may purchase your app.

Figure 9-21. An unlicensed user receives a negative response, and the app does not work

Licensing Policy

One of the key mechanisms that you can use to customize your licensing process is the licensing policy. Android LVL ships with two default policies:

- StrictPolicy
- ServerManagedPolicy

Google recommends that you use the ServerManagedPolicy because, among other things, it also handles caching of the server response. This is often useful because Google enforces limits on the number of times your application can query its servers. The StrictPolicy will always make a query to the server; and while this can be more secure by the fact that it prevents local device data tampering, it may lock your end-user out if the Google server refuses to give you a response because you reached your limits.

Both Policy objects provide two basic methods that you will be concerned with: allowAccess() and processServerResponse(). The allowAccess() method must return a Boolean value. When called, return true if you choose to permit access; otherwise, return false. Look at the sample implementation in Listing 9-9.

Listing 9-9. The allowAccess() method in the ServerManagedPolicy object (courtesy of Google)

```
public boolean allowAccess() {
        long ts = System.currentTimeMillis();
        if (mLastResponse == LicenseResponse.LICENSED) {
            // Check if the LICENSED response occurred within the validity timeout.
            if (ts <= mValidityTimestamp) {
                // Cached LICENSED response is still valid.
                return true;
            }
        } else if (mLastResponse == LicenseResponse.RETRY &&
                    ts < mLastResponseTime+MILLIS_PER_MINUTE) {
            // Only allow access if we are within the retry period or we haven't↵
 used up our
            // max retries.
            return (ts <= mRetryUntil || mRetryCount <= mMaxRetries);
        }
        return false;
    }
```

You can see that the function returns true if it receives LicenseResponse.LICENSED as its response. The function first checks whether the last response received indicated that the app was licensed. It then checks whether the date is still within the valid period. If so, then it returns true. If the date is greater than the validity period, it returns false. The function also checks whether the server has asked us to keep retrying, and it does so within reasonable retry limits and time intervals. The response object, mLastResponse,is derived from the processServerResponse() method shown in Listing 9-10. You can see that this function checks for three responses:

- LicenseResponse.RETRY

- LicenseResponse.LICENSED

- LicenseResponse.NOT_LICENSED

Accordingly, it then sets parameters that the allowAccess() method can read. You will notice one other thing. The last line in the processServerResponse() object is a commit() operation. This is the caching function where the response is obfuscated and then stored in the device's Shared Preferences. This part does not exist in the StrictPolicy because no data is cached.

Listing 9-10. The processServerResponse() method in the ServerManagedPolicy object (courtesy of Google)

```
public void processServerResponse(LicenseResponse response, ResponseData rawData) {
        // Update retry counter
        if (response != LicenseResponse.RETRY) {
            setRetryCount(0);
        } else {
            setRetryCount(mRetryCount+1);
        }

        if (response == LicenseResponse.LICENSED) {
            // Update server policy data
            Map<String, String> extras = decodeExtras(rawData.extra);
```

```
            mLastResponse = response;
            setValidityTimestamp(extras.get("VT"));
            setRetryUntil(extras.get("GT"));
            setMaxRetries(extras.get("GR"));
        } else if (response == LicenseResponse.NOT_LICENSED) {
            // Clear out stale policy data
            setValidityTimestamp(DEFAULT_VALIDITY_TIMESTAMP);
            setRetryUntil(DEFAULT_RETRY_UNTIL);
            setMaxRetries(DEFAULT_MAX_RETRIES);
        }

        setLastResponse(response);
        mPreferences.commit();
    }
```

Effective Use of LVL

It is worth the effort if you modify the LVL source code (i.e., your policy) so that it becomes something unique to your app. One mistake you can make is to use a vanilla implementation of LVL to which everyone knows the source. This makes it easier for someone to patch your app and bypass your license checking routines. Justin Case has already demonstrated this vulnerability over at the Android Police site. You can find the article at www.androidpolice.com/ 2010/08/23/exclusive-report-googles-android-market-license-verification-easily-circumvented-will-not-stop-pirates/. Granted, it is an old article, but it still demonstrates the principle that you can easily understand and modify reverse-engineered code if you know what the source looks like. In this case, Justin demonstrates how to patch and bypass LVL checking in a demo and an actual commercial app.

Another good set of guidelines comes to us from Trevor Johns over at the Android Developers blog. The article is a great read and lists a few techniques for more effective use of LVL. One particular piece of code was very interesting. Look at Figure 9-22. Trevor tells us that an attacker can guess the response of the LICENSED and NOT_LICENSED constant values, and then swap them so that an unlicensed user will receive full use of the app. To prevent this, Trevor shows us some code that will run a CRC32 check on the responses; and instead of checking for the constants, check for the result of the CRC32 check on the constant. I want to expand on this subject a little bit more. Imagine if you will, rather than running a check for a fixed value, you execute another HTTP fetch to retrieve a response from your own server.

```
public void verify(PublicKey publicKey, int responseCode, String signedData, String signature) {
    // ... Response validation code omitted for brevity ...

        // Compute a derivative version of the response code
        // Ideally, this should be placed as far from the responseCode switch as possible,
        // to prevent attackers from noticing the call to the CRC32 library, which would be
        // a strong hint as to what we're done here. If you can add additional transformations
        // elsewhere in before this value is used, that's even better.
        java.util.zip.CRC32 crc32 = new java.util.zip.CRC32();
        crc32.update(responseCode);
        int transformedResponseCode = crc32.getValue();

        // ... put unrelated application code here ...
        // crc32(LICENSED) == 3523407757
        if (transformedResponse == 3523407757) {
            LicenseResponse limiterResponse = mDeviceLimiter.isDeviceAllowed(userId);
            handleResponse(limiterResponse, data);
        }
        // ... put unrelated application code here ...
        // crc32(LICENSED_OLD_KEY) == 1007455905
        if (transformedResponseCode == 1007455905) {
            LicenseResponse limiterResponse = mDeviceLimiter.isDeviceAllowed(userId);
            handleResponse(limiterResponse, data);
        }
        // ... put unrelated application code here ...
        // crc32(NOT_LICENSED) == 2768625435
        if (transformedResponseCode == 2768625435):
            userIsntLicensed();
        }
    }
```

Figure 9-22. An alternate response verification idea

Consider the code in Listing 9-11. Instead of making a direct comparison to a number, you make an additional request to your server and retrieve the response code from there. One of the good points about this is that you can engineer your ServerVerifier object in any way you prefer. You can even set it up so that the response code changes every single time. You may even consider making use of Challenge Response in your code to vary the response each time.

Listing 9-11. The Modified Verify Function

```
public void verify(PublicKey publicKey, int responseCode, String signedData, String↵
signature) {
      // ... Response validation code omitted for brevity ...

      // Compute a derivative version of the response code
      // Rather than comparing to a static value, why not retrieve the value from↵
a server that you control?

        java.util.zip.CRC32 crc32 = new java.util.zip.CRC32();
        crc32.update(responseCode);
        int transformedResponseCode = crc32.getValue();
                ServerVerifier sv = new ServerVerifier(); // This class will make an↵
HTTP request to your server to fetch the code.
                int serverResponse = sv.retrieveLicensedCode(); // There is no limit↵
to how you can create this routine.
```

```
        // ... put unrelated application code here ...
        // crc32(LICENSED) == 3523407757 But this part is calculated on your server.
        if (transformedResponse == serverResponse) {
            LicenseResponse limiterResponse = mDeviceLimiter.isDeviceAllowed(userId);
            handleResponse(limiterResponse, data);
        }

            . . .
            . . .
            . . .
```

Alternatively, this can take place in the Policy, as well (as opposed to checking a hardcoded server response):

```
if (response == LicenseResponse.LICENSED)
```

You can have the response checked by retrieving it from one of your servers that you trust in a manner similar to this:

```
ServerVerifier sv = new ServerVerifier();
if (response == sv.getLicensedResponse())
```

Obfuscation

Obfuscation is another important point that you will want to consider. It applies to software piracy, as well as to intellectual property theft. Obfuscation is a process by which you change all class names, variable names, and method names in your source code to random, unrelated ones. You may have wondered why my decompiled app had files like a.smali, b.smali, c.smali, and so on in the directory listing. When I used BakSmali to decompile my app, I was running it on an obfuscated version of the binary. The code obfuscator made sure to change my class names like Comms, CommsEvent, CommsNotifier, and so on to ones that do not volunteer information about what they do. Additionally, if you look inside these files, you will see that the method names and member names are all obfuscated. This can be very frustrating to someone trying to reverse engineer code, and it can act as an excellent deterrent to intellectual property or code theft.

Obfuscation cannot guarantee that your code won't be stolen or pirated. It simply makes the task of reverse engineering much harder. The Android SDK ships with an obfuscator called ProGuard. You can use ProGuard for obfuscating any of your Java code. You can download it at http://proguard.sourceforge.net/; it is free and open source software. The Android developer documents strongly encourage you to obfuscate your code when you are packaging your apps for release. If you use Eclipse, then this is a straightforward task. Locate your project.properties file in your project (see Figure 9-23) and add this line (see Figure 9-24):

Figure 9-23. *The Project properties file*

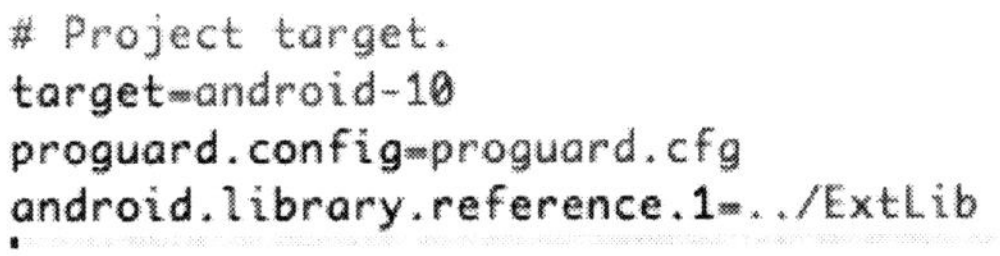

```
# Project target.
target=android-10
proguard.config=proguard.cfg
android.library.reference.1=../ExtLib
```

Figure 9-24. *Adding the proguard.config property*

```
proguard.config = proguard.cfg
```

Note that this line assumes you haven't moved the location of the proguard.cfg file from its default location.

To export either a signed or an unsigned APK file, right-click your project name, select Android Tools, and then select Export Unsigned Application Package or Export Signed Application Package (see Figure 9-25).

Figure 9-25. *Exporting the obfuscated package*

ProGuard is a free, open source Java code obfuscator. In addition to obfuscation, ProGuard also attempts to shrink, optimize, and preverify the code that you feed it. Preverification is important for mobile apps in terms of improving execution times. The preverification phase ensures that the Java class is annotated in a manner that allows the VM to read and perform some runtime checks much faster. In most cases, using the default `proguard.cfg` file should suffice. Figure 9-26 shows output from a decompiled, obfuscated class file. As you can see, the code itself is quite unreadable due to the renamed, mostly cryptic looking class and variable names. Obfuscation is not meant to stop reverse engineering; rather, it acts more as a deterrent because it could take a long time to rebuild variable and class names that are renamed. Some commercial Java obfuscators go as far as even obfuscating the strings within the class file. This makes the code even more difficult to reverse engineer.

```
protected boolean f;

protected b()
{
}

public b(a parama)
{
  this.d = parama;
  this.a = new byte[parama.b()];
  this.b = 0;
  String str = parama.a();
  int i = 1 + str.indexOf('/');
  boolean bool2;
  if ((i <= 0) || (!str.startsWith("PGP", i)))
    bool2 = false;
  else
    bool2 = bool1;
  this.f = bool2;
  if ((!this.f) && ((i <= 0) || ((!str.startsWith("CFB", i)) && (!str.startsWith("OFB", i)) && (!str.startsWith("OpenPGP", i)) && (!str.star
    bool1 = false;
  this.e = bool1;
}

private void a()
{
  for (int i = 0; i < this.a.length; i++)
    this.a[i] = 0;
  this.b = 0;
  this.d.c();
}

public final int a(int paramInt)
{
  int i = paramInt + this.b;
```

Figure 9-26. A decompiled, obfuscated class file

Summary

This chapter was dedicated to some important issues you will face when monetizing your app. While sites like Apple App Store, BlackBerry App World, and the Android Market make it easy for you to pull in revenue, you will no doubt have to face issues like software piracy and intellectual property theft. You should keep in mind that the topics discussed in this chapter aren't magic bullets. They will not protect you completely, but they will offer you an edge so that your code becomes harder to attack. In a best case scenario, an attacker will leave your app alone because he will not want to make the effort it would cost to reverse engineer it.

In this chapter, we looked at what your app can be subject to if it finds itself in a hostile environment. We looked at how your app can be reverse engineered and re-built after modifications. We showed how you can obfuscate your source code so that it becomes harder for an attacker to read your code even after reverse engineering. We then looked at how you can check licenses in your app so that you ensure your end-users aren't pirating your app. We did this by using the Android LVL. One thing to remember is to always write your own routines in the license checking libraries. This ensures that your code is fresh, new and is not well known. It makes reverse engineering harder.

Bear in mind these few steps before you release your application. You can find full descriptions of them online at `http://developer.android.com/guide/publishing/preparing.html`.

1. Choose a good package name. One that will work for the entire life of the app.

2. Turn off debugging and logging. Make sure to search for debug tracing and disable that.

3. Clean your project directories from backup files or other unnecessary files you may have created during development and testing.

4. Review your Manifest file and ensure all the required permissions exist. Ensure that your label and icon values are set as well as the correct `versionCode` and `versionName` attributes.

5. Check and optimize your application for the correct versions of Android. Make sure your app is suited to run on devices with different specifications.

6. Update your URLs within your app. This means removing any local IP addresses and testing servers. Change them to the correct production IP Addresses.

7. Implement licensing in your app.

Chapter **10**

Malware and Spyware

Like the personal computer, the mobile smartphone is susceptible to various types of malware. Throughout this chapter, I will refer to malware and spyware collectively as malware. Even though I do this, it is essential to know the difference between each of these types of hostile applications.

Malware is defined as any piece of malicious software that lives on a user's computer or smartphone whose sole task is to cause destruction of data, steal personal information, or gain access to system resources in order to gain full control of the device it is on. Malware is written with the sole intent of causing harm; and usually, malware authors will write the malware to target a specific weakness in an operating system or platform. Often, the malware author will want to maximize the spread of her malware and will look to implement a mechanism where his software can copy itself to other, similar devices.

Spyware is a term used to refer to malware that accesses and exfiltrates personal or private information from a device. For instance, in the case of mobile phone malware, the application may be after an end user's e-mail messages, contact list, SMS messages, or even photos. Spyware generally needs to be stealthy and stay on the device for long periods. Thus, spyware authors will aim to perform little or no disruptive activity on the device, so that the end user is not aware of her data being stolen. Just about anyone can use malware; it is no longer a requirement that you know how to code the malware yourself.

Many companies sell malware to individuals, large corporations, or even governments (see the case study later on in this chapter). I have seen two types of companies selling malware: the ones that sell to large organizations or governments and the ones that sell to individual retail consumers. As we will review later in this chapter, one large Middle Eastern telecommunications provider was caught spying on its entire BlackBerry subscriber base. The software that helped do this was sold by a well known US company that specializes in legal interception. It turns out that the source code was completely developed from scratch, and its sole purpose was to capture and exfiltrate e-mail messages from an infected device.

On the other end of the spectrum, you will find the malware or spyware packaged and sold to any individual who is willing to spy on someone that she knows. In most cases, the companies that sell this type of software will proclaim "Catch cheating spouses!" Apparently, this is quite appealing to some folks! I will also look at one of these versions of *retail malware* in some detail.

Four Stages of Malware

We can classify malware operations into four different, but distinct, stages. While not formal, these stages have been visible in most instances where malware has been discovered on devices.

Infection

This is the stage where the malware is introduced to the device. The holy grail of infection is one where no end-user interaction is involved. This occurs when malware can be copied to a device by something as harmless as sending a user an SMS message or compromising the device when it is on a wireless network.

The second method of infection is through a partially assisted action. The user is asked to click a link in a malicious website. Once he does this, the malware will copy itself to the device. An attacker sends this link to a user in an SMS or e-mail message. While effective, this requires user intervention; in most cases, diligent users will always be suspicious about clicking random links sent to them.

The last form of infection occurs when an attacker will physically copy the malware to the device, either through a USB port or via browsing to a website. This takes place in instances where the attacker and end user know each other, or the attacker has physical access to the end user's device. This technique is not effective if a user has password protected his device and requires a password to use it or install applications on it.

Compromise

Most often, infection and compromise go hand in hand. In this context, I am using the word compromise to describe how the malware is able to gain super-user access to the device. As a result, the malware can make changes to the device configuration in any manner it chooses to do so–and without requiring device-owner interaction.

As we saw in previous chapters, programs running on Android will require a user to grant it explicit permissions to access facilities like the Internet or read e-mail messages. During the compromise stage, the malware will use a weakness in the operating system to circumvent the permission granting process, thereby allowing it to execute any function without the user being aware.

Spread

Unless specifically targeted at an individual, a malware author will typically want to infect a large number of users. He may want to control an army of devices or just access private information from many different people. The Zeus Trojan (found on the personal computer platforms) will spread using weaknesses found in the operating system. Its sole purpose is to collect a user's keystrokes and collect credentials to banking and social networking websites.

Lately, another popular mechanism of spreading and even infection has been to use the Google Android Market (where authors can sell or freely distribute their applications). Malware authors can upload harmless looking applications like games or social network interaction tools to the Android Market. When an end user buys or downloads this app, her device is infected.

Exfiltration

Malware will often target personal or confidential information. It may log keystrokes to try to capture usernames or passwords to websites like online banking and e-mail. However, simply collecting this information is insufficient. The attacker needs to have access to this information, so malware will find a way of "phoning home" or communicating with a remote server, either to receive new instructions or to upload the captured information. This stage is called *exfiltration*. Let's take a look at a case study that illustrates how this can work.

Case Study 1: Government Sanctioned Malware

In July of 2009, a telecommunications provider for the United Arab Emirates (UAE), Etisalat, sent an SMS message to its entire subscriber base of BlackBerry device owners to download and install a system patch. This patch was purported to improve performance of the device's 3G capabilities. It turned out that this "patch" was nothing more than malware designed to read each user's outgoing e-mail.

To this day, the company maintains that the patch was meant to improve performance. Most of the researchers who examined the malware, including myself and Research In Motion (RIM), can see that there are no performance benefits whatsoever. Instead, examining the code reveals a deliberate attempt to capture all of the device owner's outgoing e-mail and send a copy of it for examination to the provider's servers.

The case title, Government Sanctioned Malware, may be a bit strong, especially when you consider that no conclusive evidence has materialized from the investigation of this case. My choice of title was based on the 11 years I spent working in the UAE (five of them for Etisalat), recent events in the media, and my knowledge of how closely the government and regulatory authorities control the media and communications infrastructure of the country.

The media events I mention took place around August of 2010, when the government of the UAE announced that it would shut down all BlackBerry services within the country if RIM did not provide a means of monitoring user messages, including e-mail and BlackBerry Messenger (a native messaging platform that allows BlackBerry users to send messages to each other). Since I'm not writing a spy novel, I'll shelve all of my theories for my next book and instead take you through some of the more factual aspects of the malware itself. In this case study, we will try to uniquely identify the stages for malware infection.

Infection

Etisalat introduced the malware onto its subscriber's devices by making use of a simple WAP-push message. This is a message that appears in the device's SMS inbox, and it contains both text and a URL. The text of the WAP-push message was as follows:

Dear Etisalat BlackBerry Customer,

Etisalat is always keen to provide you with the best BlackBerry service and ultimate experience, for that we will be sending you a performance enhancement patch that you need to install on your device. For more information, please call 101

--

Empower your Business with BlackBerry® and Mobile Solutions from Etisalat

---

Once a user clicked the accompanying URL, the device would download and install and application called Registration. The device would prompt the end user to grant the application specific permissions. Since the WAP-push message arrived from a seemingly legitimate source, most users had no reason to distrust the request and often granted the application full permissions.

Compromise

In this case, the malware did not rely on a weakness in the OS to gain access to personal information. The user, believing that the application was legitimate, granted all the necessary permissions during the installation phase.

Spread

The malware released by Etisalat was designed to remain on the device and collect information. It was not designed to spread to other devices. Rather than spreading, the malware relied on the WAP-push message. The installation would take place in one go and would not spread thereafter.

Exfiltration

This is the most important stage for the Etisalat malware. It was designed to attach itself to the sent items of the user's e-mail messages and send a copy of each outgoing message to a server inside Etisalat. This was taken care of by the built-in BlackBerry API calls.

An actual message (that the malware uses to check in with the server) is depicted in Figure 10-1. This is a message that is sent to the server every hour. The operators of the malware system can then see which devices are infected by the malware, including which of those are checking in regularly.

```
<ForwardTo>etisalat_upgr@etisalat.ae</ForwardTo>
 <Subject>I: response <PIN>21111111</PIN></Subject>
 <Content>
    <Version>4.9100</Version>
    <Copyright>Copyright (c) by Author 2008/2009 - All rights r
    <Time>Sat Jul 18 21:05:20 Asia/Dubai 2009</Time>
    <PIN>21111111</PIN>
    <PhoneNo></PhoneNo>
    <IMEI>123456.02.98765.3</IMEI>
    <IMSI>000000000000000</IMSI>
    <Reason>start</Reason>
    <s>1</s>
    <DeviceName>9000</DeviceName>
    <DeviceManufacturer>Research In Motion</DeviceManufacturer>
    <PlatformVersion>4.0.0.xxx</PlatformVersion>
    <State>running</State>
 </Content>
```

Figure 10-1. A captured "heartbeat" message as used by the Registration malware

Detection

This specific malware was only detected because it was badly written. As soon as the malware was released, the server that was supposed to receive the exfiltrated data was inundated with messages. Unable to bear the load, the server crashed. This caused the malware on the devices to constantly retry the connection to a non-responsive server. This continued set of connection attempts increased processor usage on the devices themselves.

At this point, end users began to notice sluggishness in their device performance and premature battery drain. Some users even noticed their device overheating. This prompted several researchers to investigate the Registration application, whereupon they discovered that it was really malware. Figure 10-2 shows a flowchart of how the malware operates when installed on a device. What follows is a detailed list of the characteristics of the Registration malware:

- It checks to see if it is listed as visible in the BlackBerry installed applications.

- If it is visible, it hides itself from view of the subscriber. This prevents a user from finding it and deleting it.

- It iterates over all the mail accounts on the handheld and attaches itself to each of them, looking for received e-mail messages and PIN messages.

- It intercepts and monitors the state of the handheld for network events that occur. It notifies the service-provider's server when these events occur.

- It listens for messages received from specific addresses through either e-mail or BlackBerry PIN. These are control messages that can enable or disable the interception of the subscribers' messages.

- It reports to the predefined service-provider server regularly.

- If enabled, the application will forward a copy of e-mails sent out by the subscriber to the service-provider server.

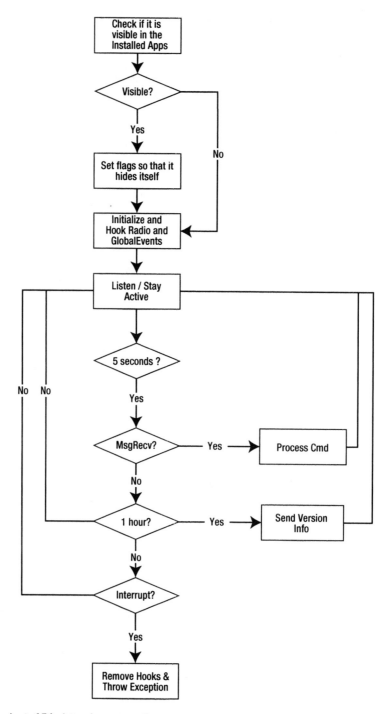

Figure 10-2. A flowchart of Etisalat malware operation

Case Study 2: Retail Malware—FlexiSPY

Now let's look at a second malware application: FlexiSPY, a type of retail malware. FlexiSPY eavesdrops on all communications when an attacker installs it on the target device. The latest version of FlexiSPY Omni offers the following features to Android users:

- Capture SMS and e-mails
- Capture call logs
- Discover GPS location through GPS and cell tower information
- Turn the phone into a listening device
- Intercept phone calls
- SIM card change notification

This seems to be sufficient coverage for spying on anyone, and I found the list of features intriguing enough to acquire a copy and analyze it.

> **Note**   In the spirit of full disclosure, I'll mention that, at the time that I reviewed FlexiSPY, I looked at the BlackBerry version because that was my primary phone. The protocols to activate and enable the device are all web-based, so they remain more or less the same, regardless of the supported device platform (including on Android, of course).

Once a buyer parts with her $349, she will receive a user manual that provides information on how the application can be installed on a target's phone. When going through the user manual, one of the first things that jumped out at me was that it provided ... *explicit instructions to set the Default Permissions of the BlackBerry handheld to Allow All*.

This means that, not just FlexiSPY, but every single application the target installs on his phone after this can gain full control (within the scope of the programming interface or API) over the handheld. Obviously, user protection is not a high priority in this case. In a similar twist, looking at the Android manual for FlexiSPY, the device itself has to be rooted before you can successfully install the malware on the device. The site offers a solution to root the device in the form of *Super One Click*. The site offers no direct links, save for this text. Finding the exploit is left up to the customer.

FlexiSPY requires activation before it can begin to spy on a target. To do this, a user has to dial the number *#900900900, which causes a hidden screen to be activated. On this screen, a user is prompted to enter the activation code. Never one to leave home without my favorite network packet sniffer, Wireshark, I sniffed the traffic that went through during the activation process. Here is the information that went across the wire:

- POST /t4l-mcli/cmd/productactivate?mode=0&ver=0302&pid=FSP_BB_
  V4.2&actcode=[Activation Code] &hash=[IMEI]&phmodel=8300(4.5.0.44)
  HTTP/1.1

This request is made to a server with the following second level domain:

`aabackup.info`

It resolves to the same IP Address as the host `djp.cc` listed previously. As you can see, the phone's IMEI is being sent back to FlexiSPY HQ. Also visible is the activation code, which returns a hash value. It appears that the phone calculates a similar algorithm and waits for a matching hash. Once the correct hash is received, the app is activated.

From this point on, it's a case of configuring the application to intercept SMS messages, e-mail messages, call logs, and so on. The application has a command channel through SMS. Thus, you have a list of eight commands, which do the following:

- Start Capture: Begin capturing events like e-mail, SMS, location, and so on.
- Stop Capture: Stop an already started capture.
- Send Immediate: Send all collected events to the central logging host.
- Send Diagnostics: Send diagnostic info.
- Start SIM Monitor: Watch for any attempt at changing the SIM card.
- Stop SIM Monitor: Stop monitoring the SIM card.
- Start Mic Monitor: Wait for calls from a trigger number.
- Stop Mic Monitor: Stop monitoring calls from that trigger number.

The funny thing is that the command channel SMS messages cannot be deleted, so the manual advises a user to select short phrases like "Good morning" or similar to begin capturing information. The phrases should be chosen so as not to arouse the target's suspicion.

Bear in mind that I performed the preceding checks on a BlackBerry version of FlexiSPY. Given the similarities of each platform running Java, Android would behave in a similar manner.

Anti-Forensics

Currently, the most widely used detection mechanism is signature based. This means that any anti-malware company writing removal or detection capabilities needs to know about the malware *beforehand*. If it encounters it, then it can remove it. Consequently, a new strain of malware is unlikely to be detected. This is unfortunate because, if the anti-malware companies are unable to keep up with the evolution of malware, then there is always a lag from the point when malware is released, to the point when it is discovered and addressed. During this lag period, all users are at risk.

As a developer, you have no direct control of whether a user chooses to install anti-malware applications. Your responsibility lies in making sure that your application handles its data securely. We've covered most of these techniques in our previous chapters, but I wanted to highlight another available, yet unorthodox, option: anti-forensics.

Anti-forensics is a technique that is used to defeat forensic analysis of computers or mobile devices by reducing the quality of information that can be gathered. Forensic analysis involves examining such devices for evidence. Most often, the evidence that has to be gathered is very fragile. Anti-forensics seeks to destroy this information by using automated tools running at periodic intervals. Then, when a forensic analysis takes place, the investigator will only find garbled or useless data. This considerably lowers the quality of information that can be retrieved. We can use a similar technique to thwart the actions of malware.

I will start with a simple example: let's say your application reads and writes to a device's message stores. Since you have access to this data, you can artificially generate e-mail messages and delete them at will. Assume that there is a malware application installed on the device waiting to copy messages entering the inbox. By generating many fake messages and later deleting them on a periodic basis, you are feeding the malware low quality, useless data that will exfiltrate. If done correctly, this process can make it tedious for a malware author to extract valid information. This concept is illustrated in Figures 10-3 and 10-4.

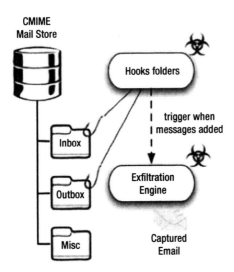

Figure 10-3. Malware intercepting mail messages

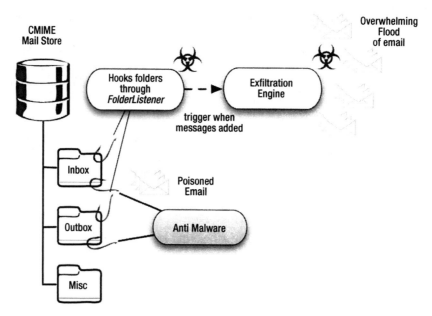

Figure 10-4. Generating fake messages

This technique can be considered a bit aggressive; and obviously, an end user should consent to this type of behavior from your application. I have mentioned it here as another technique to consider. I will leave it up to your imagination as to how to come up with additional mechanisms of defeating malware. However, unless your primary goal is to develop such anti-malware applications, you may choose to skip them.

Summary

In this chapter, we looked at malware and spyware and what they are. We also examined the various stages of malware and how we can classify them into broad categories. We learned that malware can be used by anyone and that there are many commercial entities that offer malware to both individual and corporate consumers. Our case study involved a real-world malware infection that took place in 2009 when Etisalat, one of the telecom providers for the UAE, subjected its entire subscriber base of BlackBerry users to a spyware application.

We've seen that, as an application developer, you are generally limited in your abilities to control what malware is introduced onto the device. Instead, your goal is to handle your application's data (and end-user data) securely. We very briefly covered a topic that looks at how some anti-forensics techniques can be used to purposely feed malware with useless data, thus forcing the malware author to wade through these messages to find the real ones. While this is by no means a foolproof solution, this technique mostly acts as a deterrent. Unless a malware author specifically targets you, he is unlikely to waste his time sifting through useless data. Instead, he will simply move onto the next person he has infected.

Android Permission Constants

For reference purposes, this appendix provides a complete list of Android permission constants. Permissions and their use are discussed throughout the book, particularly in Chapter 3.

Permission Constant	Description
ACCESS_CHECKIN_PROPERTIES	Allows read/write access to the `properties` table in the checkin database, enabling the ability to change values that get uploaded
ACCESS_COARSE_LOCATION	Allows an application to access coarse (e.g., Cell-ID, WiFi) location
ACCESS_FINE_LOCATION	Allows an application to access fine (e.g., GPS) location
ACCESS_LOCATION_EXTRA_ COMMANDS	Allows an application to access extra location provider commands
ACCESS_MOCK_LOCATION	Allows an application to create mock location providers for testing
ACCESS_NETWORK_STATE	Allows applications to access information about networks
ACCESS_SURFACE_FLINGER	Allows an application to use SurfaceFlinger's low-level features
ACCESS_WIFI_STATE	Allows applications to access information about Wi-Fi networks
ACCOUNT_MANAGER	Allows applications to call into AccountAuthenticators
AUTHENTICATE_ACCOUNTS	Allows an application to act as an AccountAuthenticator for the AccountManager
BATTERY_STATS	Allows an application to collect battery statistics
BIND_APPWIDGET	Allows an application to tell the AppWidget service which application can access AppWidget's data
BIND_DEVICE_ADMIN	Must be required by device administration receiver, to ensure that only the system can interact with it

(continued)

Permission Constant	Description
BIND_INPUT_METHOD	Must be required by an InputMethodService to ensure that only the system can bind to it
BIND_REMOTEVIEWS	Must be required by a RemoteViewsService to ensure that only the system can bind to it
BIND_WALLPAPER	Must be required by a WallpaperService to ensure that only the system can bind to it
BLUETOOTH	Allows applications to connect to paired bluetooth devices
BLUETOOTH_ADMIN	Allows applications to discover and pair bluetooth devices
BRICK	Required to be able to disable the device (very dangerous!)
BROADCAST_PACKAGE_REMOVED	Allows an application to broadcast a notification that an application package has been removed
BROADCAST_SMS	Allows an application to broadcast an SMS receipt notification
BROADCAST_STICKY	Allows an application to broadcast sticky intents
BROADCAST_WAP_PUSH	Allows an application to broadcast a WAP PUSH–receipt notification
CALL_PHONE	Allows an application to initiate a phone call without going through the Dialer user interface for the user to confirm the call being placed
CALL_PRIVILEGED	Allows an application to call any phone number, including emergency numbers, without going through the Dialer user interface for the user to confirm the call being placed
CAMERA	Required to be able to access the camera device
CHANGE_COMPONENT_ENABLED_STATE	Allows an application to change whether an application component (other than its own) is enabled or not
CHANGE_CONFIGURATION	Allows an application to modify the current configuration, such as locale
CHANGE_NETWORK_STATE	Allows applications to change network connectivity state
CHANGE_WIFI_MULTICAST_STATE	Allows applications to enter Wi-Fi Multicast mode
CHANGE_WIFI_STATE	Allows applications to change Wi-Fi connectivity state
CLEAR_APP_CACHE	Allows an application to clear the caches of all installed applications on the device
CLEAR_APP_USER_DATA	Allows an application to clear user data
CONTROL_LOCATION_UPDATES	Allows enabling/disabling location update notifications from the radio
DELETE_CACHE_FILES	Allows an application to delete cache files
DELETE_PACKAGES	Allows an application to delete packages
DEVICE_POWER	Allows low-level access to power management
DIAGNOSTIC	Allows applications to RW to diagnostic resources

Permission Constant	Description
DISABLE_KEYGUARD	Allows applications to disable the keyguard
DUMP	Allows an application to retrieve state dump information from system services
EXPAND_STATUS_BAR	Allows an application to expand or collapse the status bar
FACTORY_TEST	Run as a manufacturer test application, running as the root user
FLASHLIGHT	Allows access to the flashlight
FORCE_BACK	Allows an application to force a BACK operation on whatever is the top activity
GET_ACCOUNTS	Allows access to the list of accounts in the Accounts Service
GET_PACKAGE_SIZE	Allows an application to find out the space used by any package
GET_TASKS	Allows an application to get information about the currently or recently running tasks: a thumbnail representation of the tasks, what activities are running in it, and so on
GLOBAL_SEARCH	Can be used on content providers to allow the global search system to access their data
HARDWARE_TEST	Allows access to hardware peripherals
INJECT_EVENTS	Allows an application to inject user events (e.g., keys, touch, and trackball) into the event stream and deliver them to ANY window
INSTALL_LOCATION_PROVIDER	Allows an application to install a location provider into the Location Manager
INSTALL_PACKAGES	Allows an application to install packages
INTERNAL_SYSTEM_WINDOW	Allows an application to open windows that are for use by parts of the system user interface
INTERNET	Allows applications to open network sockets
KILL_BACKGROUND_PROCESSES	Allows an application to call `killBackgroundProcesses(String)`
MANAGE_ACCOUNTS	Allows an application to manage the list of accounts in the AccountManager
MANAGE_APP_TOKENS	Allows an application to manage (e.g., `create`, `destroy`, and Z-order) application tokens in the window manager
MASTER_CLEAR	
MODIFY_AUDIO_SETTINGS	Allows an application to modify global audio settings
MODIFY_PHONE_STATE	Allows modification of the telephony state—power on, mmi, and so on
MOUNT_FORMAT_FILESYSTEMS	Allows formatting file systems for removable storage

(continued)

Permission Constant	Description
MOUNT_UNMOUNT_FILESYSTEMS	Allows mounting and unmounting file systems for removable storage
NFC	Allows applications to perform I/O operations over NFC
PERSISTENT_ACTIVITY	This constant is deprecated. This functionality will be removed in the future; please do not use it. Allows an application to make its activities persistent.
PROCESS_OUTGOING_CALLS	Allows an application to monitor, modify, or abort outgoing calls
READ_CALENDAR	Allows an application to read the user's calendar data
READ_CONTACTS	Allows an application to read the user's contacts data
READ_FRAME_BUFFER	Allows an application to take screen shots and more generally get access to the frame buffer data
READ_HISTORY_BOOKMARKS	Allows an application to read (but not write) the user's browsing history and bookmarks
READ_INPUT_STATE	Allows an application to retrieve the current state of keys and switches
READ_LOGS	Allows an application to read the low-level system log files
READ_PHONE_STATE	Allows read only access to phone state
READ_SMS	Allows an application to read SMS messages
READ_SYNC_SETTINGS	Allows applications to read the sync settings
READ_SYNC_STATS	Allows applications to read the sync stats
REBOOT	Required to be able to reboot the device
RECEIVE_BOOT_COMPLETED	Allows an application to receive the `ACTION_BOOT_COMPLETED` that is broadcast after the system finishes booting
RECEIVE_MMS	Allows an application to monitor incoming MMS messages and to record or perform processing on them
RECEIVE_SMS	Allows an application to monitor incoming SMS messages and to record or perform processing on them
RECEIVE_WAP_PUSH	Allows an application to monitor incoming WAP push messages
RECORD_AUDIO	Allows an application to record audio
REORDER_TASKS	Allows an application to change the Z-order of tasks
RESTART_PACKAGES	This constant is deprecated. The `restartPackage(String)` API is no longer supported
SEND_SMS	Allows an application to send SMS messages
SET_ACTIVITY_WATCHER	Allows an application to watch and control how activities are started globally in the system

Permission Constant	Description
SET_ALARM	Allows an application to broadcast an Intent to set an alarm for the user
SET_ALWAYS_FINISH	Allows an application to control whether activities are immediately finished when put in the background
SET_ANIMATION_SCALE	Modifies the global animation scaling factor
SET_DEBUG_APP	Configures an application for debugging
SET_ORIENTATION	Allows low-level access to setting the orientation (actually, rotation) of the screen
SET_POINTER_SPEED	Allows low-level access to setting the pointer speed
SET_PREFERRED_APPLICATIONS	This constant is deprecated and no longer useful; see `addPackageToPreferred(String)` for details
SET_PROCESS_LIMIT	Allows an application to set the maximum number of (not needed) application processes that can be running
SET_TIME	Allows applications to set the system time
SET_TIME_ZONE	Allows applications to set the system time zone
SET_WALLPAPER	Allows applications to set the wallpaper
SET_WALLPAPER_HINTS	Allows applications to set the wallpaper hints
SIGNAL_PERSISTENT_PROCESSES	Allow an application to request that a signal be sent to all persistent processes
STATUS_BAR	Allows an application to open, close, or disable the status bar and its icons
SUBSCRIBED_FEEDS_READ	Allows an application to allow access the subscribed feeds `ContentProvider`
SUBSCRIBED_FEEDS_WRITE	
SYSTEM_ALERT_WINDOW	Allows an application to open windows using the type `TYPE_SYSTEM_ALERT`—shown on top of all other applications
UPDATE_DEVICE_STATS	Allows an application to update device statistics
USE_CREDENTIALS	Allows an application to request authtokens from the AccountManager
USE_SIP	Allows an application to use SIP service
VIBRATE	Allows access to the vibrator
WAKE_LOCK	Allows using PowerManager WakeLocks to keep processor from sleeping or screen from dimming
WRITE_APN_SETTINGS	Allows applications to write the apn settings
WRITE_CALENDAR	Allows an application to write (but not read) the user's calendar data
WRITE_CONTACTS	Allows an application to write (but not read) the user's contacts data

(continued)

Permission Constant	Description
WRITE_EXTERNAL_STORAGE	Allows an application to write to external storage
WRITE_GSERVICES	Allows an application to modify the Google service map
WRITE_HISTORY_BOOKMARKS	Allows an application to write (but not read) the user's browsing history and bookmarks
WRITE_SECURE_SETTINGS	Allows an application to read or write the secure system settings
WRITE_SETTINGS	Allows an application to read or write the system settings
WRITE_SMS	Allows an application to write SMS messages

Content Provider Classes

Class Name	Description
AlarmClock	The AlarmClock provider contains an Intent action and extras that can be used to start an Activity to set a new alarm in an alarm clock application
Browser	
Browser.BookmarkColumns	Column definitions for the mixed bookmark and history items available at BOOKMARKS_URI
Browser.SearchColumns	Column definitions for the search history table, available at SEARCHES_URI
CallLog	The CallLog provider contains information about placed and received calls
CallLog.Calls	Contains the recent calls
ContactsContract	The contract between the contacts provider and applications
ContactsContract.AggregationExceptions	Constants for the contact aggregation exceptions table, which contains aggregation rules overriding those used by automatic aggregation
ContactsContract.CommonDataKinds	Container for definitions of common data types stored in the ContactsContract.Data table
ContactsContract.CommonDataKinds.Email	A data kind representing an email address
ContactsContract.CommonDataKinds.Event	A data kind representing an event
ContactsContract.CommonDataKinds.GroupMembership	Group Membership

Class Name	Description
ContactsContract.CommonDataKinds.Im	A data kind representing an IM address You can use all columns defined for `ContactsContract.Data`, as well as the following aliases
ContactsContract.CommonDataKinds.Nickname	A data kind representing the contact's nickname
ContactsContract.CommonDataKinds.Note	Notes about the contact
ContactsContract.CommonDataKinds.Organization	A data kind representing an organization
ContactsContract.CommonDataKinds.Phone	A data kind representing a telephone number
ContactsContract.CommonDataKinds.Photo	A data kind representing a photo for the contact
ContactsContract.CommonDataKinds.Relation	A data kind representing a relation
ContactsContract.CommonDataKinds.SipAddress	A data kind representing a SIP address for the contact
ContactsContract.CommonDataKinds.StructuredName	A data kind representing the contact's proper name
ContactsContract.CommonDataKinds.StructuredPostal	A data kind representing a postal addresses
ContactsContract.CommonDataKinds.Website	A data kind representing a website related to the contact
ContactsContract.Contacts	Constants for the contacts table, which contains a record per aggregate of raw contacts representing the same person
ContactsContract.Contacts.AggregationSuggestions	A *read-only* subdirectory of a single contact aggregate that contains all aggregation suggestions (e.g., other contacts)
ContactsContract.Contacts.Data	A subdirectory of a single contact that contains all of the constituent raw `contactContactsContract.Data` rows
ContactsContract.Contacts.Entity	A subdirectory of a contact that contains all of its `ContactsContract.RawContacts`, as well as `ContactsContract.Data` rows
ContactsContract.Contacts.Photo	A *read-only* subdirectory of a single contact that contains the contact's primary photo
ContactsContract.Data	Constants for the data table, which contains data points tied to a raw contact
ContactsContract.Directory	A Directory represents a contacts corpus
ContactsContract.Groups	Constants for the groups table

(continued)

Class Name	Description
ContactsContract.Intents	Contains helper classes used to create or manage Intents that involve contacts
ContactsContract.Intents.Insert	Convenience class that contains string constants used to create contact Intents
ContactsContract.PhoneLookup	A table that represents the result of looking up a phone number (e.g., for caller ID)
ContactsContract.QuickContact	Helper methods to display QuickContact dialogs that allow users to pivot on a specific Contacts entry
ContactsContract.RawContacts	Constants for the raw contacts table, which contains one row of contact information for each person in each synced account
ContactsContract.RawContacts. Data	A subdirectory of a single raw contact that contains all of its ContactsContract.Data rows
ContactsContract.RawContacts. Entity	A subdirectory of a single raw contact that contains all of its ContactsContract.Data rows
ContactsContract. RawContactsEntity	Constants for the raw contacts entities table, which can be thought of as an outer join of the raw_contacts table with the data table
ContactsContract.Settings	Contacts-specific settings for various Accounts
ContactsContract.StatusUpdates	A status update is linked to a ContactsContract.Data row and captures the user's latest status update via the corresponding source
ContactsContract.SyncState	A table provided for sync adapters to use for storing private sync state data
LiveFolders	A LiveFolder is a special folder whose content is provided by a ContentProvider
MediaStore	The Media provider contains metadata for all available media on both internal and external storage devices
MediaStore.Audio	Container for all audio content
MediaStore.Audio.Albums	Contains artists for audio files
MediaStore.Audio.Artists	Contains artists for audio files
MediaStore.Audio.Artists.Albums	A subdirectory of each artist containing all albums on which a song by the artist appears
MediaStore.Audio.Genres	Contains all genres for audio files
MediaStore.Audio.Genres.Members	A subdirectory of each genre containing all members
MediaStore.Audio.Media	
MediaStore.Audio.Playlists	Contains playlists for audio files
MediaStore.Audio.Playlists.Members	A subdirectory of each playlist containing all members

Class Name	Description
MediaStore.Files	Media provider table containing an index of all files in the media storage, including non-media files
MediaStore.Images	Contains metadata for all available images
MediaStore.Images.Media	
MediaStore.Images.Thumbnails	This class allows developers to query and get two kinds of thumbnails: MINI_KIND: 512 x 384 thumbnail and MICRO_KIND: 96 x 96 thumbnail
MediaStore.Video	
MediaStore.Video.Media	
MediaStore.Video.Thumbnails	This class allows developers to query and get two kinds of thumbnails: MINI_KIND: 512 x 384 thumbnail and MICRO_KIND: 96 x 96 thumbnail
SearchRecentSuggestions	This is a utility class providing access to SearchRecentSuggestionsProvider
Settings	The Settings provider contains global system-level device preferences
Settings.NameValueTable	Common base for tables of name/value settings
Settings.Secure	Secure system settings, which contain system preferences that applications can read, but are not allowed to write
Settings.System	System settings, which contain miscellaneous system preferences
SyncStateContract	The ContentProvider contract for associating data with any data array account
SyncStateContract.Constants	
SyncStateContract.Helpers	
UserDictionary	A provider of user-defined words for input methods to use for predictive text input
UserDictionary.Words	Contains the user-defined words

Index

A

CPSIA information can be obtained at www.ICGtesting.com
Printed in the USA
LVOW11s1355201113

362095LV00008B/375/P